Stream Guardians Aquatic Conservation Biomonitoring

by

Kevin Bryce Lunde

Copyright © 2024 by Kevin Bryce Lunde

All rights reserved. No part of this book may be reproduced in any manner whatsoever without written permission except in the case of brief quotations embodied in critical articles and reviews.

First Printing, 2024

Abstract

Changes to hydrology, water chemistry, physical habitat, and the landscape surrounding aquatic ecosystems can have profound effects on their biological communities, potentially reducing important ecosystem services and functions provided to wildlife and humans. In this dissertation, I examine how environmental variables, human activities, and management practices have affected stream and wetland biota throughout Northern California.

The parasitic trematode *Ribeiroia ondatrae* has been shown to cause limb malformations in amphibian species through laboratory studies, but these small-scale experiments lacked important ecological co-factors that could alter parasite transmission rates and host susceptibility. Therefore, I conducted a multi-year, nested experiment at Hog Lake in Mendocino County to test host responses to *Ribeiroia* infection. The addition of *Ribeiroia*-infected snails to half of Hog Lake caused an increase in severe limb malformations in Pacific chorus frogs (*Pseudacris regilla*) and monitoring at different spatial scales revealed unique dose-response relationships because of ecological interactions and environmental co-factors. To determine if the parasite might contribute to population declines, I monitored juvenile and adult *P. regilla* at Hog Lake and a second wetland for four years. The consistently low (< 5%) malformation prevalence in adult frogs despite a generally high malformation prevalence (30-50%) in juvenile frogs confirmed that malformed amphibians do not survive to adulthood, indirect evidence that *Ribeiroia* may cause population declines. Multi-year surveys at 17 Northern California wetlands showed a strong dose-response relationship among the parasite and *P. regilla* malformation levels, providing evidence that *Ribeiroia* is an important cause of limb malformations in this region.

Effective conservation of wetland species depends on understanding how anthropogenic stress, natural environmental variables, and management activities affect biological communities. To identify which of these explanatory variables were most influential and determine the conservation value of created wetlands, I sampled amphibians and insects from a total of 49 stormwater ponds, stockponds, and natural ponds in Northern California. Overall, landscape variables (i.e., percent urban and natural, number of ponds within 1 km, and elevation) were associated with differences in macroinvertebrate community structure, but specific conductance and percent littoral vegetation present were important co-factors. Compared to natural ponds, stockponds supported the most similar invertebrate assemblages and greater amphibian species richness. Light cattle-grazing of areas surrounding natural ponds and stockponds was associated with increased amphibian richness, whereas the addition of exotic fishes was associated with mild differences in invertebrate populations. This research showed that stockponds are conservation resources for amphibians and invertebrates but that proper management is necessary to maximize this potential.

To objectively quantify the ambient condition of wetlands, ecologists use the plants and animals found in aquatic habitats as biological indicators. Because no biological indicator has been developed for wetlands in California, I designed an index of biotic integrity (IBI) to determine the ecological condition of the wetland based on macroinvertebrate community structure. Eight metrics that showed significant responses to urbanization, had adequate range, and lacked redundancy with each other were incorporated into the IBI. The IBI was successfully validated and showed no bias along natural gradients (e.g., ecoregion, elevation, and precipitation), except that non-perennial and perennial ponds did support slightly different communities, indicating that the IBI is applicable across this region.

Although biomonitoring data have been successfully used to quantity the ecological condition of perennial streams in many regions of California, no analysis tool (e.g., IBI) has been developed for the San Francisco Bay Area, a region which contains a large proportion of non-perennial streams. To identify least-disturbed reference sites in a highly urban region and examine how inter-site and temporal variability affect bioassessment data, I analyzed a large (> 400 sites) stream bioassessment dataset. I found that using geographic information system (GIS) watershed analysis and local physical habitat data were both necessary to identify least-disturbed reference sites. Among reference sites, the macroinvertebrate assemblages of perennial streams were different from non-perennial streams, a result which demonstrates the need for separate IBIs for these two habitat types. Interannual variability was moderate across 2000 to 2007, with index scores ranging from 10-15 out of 100 points, but some sites showed extreme variation of more than 50 points.

In summary, this dissertation shows that effective management of wetlands and streams can be accomplished with the use of biomonitoring data to infer ecological condition and that stockponds are valuable conservation resources when properly managed.

TABLE OF CONTENTS

Introduction..

CHAPTER 1: A practical guide for the study of malformed amphibians and their causes 1

CHAPTER 2: Beyond laboratory experiments: Using an ecosystem-level manipulation to
understand host-parasite dynamics 31

CHAPTER 3: Macroinvertebrate and amphibian assemblages in stormwater ponds, stockponds,
and natural ponds in Northern California: The conservation value of created wetlands...68

CHAPTER 4: Development and validation of a macroinvertebrate index of biotic integrity (IBI) for
assessing urban impacts to Northern California freshwater wetlands 100

CHAPTER 5: Identifying reference sites and quantifying biological variability within the benthic
macroinvertebrate community at Northern California streams 138

CHAPTER 6: Conclusions and future research 168

ACKNOWLEDGMENTS

I would have not been able to complete this dissertation without the help of many individuals. First and foremost, I want to thank my advisor, Vince Resh. He has been a superb mentor during my tenure at UC Berkeley. His encouragement and support were invaluable in helping me write this dissertation. He allowed me the freedom to explore my ideas and provided the emotional, intellectual, and financial support I needed to complete this research. His dedication to teaching and mentoring undergraduate and graduate students was an inspiration. I would also like to thank my orals committee members Joe McBride (chair), Bob Lane, Adina Merenlender and Matt Kondolf for guiding me to important papers in their respective fields and helping me develop my prospectus, which formed the basis of this dissertation research. I want to thank my dissertation committee members Adina Merenlender and Matt Kondolf for providing valuable feedback on my dissertation chapters.

I thank my long-time colleague and friend Pieter Johnson (University of Colorado Boulder) for his intellectual involvement with Chapters 1 and 2. His advice and encouragement were an immense help during graduate school. I am indebted to many Resh Lab graduate students for their support, advice, and friendship. I thank Leah Béche for being a role model when I started graduate school, Rafi Mazor for his statistical advice and encouragement to delve further into the data, Tina Mendez for being a "big sister", Chris Solek for helping me apply the results of my dissertation, Matt Cover for getting me hooked on bioassessment research and for connecting me with the Water Board Surface Water Ambient Monitoring Program, Alison Purcell for teaching me ordination methods to analyze biomonitoring data, Wendy Renz for her insights on vernal pool and pond ecosystems, Kaua Fraiola for his infectious excitement about ecology and his company, Joanie Ball for her assistance with GIS analyses, Justin Lawrence for our research collaborations, and Lisa Hunt for sharing her knowledge regarding how science work in the real world. I also thank "honorary" lab mates Igor Lacan and Matt Deitch for their scientific advice and friendship. I also benefited from conservations and input from Adina Merenlender's graduate students: Ted Grantham, Mary Matella, and Justin Kitzes.

A number of undergraduate students assisted with many aspects of my research. In particular, Mohammad Aghaee worked with me for three years and contributed greatly to Chapter 2, Kevin Yao and Sahar Osman contributed greatly to Chapters 3 and 4. In addition, I thank Addie Cuneo, Annie Strother, Bryson Marks, Catherine Dunn, Chennie Castañon, Daisy Guardado, Jenny Baumauer, Jessica Dugan, Jianni Xin, Jinlin Wang, Kate Thi, Katherine He, Lancelle Lipana, Luis Gomez, Maggie Groff, Marvin Miranda, Michelle Baragona, Mike Li, Mollie McKillop, and Steven Ly for their assistance.

Additionally, I thank Jim Carter (US Geological Survey) for input on subsampling invertebrates, Shane Fierer (Hopland Research and Extension Center) for his assistance with GIS analyses, and Bob Keiffer (Hopland Research and Extension Center) for facilitating the research at Hog Lake.

I thank the various funding sources which enabled me to complete this research. I was largely funded through the Environmental Protection Agency (EPA) STAR Fellowship Program, National Science Foundation (NSF) Graduate Research Fellowship Program, and UC Berkeley Graduate Division. Additional funding for the research was from the Alameda Countywide Clean Water Program, UC Berkeley Committee on Research Faculty Research Grant, UC Berkeley Margaret C. Walker Fund in Insect Systematics, and UC Berkeley Entomological Student Organization Travel Grants.

Finally, I thank my friends and family for their support and companionship during this monumental endeavor called graduate school. I thank my parents Pat and Stan for nurturing my intellectual development and my brother for his sage advice on graduate school. I thank my son Anders, for being the ticking clock that moved my dissertation into high gear. Last but not least, I am indebted my wife Becky for her love, her encouragement, and her keen editing skills, all of which were necessary to complete this dissertation.

INTRODUCTION

INVESTIGATIONS OF ALTERED AQUATIC ECOSYSTEMS: BIOMONITORING, DISEASE, AND CONSERVATION

Investigation of altered aquatic ecosystems: biomonitoring, disease, and conservation

Freshwater ecosystems provide vital services to humans valued at over $6 trillion and support high biological diversity (Costanza et al., 1997; Jackson et al., 2001). However, these systems are under severe stress (Brinson and Malvarez, 2002; Dudgeon et al., 2006). Rivers, lakes and wetlands provide invaluable resources to people including food, drinking water, recreation opportunities, energy, and transportation. However, these services can be, and are often, negatively affected by each of these uses and other human activities. For example, urbanization may reduce water quality and alter the hydrologic regime (Paul and Meyer, 2001). Agricultural practices can result in pesticide and nutrient runoff leading to toxic conditions or eutrophication (Kemp et al., 2005; Smith et al., 1999b; Solomon et al., 1996). Overexploitation (i.e. overharvesting species) can have direct consequences on vertebrate populations, especially fishes (e.g., Hilborn et al., 2003). Deliberate and accidental introductions of species can lead to complex ecosystems shifts in aquatic habitats, resulting in already stressed ecosystems being more likely to have successful invaders (Koehn 2004). Flow modifications to running waters (e.g., dams, water withdrawals, impervious watersheds) lead to changes in flow magnitude, frequency, timing, duration, and rate of change that affect both aquatic and riparian species, as well as habitat conditions (Poff et al., 1997). Although freshwater ecosystems (e.g., rivers, lakes, wetlands) only occupy less than 1% of the world's surface, they support over 25% of the global vertebrate biodiversity and 6% of total biodiversity (Gleick, 1996). Yet extinction rates in freshwater systems are higher than in all other habitats (Sala et al., 2000), which underscores the need to better understand aquatic species and their stressors.

Rivers, lakes, and wetlands have been severely degraded in California, similar to other regions with a mediterranean climate (Gasith and Resh, 1999). Because of the strong wet and dry season dynamics in California's mediterranean climate, dams have been constructed on most of the large rivers to prevent flooding and provide water for agriculture and domestic use in the dry season (Carle, 2009). Moreover, a large proportion of alpine lakes have been impacted by the stocking of invasive fish across the national forest and national park lands (Vredenburg, 2004). Even in protected areas, the drifting of agro-chemicals can move more than 100 km and pollute lakes and wetlands (Davidson et al., 2002). In addition, nearly 90% of historic wetlands have been drained and filled in California (Dahl, 1990).

Biomonitoring is used worldwide to assess the ecological condition of streams and rivers based on the presence or abundance of aquatic organisms. With this approach, government agencies, citizen groups, and research institutions can determine the cumulative effect of multiple stressors (e.g., urbanization, agriculture, logging, hydropower operations) on ecological condition by developing responsive indicators based on aquatic biological communities (Karr, 1999; Resh, 2007; Resh and Rosenberg, 1989). Of the potential organism assemblages used for assessments in aquatic habitats (e.g., diatoms, benthic macroinvertebrates, zooplankton, and fish (Hellawell, 1986)), benthic macroinvertebrates (e.g., insects, crustaceans and snails) are the most widely used to assess stream condition because they are ubiquitous, diverse, and species have unique responses to specific stressors (Resh, 2008).

Biological monitoring has been successfully used to evaluate ecological integrity within a broad array of aquatic ecosystems and is an important component of programs that have previously focused on physical or chemical assessments (Resh, 2007; Yoder and Rankin, 1998). Biomonitoring is effective because aquatic organisms are cumulative indicators of overall environmental conditions, responding not only to pollutants but to changes in physical habitat conditions, which are difficult to assess with traditional chemical and toxicity monitoring tools (e.g., Rosenberg and Resh, 1993). Programs to detect ecological impacts to streams and rivers that utilize biomonitoring methods have become well established world-wide (Barbour et al., 1999; Hering et al., 2004; Resh, 2007; Smith et al., 1999a). A common approach has been to develop multimetric indicators commonly referred to as an index of biotic integrity (IBI) (Barbour et al., 1999; Carter et al., 2006; Karr and Chu, 1999). These indicators, although only looking at a single assemblage, are considered overall indicators for the ecological condition of the habitat.

Another threat to biodiversity in aquatic habitats is disease. Novel and re-emerging wildlife diseases have increased over the past decade (Daszak et al., 2000). The growing interactions between humans and wildlife increase the chance that pathogens also can infect human populations. Furthermore, wildlife diseases can take a significant toll on aquatic species. For example, chytrid fungus (*Batrachochytrium dendrobatidis*) has caused extinctions and declines in amphibians species around the world, including in the Sierra Nevada mountain range of California (Skerratt et al., 2007; Wake and Vredenburg, 2008). Anthropogenic activities can play a significant role in altering the abundance and distribution of aquatic diseases (Daszak et al., 2000). For example, chronic stress to aquatic ecosystems (e.g., poor water quality) can facilitate the success of ecological invaders including pathogens (e.g., viruses, bacteria, trematodes) or reduce immune response to prevent morbidity or mortality.

In this dissertation, I explore disease dynamics of a multi-host parasite (*Ribeiroia ondatrae*) that can cause severe limb malformations among frog and salamander hosts (Fig. 1). Populations of the parasitic trematode *Ribeiroia ondatrae* (hereafter *Ribeiroia*) can be altered through nutrient enrichment and eutrophication, which increase snail populations and parasite output from infected snails, and from landscape-scale factors such as wetland loss that concentrates the three required hosts to the same water body (Johnson et al., 2007; Johnson and Lunde, 2005). Chapters 1 and 2 focus host-parasite dynamics of *Ribeiroia*, which causes extra, missing, and misshapen limbs in frogs, toads, and salamanders (Johnson et al., 2010). Aquatic ecology can be a useful tool to determine the biological condition of rivers, lakes, and wetlands based on the abundance or composition of resident taxa (e.g., macroinvertebrates). Chapters 3 and 4 describe research using biomonitoring data in ponds and wetlands in Northern California, while Chapter 5 describes the process of identifying reference sites using a large stream biomonitoring dataset in Northern California.

Chapter 1 describes how to study malformed frogs and the trematode *Ribeiroia*. The chapter makes a number of important contributions to the literature on this topic. In particular, it defines an expected or "normal" abnormality prevalence in any given population, and describes statistical tests and sample sizes needed to demonstrate that a population has above baseline levels. This chapter describes how to determine if a given agent (parasite or other) is causing a high prevalence of limb malformations within a population by using epidemiological approaches. It proposes using indicator amphibians that are both common and abundant over wide geographic areas to help compare malformation hotspots across states and ecoregions in order to prioritize problem wetlands or regions. In addition, it describes appropriate amphibian and snail field-based sampling techniques as well as laboratory methods to quantify and identify *Ribeiroia* in both snail and amphibian hosts.

Chapter 2 describes a multi-scale study to document how host-parasite interactions within the *Ribeiroia*-snail-amphibian model vary as a function of temporal and spatial scale. The first objective of this chapter was to document the relationship between *Ribeiroia* infection and amphibian malformations from 17 wetlands in northern California and to evaluate the variability in this relationship to assist in contextualizing experimental results. The second objective was to experimentally test the influence of *Ribeiroia* infection on amphibian malformations and mortality within field settings by manipulating parasite levels at the ecosystem scale (1600 m^2), and to examine how experimental venue affects parasite-host dynamics. I conducted the large-scale manipulation of *Ribeiroia* parasite levels by adding over 500 infected snails to one half of a wetland that I previously divided into two halves with an impermeable barrier. I used the other half wetland as an experimental control unit. The third objective was to examine the conservation implications of parasite infection on amphibian hosts by comparing malformation prevalence between juveniles from one year and returning adults from the following year. This chapter makes a number of important contributions because it was the first study to test if *Ribeiroia* could cause severe limb malformations in an experimental field setting. It was also the first to nest a replicated cage study within the larger ecosystem manipulation and compare parasite pathology across spatial scales. Lastly, the chapter validates the use of fine mesh cages as a field-method to test if parasite infection is a suspected cause. The spatial monitoring data also contribute to our knowledge about background rates of limb abnormalities in populations where *Ribeiroia* is absent.

Chapter 3 is a natural history-based study describing the biological communities of both macroinvertebrates and amphibians observed at 49 stormwater ponds, stockponds, and natural ponds throughout Northern California. A main objective of this chapter was to evaluate the conservation value of constructed ponds (i.e., stormwater ponds and stockponds) and understand if created wetlands can potentially help offset losses in biodiversity from historic wetland loss, and if so, what conditions at those ponds encourage a biological community similar to natural ponds. A second objective was to determine important environmental variables that affect macroinvertebrate community structure and amphibian richness. Third, the chapter examines how two important uses of ponds, cattle grazing and fish stocking, affect resident macroinvertebrate and amphibian populations.

Chapter 4 uses the dataset generated from the previous chapter to develop an index of biotic integrity (IBI) based on the macroinvertebrate community found in created and natural ponds. Although some states within the U.S. have developed biological indicators for wetlands and ponds, no such tools have been developed in California. This chapter proposes a standardized protocol for sampling macroinvertebrates in depressional wetlands, which was needed because sampling methods vary between bioassessment programs in other regions. The main objective of this chapter was to determine if a biomonitoring approach could be used to evaluate the condition of wetlands based on macroinvertebrate populations. Therefore, I classified sites as reference-quality based on low levels of urbanization and then examined metrics (univariate descriptors of the biological community) from the literature that have been associated with anthropogenic stress in other regions. Metrics that were responsive to stress, and that had adequate range and lacked redundancy with other metrics were combined into a multimetric IBI. To demonstrate the ability of the IBI to work in new wetlands, I tested if the IBI could discriminate between reference and impacted sites in the validation dataset, which included 14 of the original 49 sites sampled that were not used to create the IBI. The accuracy, bias, and precision of the IBI was tested across environmental gradients to examine it's applicability in the region. Lastly, I compare the macroinvertebrate IBI against amphibian species richness at these same ponds to examine how a macroinvertebrate assemblage represents the wetland as an overall indicator. This chapter resulted in the development of an IBI that may be used the State Water Resources Control Board as an intensive indicator for depressional wetlands. The collection methods and IBI are being tested in Southern California to examine how applicable it might be in that region.

Chapter 5 describes the process of identifying reference sites using a large stream-based biomonitoring dataset in Northern California. The data were collected by stormwater agencies, state agencies, and non profit groups between 2000 and 2007 at over 400 locations. The purpose of this study was to examine how reference-selection methods and inter-site variability between reference sites and interannual variability could influence interpretations of stream macroinvertebrate biomonitoring data. The first objective was to determine what process and data were necessary to select high-quality reference sites in this region with widespread urban development. Second, I sought to quantify the extent of inter-site variability in the reference pool, and to determine whether this variability could be reduced by grouping sites into classes of similar stream types (e.g., hydroperiod). Third, I wanted to determine if the interannual variability of macroinvertebrate communities could significantly affect IBI scores and, if so, to determine if the sources of interannual variability were associated with disturbance or common environmental gradients. This chapter provides important results that will be used by the state of California State Water Resources Control Board as it develops biological objectives for bioassessment data from perennial streams. This study also contributes to a small set of studies that compare the biological communities in perennial and non-perennial streams.

In summary, my dissertation research incorporates applied aquatic ecology through the use of bioassessment to document the condition of streams and wetlands, and the use of traditional aquatic ecology to study of malformed amphibians caused by a multi-host parasite. Although limnology and aquatic ecology have a long history, the research has traditionally focused on natural or "pristine" habitats as places to examine how species interact with each other and their environments. However, I argue that few aquatic ecosystems in the world are unaltered, and what we need is more information on how impacted, degraded, and created aquatic ecosystems function. Thus, I have intentionally studied streams and ponds in highly disturbed areas to document relationships between anthropogenic stress and resident biota, to examine how management of these resources affects community structure, and to describe how we can use biota as indicators of particular stressors. The dissertation contributes to a new and growing body of literature on "novel" ecosystems, which focus on understanding the ecology of altered and created habitats (Hobbs et al., 2006). A greater understanding of the interplay between aquatic species and their novel environments can lead to improved conservation of this vital resource.

LITERATURE CITED

BARBOUR, M. T., J. GERRITSEN, B. D. SNYDER, AND J. B. STRIBLING. 1999. Rapid Bioassessment Protocols for Use in Streams and Wadeable Rivers: Periphyton, Benthic Macroinvertebrates and Fish, Second Edition. EPA 841-B-99-002. Office of Water, U.S. Environmental Protection Agency, Washington, DC, USA.

BRINSON, M. M., AND A. I. MALVAREZ. 2002. Temperate freshwater wetlands: types, status, and threats. Environmental Conservation 29:115-133.

CARLE, D. 2009. Introduction to Water in California. University of California Press, Berkeley, CA.

CARTER, J. L., V. H. RESH, M. J. HANNAFORD, M. J. MYERS, F. R. HAUER, AND G. A. LAMBERTI. 2006. Macroinvertebrates as biotic indicators of environmental quality. Pp. 805-833. *In* F. R. Hauer, and G. A. Lamberti (Eds.), Methods in Stream Ecology. Second Edition. Academic Press/Elsevier, San Diego, CA, USA.

COSTANZA, R., R. DARGE, R. DEGROOT, S. FARBER, M. GRASSO, B. HANNON, K. LIMBURG, S. NAEEM, R. V. ONEILL, J. PARUELO, R. G. RASKIN, P. SUTTON, AND M. VANDENBELT. 1997. The value of the world's ecosystem services and natural capital. Nature 387:253-260.

DAHL, T. E. 1990. Wetland losses in the United States - 1780's to 1980's. U.S. Department of the Interior, Fish and Wildlife Service, Washington DC, Jamestown, ND: Northern Prairie Wildlife Research Center Online.
http://www.npwrc.usgs.gov/resource/wetlands/wetloss/index.htm.

DASZAK, P., A. A. CUNNINGHAM, AND A. D. HYATT. 2000. Wildlife ecology - Emerging infectious diseases of wildlife - Threats to biodiversity and human health. Science 287:443-449.

DAVIDSON, C., H. B. SHAFFER, AND M. R. JENNINGS. 2002. Spatial tests of the pesticide drift, habitat destruction, UV-B, and climate-change hypotheses for California amphibian declines. Conservation Biology 16:1588-1601.

DUDGEON, D., A. H. ARTHINGTON, M. O. GESSNER, Z. I. KAWABATA, D. J. KNOWLER, C. LEVEQUE, R. J. NAIMAN, A. H. PRIEUR-RICHARD, D. SOTO, M. L. J. STIASSNY, AND C. A. SULLIVAN. 2006. Freshwater biodiversity: importance, threats, status and conservation challenges. Biological Reviews 81:163-182.

GASITH, A., AND V. H. RESH. 1999. Streams in Mediterranean climate regions: Abiotic influences and biotic responses to predictable seasonal events. Annual Review of Ecology and Systematics 30:51-81.

GLEICK, P. H. 1996. Water resources. Pp. 817-823. *In* S. H. Schneider (Ed.), Encyclopedia of Climate and Weather. Oxford University Press, New York, NY, USA.

HELLAWELL, J. M. 1986. Biological Indicators of Freshwater Pollution and Environmental Management. Elsevier Applied Science Publishers, New York, NY.

HERING, D., O. MOOG, L. SANDIN, AND P. F. M. VERDONSCHOT. 2004. Overview and application of the AQEM assessment system. Hydrobiologia 516:1-20.

HILBORN, R., T. A. BRANCH, B. ERNST, A. MAGNUSSON, C. V. MINTE-VERA, M. D. SCHEUERELL, AND J. L. VALERO. 2003. State of the world's fisheries. Annual Review of Environment and Resources 28:359-399.

HOBBS, R. J., S. ARICO, J. ARONSON, J. S. BARON, P. BRIDGEWATER, V. A. CRAMER, P. R. EPSTEIN, J. J. EWEL, C. A. KLINK, A. E. LUGO, D. NORTON, D. OJIMA, D. M. RICHARDSON, E. W. SANDERSON, F. VALLADARES, M. VILA, R. ZAMORA, AND M. ZOBEL. 2006. Novel ecosystems: theoretical and management aspects of the new ecological world order. Global Ecology and Biogeography 15:1-7.

JACKSON, R. B., S. R. CARPENTER, C. N. DAHM, D. M. MCKNIGHT, R. J. NAIMAN, S. L. POSTEL, AND S. W. RUNNING. 2001. Water in a changing world. Ecological Applications 11:1027-1045.

JOHNSON, P. T. J., J. M. CHASE, K. L. DOSCH, R. B. HARTSON, J. A. GROSS, D. J. LARSON, D. R. SUTHERLAND, AND S. R. CARPENTER. 2007. Aquatic eutrophication promotes pathogenic infection in amphibians. Proceedings of the National Academy of Sciences of the United States of America 104:15781-15786.

JOHNSON, P. T. J., AND K. B. LUNDE. 2005. Parasite infection and limb malformations: a growing problem in amphibian conservation. Pp. 124-138. *In* M. J. Lannoo (Ed.), Amphibian declines: the conservation status of United States species. University of California Press, Berkeley, CA.

JOHNSON, P. T. J., M. K. REEVES, S. K. KREST, AND A. E. PINKNEY. 2010. A decade of deformities. Advances in our understanding of amphibian malformations and thier implications. Pp. 511-536. *In* Donald W. Sparling, Greg Linder, Christine A. Bishop, and S. K. Krest (Eds.), Ecotoxicology of Amphibians and Reptiles, Second Edition. Soceity for Environmental Toxicology and and Contaminants (SETAC), Pensacoloa, Florida, USA.

KARR, J. R. 1999. Defining and measuring river health. Freshwater Biology 41:221-234.

KARR, J. R., AND E. W. CHU. 1999. Restoring Life in Running Waters. Island Press, Washington, DC.

KEMP, W. M., W. R. BOYNTON, J. E. ADOLF, D. F. BOESCH, W. C. BOICOURT, G. BRUSH, J. C. CORNWELL, T. R. FISHER, P. M. GLIBERT, J. D. HAGY, L. W. HARDING, E. D. HOUDE, D. G. KIMMEL, W. D. MILLER, R. I. E. NEWELL, M. R. ROMAN, E. M. SMITH, AND J. C. STEVENSON. 2005. Eutrophication of Chesapeake Bay: historical trends and ecological interactions. Marine Ecology-Progress Series 303:1-29.

PAUL, M. J., AND J. L. MEYER. 2001. Streams in the urban landscape. Annual Review of Ecology and Systematics 32:333-365.

POFF, N. L., J. D. ALLAN, M. B. BAIN, J. R. KARR, K. L. PRESTEGAARD, B. D. RICHTER, R. E. SPARKS, AND J. C. STROMBERG. 1997. The natural flow regime. Bioscience 47:769-784.

RESH, V. H. 2007. Multinational, freshwater biomonitoring programs in the developing world: Lessons learned from African and Southeast Asian river surveys. Environmental Management 39:737-748.

RESH, V. H. 2008. Which group is best? Attributes of different biological assemblages used in freshwater biomonitoring programs. Environmental Monitoring and Assessment 138:131-138.

RESH, V. H., AND D. M. ROSENBERG. 1989. Spatial-temporal variability and the study of aquatic insects. Canadian Entomologist 121:941-963.

ROSENBERG, D. M., AND V. H. RESH. 1993. Freshwater Biomonitoring and Benthic Macroinvertebrates. Chapman & Hall, New York, NY, USA.

SALA, O. E., F. S. CHAPIN, J. J. ARMESTO, E. BERLOW, J. BLOOMFIELD, R. DIRZO, E. HUBER-SANWALD, L. F. HUENNEKE, R. B. JACKSON, A. KINZIG, R. LEEMANS, D. M. LODGE, H. A. MOONEY, M. OESTERHELD, N. L. POFF, M. T. SYKES, B. H. WALKER, M. WALKER, AND D. H. WALL. 2000. Biodiversity - Global biodiversity scenarios for the year 2100. Science 287:1770-1774.

SKERRATT, L. F., L. BERGER, R. SPEARE, S. CASHINS, K. R. MCDONALD, A. D. PHILLOTT, H. B. HINES, AND N. KENYON. 2007. Spread of chytridiomycosis has caused the rapid global decline and extinction of frogs. Ecohealth 4:125-134.

SMITH, M. J., W. R. KAY, D. H. D. EDWARD, P. J. PAPAS, K. S. RICHARDSON, J. C. SIMPSON, A. M. PINDER, D. J. CALE, P. H. J. HORWITZ, J. A. DAVIS, F. H. YUNG, R. H. NORRIS, AND S. A. HALSE. 1999a. AusRivAS: using macroinvertebrates to assess ecological condition of rivers in Western Australia. Freshwater Biology 41:269-282.

SMITH, V. H., G. D. TILMAN, AND J. C. NEKOLA. 1999b. Eutrophication: impacts of excess nutrient inputs on freshwater, marine, and terrestrial ecosystems. Environmental Pollution 100:179-196.

SOLOMON, K. R., D. B. BAKER, R. P. RICHARDS, D. R. DIXON, S. J. KLAINE, T. W. LAPOINT, R. J. KENDALL, C. P. WEISSKOPF, J. M. GIDDINGS, J. P. GIESY, L. W. HALL, AND W. M. WILLIAMS. 1996. Ecological risk assessment of atrazine in North American surface waters. Environmental Toxicology and Chemistry 15:31-74.

VREDENBURG, V. T. 2004. Reversing introduced species effects: Experimental removal of introduced fish leads to rapid recovery of a declining frog. Proceedings of the National Academy of Sciences of the United States of America 101:7646-7650.

WAKE, D. B., AND V. T. VREDENBURG. 2008. Are we in the midst of the sixth mass extinction? A view from the world of amphibians. Proceedings of the National Academy of Sciences of the United States of America 105:11466-11473.

YODER, C. O., AND E. T. RANKIN. 1998. The role of biological indicators in a state water quality management process. Environmental Monitoring and Assessment 51:61-88.

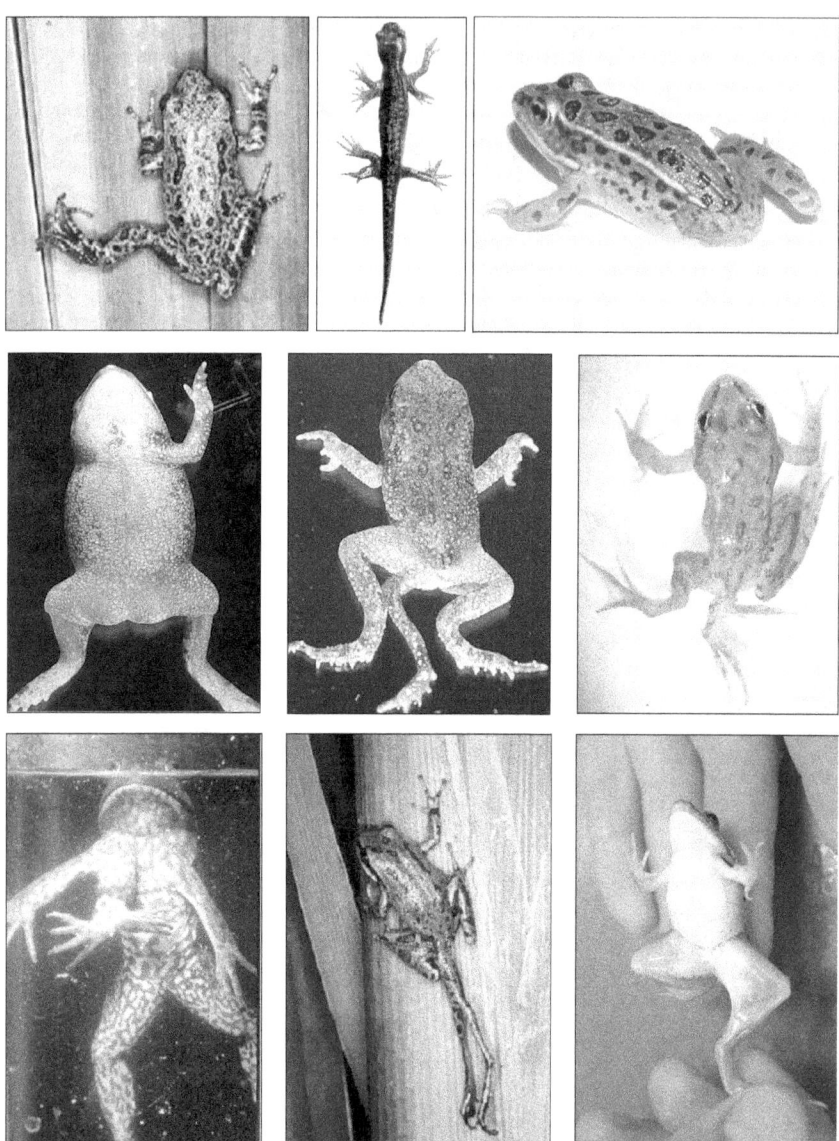

Fig. 1. Photographs of frogs, toads, and salamanders with limb malformations caused by *Ribeiroia ondatrae*.

CHAPTER 1

A PRACTICAL GUIDE FOR THE STUDY OF MALFORMED AMPHIBIANS AND THEIR CAUSES

A practical guide for the study of malformed amphibians and their causes

Abstract

Reports of severely malformed amphibians in the 1990s prompted researchers to examine the causes and extent of the issue. However, disparities in survey methods and a shortage of baseline data have hindered standardization among investigations, including inconsistencies in identifying "affected" or "hotspot" sites where malformation prevalence is elevated. Here, I review field-based surveys and experimental approaches used over the last decade to address this complex ecological issue. I offer specific recommendations regarding amphibian-sampling techniques, including methods to capture and examine amphibians, with the aim of enhancing the accessibility of this topic to scientists, students, and educators of diverse backgrounds. A quantitative evaluation of USFWS amphibian abnormality surveys suggests that the typical amphibian population has an abnormality prevalence of 3.3% (95% CI: 3.0-3.6%). Using a statistically-based framework, I therefore suggest that sites with malformation frequencies significantly > 5% should be conservatively considered 'higher-than baseline' whereas sites with > 10% abnormal individuals should be considered 'hotspots'. Based on established approaches from epidemiology, I provide recommendations regarding methods to identify proximate causes(s) of abnormalities with a focus on using 'multiple lines of evidence', including large-scale field surveys, comparisons of malformation 'signatures' between field and laboratory studies, and the use of manipulative experiments at multiple spatial scales. As an example, I describe methods to examine the causal influence of infection by the trematode parasite – *Ribeiroia ondatrae* – including quantifying presence and abundance within amphibian and snail host populations with adequate power of detection. I conclude by identifying priority research questions with the goal of stimulating additional information to evaluate the causes and consequences of amphibian malformations.

Key words: abnormalities, amphibian decline, anuran, deformities, disease ecology, educational outreach, etiology, field methods, *Ribeiroia*, teratology

INTRODUCTION

In August of 1958, Dr. Royal Bruce Brunson, a biologist at Montana State University, made an alarming discovery: a pond with large numbers of severely deformed Pacific Chorus Frogs (*Pseudacris regilla*) in Montana. Approximately 20% of emerging frogs exhibited severely malformed limbs, including extra limbs, missing limbs, and a variety of twisted and otherwise misshapen limbs (Hebard and Brunson, 1963). Dr. Brunson again noted high frequencies of malformed Chorus Frogs at this pond in 1959, 1960, 1961, and 1964 (R. Brunson 1999, personal communication), while others found deformities at the same site through the 1970s and into the 1990s (Miller, 1975; Anderson, 1977; J. Werner, personal communication). Given the rise of nuclear power, some feared such deformities were caused by radiation whereas others suggested pesticides used for mosquito control. However, no evidence was available to support these hypotheses. Investigators generally assumed that, while remarkable, the phenomenon was an isolated or at least very rare occurrence (e.g., Hebard and Brunson, 1963), such that real cause would remain unknown for many years to come.

Four decades later, discoveries that multiple wetlands across the United States had large numbers malformed amphibians clearly demonstrated that this phenomenon was neither isolated nor rare (Sessions and Ruth, 1990; Helgen et al., 1998; Johnson et al., 1999; Kaiser, 1999a,b; Converse et al., 2000; Hoppe, 2000; Souder, 2000; Johnson et al., 2002; Kiesecker, 2002; Eaton-Poole et al., 2003; Johnson et al., 2003; Lannoo et al., 2003; McCallum and Trauth, 2003; Vandenlangenberg et al., 2003; Hoppe, 2005; NARCAM, 2010). These reports often documented populations in which greater than 10% and even up to 95% of amphibians suffered from severe limb malformations. Malformations primarily affected the limbs of recently emerged individuals, typically from lentic habitats such as ponds and lakes. Particularly troubling was evidence from museum-based and historical studies suggesting that, over the last several decades, malformations in amphibians have become more widespread, more severe, and often affect a higher proportion of individuals in a population than observed historically (Gray, 2000; Hoppe, 2000; Johnson et al., 2003; Johnson and Lunde, 2005).

Research conducted by academic groups as well as local, state and federal agencies has identified important causes of amphibian malformations. Although dozens of agents can potentially induce amphibian malformations in laboratory settings (reviewed by Ouellet, 2000; Stopper et al., 2002), four factors emerged as the most likely candidates to explain contemporary observations of limb abnormalities in wild populations: (1) pesticides, (2) UV-B radiation, (3) injury from predators, and (4) parasites (see reviews by Blaustein and Johnson, 2003; Sessions, 2003; Ankley et al., 2004; Johnson et al., 2010). Substantial progress has been made in understanding the role of these four causes in causing limb malformations in North American amphibians. Research conducted by the EPA, for example, argued against UV-B as a cause of deformities because elevated exposure resulted in bilaterally symmetric malformations, which are rare in natural populations (Ankley et al., 2004). Research on contaminants such as pesticides has suggested a linkage between abnormality levels and land use (e.g., Ouellet et al., 1997; Kiesecker, 2002; Taylor et al., 2005; Reeves et al., 2008; Reeves et al., 2010), yet no particular pesticide or chemical has been identified as a direct cause. Efforts are underway to identify potential compounds using field and laboratory experiments (e.g., Bridges et al., 2004). A series of recent studies have further revealed that aquatic predators can cause amphibian limb abnormalities, including missing and shortened limb abnormalities in Oregon, the Northeast, and Alaska (Ballengée and Sessions, 2009; Bowerman et al., 2010; Reeves et al., 2010).

One of the most well-studied recent causes of amphibian malformations is infection by the digenetic trematode, *Ribeiroia ondatrae*. Experimental exposures involving field-based levels of *Ribeiroia* infection cause skin webbings, bony triangles, partially- and completely-missing limbs, extra limbs, and otherwise abnormal limbs in frogs, toads, and salamanders (Johnson et al., 1999, 2001, 2006, 2008; Sessions et al., 1999; Kiesecker, 2002, Stopper et al., 2002, Schotthoefer et al., 2003). *Ribeiroia* infection has been linked to both contemporary and historical accounts of 'mass malformations' in naturally occurring amphibian populations, including Dr. Brunson's long-enigmatic Jette Pond in Montana (Kiesecker, 2002; Lannoo et al., 2003; Johnson et al., 2002, 2003, 2006; Sutherland, 2005; Johnson and Hartson, 2009). However, infection by this parasite cannot explain all types of malformations, nor is it present at all sites with large numbers of malformed amphibians. For example, *Ribeiroia* was not present at several sites with high levels of missing legged frogs in Minnesota (Lannoo et al., 2003; Lannoo, 2008), nor at any sites with malformations in Alaska (Reeves et al., 2008; Reeves et al., 2010). In addition to *Ribeiroia*, other parasites have been suggested or shown to cause morphological abnormalities in amphibians, including monogeneans (Rajakaruna et al., 2008), parasitic arthropods (Murphy, 1965; Kupferberg et al., 2009) and viruses (Ouellet, 2000).

Although our understanding of the amphibian malformation issue has progressed considerably over the past decade, a number of factors still hinder scientific advancement. First, field sampling methods differ substantially among research groups, preventing standardized comparisons across studies. Second, there have been few methodologically oriented papers that discuss approaches to sampling amphibians, and no paper to date has attempted to evaluate what lessons can be learned from various approaches or recommend overall guidelines for conducting large-scale malformation surveys. Third, field surveys have suffered from a lack of information regarding the expected baseline levels for malformation prevalence, limiting the ability of researchers to classify and identify which wetlands or regions are exhibiting unusual levels of abnormalities. Finally, there has been little discussion regarding what data are necessary to determine the causative agent(s) at sites with a large percentage of malformed amphibians or how to collect and analyze such data.

The purpose of this article is to provide background on amphibian malformations, critically examine survey methods and approaches to analysis to improve the detection of malformation types and rates in the field, and review the causes of malformations and consequences for amphibian decline. In particular, I describe the statistical tools necessary to classify sites with a higher than expected prevalence of abnormalities and discuss issues regarding sample size and site selection. I further discuss what data are required to evaluate the influence of potential causes by drawing upon example models from disease ecology and epidemiology. I outline field and laboratory protocols to examine populations of amphibians and snails for *Ribeiroia* parasites. Lastly, I discuss the need for integrated research to investigate malformation co-factors of and how malformations might contribute to amphibian declines. It is our hope that such information will allow researchers to better communicate with each other, facilitate broad scale meta-analyses, and investigate the issue in a rigorous and scientifically defensible manner.

I. A PRACTICAL GUIDE FOR FIELD SURVEYS OF MALFORMED AMPHIBIANS

Two major goals of this section are to make the study of amphibian malformations more accessible to scientists of diverse backgrounds and to develop more consistent methods by offering recommendations on how to sample amphibians and analyze the resulting data. To this end, I have synthesized information on field protocols and statistical techniques to establish an informed methodology for studying malformations and encourage new research to answer many pressing questions. Fundamental to this discussion is consistent use of terminology, which is based on Meteyer (2000), Johnson et al. (2001b), and USFWS (2008). In this paper, I use the term "abnormality" to refer to any deviation from normal morphology, independent of whether its origin was developmental or acquired after proper development (i.e., injury). I use "malformation" to refer to a deviation from normal morphology resulting from improper development, which might be due to teratogens, genetic anomalies, or developmental errors.

Amphibian populations with a high prevalence of limb abnormalities have also been reported historically and currently in regions beyond North America, including Eurasia (Rostand, 1949; Woitkewitsch, 1959; Dubois, 1979; Henle, 1981; Borkin and Pikulik, 1986; Veith and Viertel, 1993; Van Gelder and Strijbosch, 1995, Bohl, 1997), India (Gurushankara et al., 2007), Japan (Meyer-Rochow and Asashima, 1998), Bermuda (Bacon et al., 2006), and Australia (Tyler 1998; Spolyarich et al., 2011). Although, the methods, taxa, and wetland types discussed in this paper are designed to be most applicable for surveys in North America, the lessons and study goals apply to researchers in temperate and tropical regions.

How to Select Study Sites

Most malformation reports involve amphibian species with larvae that develop in ponds, streams, or lakes (Johnson et al., 2010). Wetlands reported to support the largest populations of malformed frogs tend to be small, lentic (still-water) habitats that are either anthropogenic in origin or heavily altered by human activity. For example, cattle ponds and farm ponds are common malformation hotspots in the western and midwestern USA, respectively (Johnson et al., 2002; Lannoo et al., 2003). As of 1999, amphibian abnormalities had been documented in 44 states (Kaiser, 1999b), suggesting malformation surveys are warranted in any region, state, or locality. Moreover, amphibian abnormalities have been documented in 71 species and the most commonly affected groups are frogs and toads (Lannoo, 2008).

Because of the diversity of sites and species involved, the sampling design used to include sites (e.g., wetlands, streams, ponds) in a malformation survey can influence what conclusions may be derived from the data. The majority of initial deformed frog surveys targeted wetlands with recent or historical reports of malformations (Sessions and Ruth, 1990; Gardiner and Hoppe, 1999; Johnson et al., 2002). Such targeted designs are likely to encounter a large number of sites with high levels of malformations and are thus useful to identify agents causing malformations, to determine which amphibian species are most susceptible to malformations and which malformation types are most common, or to examine the effects of malformations on amphibian population dynamics. Surveys targeting malformation sites can also incorporate a case-control design by pairing targeted sites to nearby wetlands with no known history of malformations (e.g., Johnson et al., 2002; Vandenlangenberg et al., 2003). Such a survey design allows for a comparison between malformation prevalence and levels of suspected causative agents between the two types of sites. A third type of survey design involves using a probabilistic design, in which sample sites are drawn from a larger, previously identified pool of suitable sites (Olsen and Peck, 2008). This design can be used to determine associations between malformations and factors such as ecoregion or land use (e.g., Schoff et al., 2003; Reeves et al., 2008). This same survey design can also be used to provide baseline data for future surveys to determine whether malformation levels are increasing over time. One weakness of a probabilistic design is that some selected wetlands may not support amphibians, and a large number of wetlands must be surveyed if only a small proportion are expected to have significant numbers of amphibian with malformations.

Which Species and Life Stage to Examine

Whether malformations are detected at a given wetland can be strongly influenced by what amphibian life stage and species are sampled. Abnormalities are most common in late stage larval- and recently metamorphosed amphibians, but nearly absent in adult populations (Johnson et al., 2010). It has been suggested that this difference results from reduced survivorship among the malformed metamorphic frogs, possibly from increased predation or inability to capture prey (Goodman and Johnson, in press). Therefore, among anurans (frogs and toads), targeted sampling at the metamorphic stage (just prior to or recently after metamorphosis) is optimal because: 1) it allows researchers to non-lethally inspect large sample sizes in the field and 2) all skeletal features have developed by metamorphosis, such that any external malformations will be visible. In contrast, inspection of abnormalities among anuran larvae is most reliably performed with a stereo dissection microscope, which requires either anesthetizing or euthanizing large number of individuals for transportation to a laboratory facility. Although field inspections of late-stage larvae (i.e., after Gosner (1960) stage 42) may be feasible for large species, this approach is likely to underreport small and early-stage abnormalities among small anurans. Furthermore, lab-held animals should not generally be returned to field sites without careful examination for pathogens acquired in captivity. If the target species is a salamander or newt, sampling near-metamorphic individuals is optimal because the limbs and digits have fully developed and capture success tends to be high. Adult amphibians should not be targeted for malformation surveys because: 1) they rarely exhibit malformations above baseline levels, even when 50% of the cohort's metamorphic frogs are malformed (See Dissertation Chapter 2); 2) the present location of an adult may not represent their natal pond or stream; and 3) collection of this life stage is likely to have the greatest impact on the amphibian populations.

Although field surveys may be designed to sample multiple species of amphibians per wetland, to facilitate comparisons among study sites and geographic regions, researchers can use a "focal amphibian species" or genus that is likely to be present across the range of a given monitoring program and is known to be affected with malformations. The focal species should be common, have a large geographic range, and be abundant when present. In the western United States, the Pacific Chorus Frog (*Pseudacris regilla*) fits these criteria (Rorabaugh and Lannoo, 2005). In addition, owing to their small size, *P. regilla* are easy to catch by hand, regardless of abnormality status, which limits sampling bias. In the midwestern and northeastern United States, the northern Leopard Frog (*Lithobates pipiens*) is an ideal focal species in light of its large geographic range, which includes a third of the United States as well as southern Canada (Rorabaugh, 2005). Monitoring of these focal taxa when present allows researchers to make valid statistical comparisons of malformation prevalence among sites and among studies. It is important to stress, however, that the suggestion to include a focal species is not an argument to study only these species. Certainly, studies are needed to document malformations among rarer species and those in decline.

How and When to Sample for Amphibian Malformations

The best methods for capturing amphibians depend on the species and life history stage of interest. Larval amphibians can be sampled using active sweeps with a dip net as documented in sampling guides (Heyer et al., 1994; Olson et al., 1997; Dodd, 2010). For metamorphic anurans, I recommend using species-specific, fixed time-transects, while recording the area covered and the estimated percentage capture efficiency to allow for density estimates and comparisons among observers. Toad metamorphs are often easily captured by hand while searching around the wetland shoreline or among cracks in the drying soil. Hylid and ranid frog metamorphs can be captured by hand or with a dip net along the shoreline. Although most species can be sampled during the day, some may be easier to capture at night with the aid of a headlamp.

During each transect, captured animals of the same species can be stored in a moistened Ziploc bag, plastic bucket, or pillow case. Care should be taken to ensure that animals do not become overcrowded or overheated, which will depend on the species being collected, the container size, and ambient temperatures. For small wetlands, all transects can be completed prior to inspections such that no animal is sampled twice. Recapture of the same individual is unlikely in larger wetlands (> 5 ha) where transects areas can be distributed along the shoreline. If infection by chytrid fungus (*Batrachochytrium dendrobatidis*) or another pathogen is of concern or if the targeted species is threatened, each individual should be inspected immediately using a clean pair of nitrile gloves to reduce the potential of disease transfer or handling stress. To prevent spread of disease and unintentional species introductions, all sampling equipment (nets, trays, waders) should be rigorously sterilized between sampling sites following established protocols, such as a 15 minute soak in 4% bleach solution (Speare et al., 2004).

How to Detect and Describe Abnormalities

There are many approaches to identifying morphological abnormalities in amphibians, including gross visual inspections (e.g., Ouellet et al., 1997), microscopy (e.g., Johnson et al., 2001b; Johnson et al., 2002), radiographs of skeletal structure (Meteyer et al., 2000; Lannoo et al., 2003), clearing and staining to visualize skeletal structure (methods described in Dingerkus and Uhler, 1977; Kelly and Bryden, 1983) (e.g., Sessions and Ruth, 1990; Kiesecker, 2002), dissections to inspect internal organs, and histology (e.g., Hayes et al., 2002). The choice of one or more of these methods will depend on the study objective. Overall, limb abnormalities have been the most common class of amphibian abnormality reported in the United States (Blaustein and Johnson, 2003; Ankley et al., 2004; Johnson et al., 2010). Therefore, I discuss approaches to best identify, describe, and quantify limb abnormalities.

I advocate using visual field inspections to identify limb abnormalities because they: 1) allow researchers to sample and release amphibians in a non-lethal manner; 2) are inexpensive; and 3) provide immediate feedback to the researcher regarding abnormality status at the site. Although field-based inspections may miss internal and perhaps some minor external abnormalities, common limb abnormalities can often be observed with the naked eye and described in the field (USFWS, 2008). Laboratory-based techniques, such as those requiring stereo dissection microscope examination, radiography, or clearing and staining, can be used on previously identified abnormal amphibians to more thoroughly describe the bone or tissue abnormalities (Lannoo, 2008; Green et al., 2010). The use of laboratory-based inspection methods to determine the proportion of abnormal amphibians, however, has the disadvantage of requiring euthanasia of each inspected individual.

For every metamorphic amphibian examined, each limb and digit should be carefully inspected and examined for overall symmetry, and then describing or photographing each abnormality in the field. Some abnormalities (e.g., skin webbings) are only visible when limbs are manually extended. It is important to handle the animal gently, keep one's hands or gloves moist while inspecting and ensuring that animals do not overheat on warm days. A detailed discussion of abnormality classification systems and terminology is beyond the scope of this paper, but can be found in articles by Johnson et al. (2001b), Meteyer (2000), Meteyer et al. (2000), and especially in USFWS (2008).

A given individual may suffer from more than one abnormality, which has been termed abnormality severity, and calculated by summing the number of abnormalities on each abnormal amphibian (detailed in Johnson et al., 2001b). One bias of this scoring system is that it weights extra limbs heavier than missing limbs; for instance, frogs with up to eight extra limbs have been observed yet an individual can only be missing up to four limbs. Similarly, it is unlikely that a single missing digit is as severe as a completely missing limb, yet each are scored as one abnormality. This simple severity index could be improved by incorporating the degree to which each abnormality type limits locomotion, increases risk of predation, or affects overall survival, when such data become available.

How Many Malformations are Expected in a Population

One of the most important challenges in studying amphibian abnormalities is determining whether observed malformations are outside the realm of what is expected in a given population. To draw a parallel with epidemiology, this is analogous to differentiating between 'endemic' (or expected) and 'epidemic' levels of a given disease. Such a dichotomous classification scheme involves determining whether the prevalence of abnormalities (total number of abnormal frogs / total number of frogs inspected) is within or greater than the expected baseline range. However, how the expected proportion of abnormal frogs in a population is defined can strongly influence data analyses and conclusions, especially when evaluating evidence of causation or whether malformations are increasing over time.

All populations of organisms can be expected to exhibit some morphological abnormalities resulting from genetic defects, developmental problems, and trauma. For example, in epidemiology, researchers determine whether a disease is above expected levels by comparing the disease prevalence in a given population to the endemic (background) levels (Merrill, 2009). If the disease prevalence is significantly greater than expected, it is classified as an "epidemic" in humans or an "epizootic" in animals (Merrill, 2009). I advocate using the same approach to determine whether an amphibian population exhibits an unusually high prevalence of abnormalities. However, such a comparison requires knowledge of the expected or baseline abnormality prevalence for amphibians. In humans, for example, survey data of more than 1 million births have found the expected baseline level of congenital (at birth) limb malformations is 0.06–0.07% (Froster-Iskenius and Baird, 1989; McGuirk et al., 2001) and around 3% for overall birth defects (CDC, 2006)

Currently, the preponderance of data indicate that the expected morphological abnormality prevalence in recently metamorphosed anurans ranges between 2 and 5%, likely with some variation by geographic region and species under study (Table 1.1). For example, 21 reference ponds in the western United States had an average abnormality prevalence for *P. regilla* of 2.4% (data from Johnson et al., 2002). Large-scale field surveys across the United States and Canada have identified similar mean abnormality levels ranging from 0.3% to 4.3% (Table 1.1). In a review, Ouellet (2000) estimated baseline malformation prevalence between 0 and 2% based on a field studies with large sample sizes. One challenge in determining an unbiased baseline is that surveys across land use gradients will inevitably include some sites that are highly altered by agriculture, urbanization, or other anthropogenic stressors. These sites, therefore, may not be representative of the least-disturbed or reference wetland conditions. Further, differences in focal species, life stage, malformation classification system and malformation scope (e.g., all morphology or only limb morphology) hinders the comparison across regions and species.

The US Fish and Wildlife Service recently reported results from a 10-year survey of amphibian abnormalities across the nation using standardized monitoring of wetlands on National Wildlife Refuges (USFWS 2011). The USFWS survey sampled more than 70,000 anurans representing 672 wetlands, 37 species and 45 states. This dataset represents the best available source of information to evaluate regional estimates of baseline malformation prevalence and to identify local areas or wetlands that exceed this baseline (see USFWS, 2008, 2011; Reeves et al., 2008). This study identified a nation-wide morphological abnormality prevalence of skeletal abnormalities averaging 3.3% (95% CI: 3.0–3.6) (Fig. 1.1). The major types of skeletal abnormalities observed in this study were ectromelia (missing part of a limb, 11.3%), brachydactyly (short digit, 9.1%), and ectrodactyly (missing digit, 4.8%) (USFWS, 2011). These data suggest that populations with significantly more abnormalities than this should be considered above-baseline. Yet, because of the variability in expected abnormality prevalence in the national survey by USFWS and other published studies as well as a lack of information as to how this figure might vary by species, I suggest a conservative threshold of 5% (70th percentile) as a standard or expected baseline prevalence for limb malformations. Using the upper end of the observed prevalence range will reduce the risk of over-classifying epidemic sites and focus attention on the most impacted wetlands. It would be reasonable to modify the expected baseline level for a given survey based on locally derived species-specific data.

<u>How to Determine Whether a Population Exhibits Above-baseline Levels of Malformations</u>

Continuing to adapt epidemiological methods to the amphibian malformation issue, I suggest that a statistical approach should be used to determine whether the sampled abnormality prevalence is greater than the established baseline prevalence (e.g., 5%). Statistical tests are necessary for this comparison because researchers are inferring population-level data (i.e., assuming abnormality prevalence for all individuals at the entire wetland) based on a small subsample of those amphibians (i.e., the number of individuals inspected). As a result of the dichotomous nature of the data (i.e., abnormal or normal), statistical confidence intervals around the prevalence estimate follow a binomial distribution (Zar, 1999). Therefore, a Fisher's exact test, Chi-squared test, or G-test can provide estimates of whether the observed malformation prevalence is significantly greater than the expected baseline range (Zar, 1999). If the lower 95% confidence interval exceeds 5%, then the observed amphibian sample has a higher-than-baseline prevalence and further investigations may be warranted to determine a site-specific cause. This is not to say that all wetlands with > 5% abnormalities are necessarily a "problem" or that all of those with < 5% are "healthy," but it does provide a well-defined, null hypothesis framework from which to build upon.

The term "hotspot" has been used in the scientific literature and common media to describe wetlands with high abnormality prevalence. However, an exact prevalence, or even range of prevalence, has yet to be associated with this term. A hotspot site should have an uncommonly high abnormality prevalence (e.g., 95th percentile among all populations) and amphibians that exhibit severe malformation types likely to reduce survivorship, such as completely missing or extra limbs. Based on the standardized monitoring of National Wildlife

Refuges across the United States, 5% of the sample events (95th percentile) had an abnormality prevalence of 8.1% or higher (Fig. 1.1). Because the 8.1% prevalence estimate is based solely on skeletal abnormalities, I recommend 10% as a conservative threshold to help classify sites with overall elevated abnormality prevalence levels as hotspots. Similar to comparisons to baseline, statistical comparisons can be used to determine if an observed prevalence significantly exceeds 10%. Classification of amphibian populations at wetlands into either above-baseline or hotspot categories using statistical criteria will help focus the requisite research attention on the wetlands and amphibians most affected by this phenomenon.

Issues with Malformation Prevalence: Sample Size, Statistical Confidence, and Bias

Abnormality prevalence, calculated at each site and from each species, is a valuable and important parameter to collect during a field study. Sample size plays a pivotal role in determining the confidence of estimate, whereby increasing sample size reduces uncertainty in the prevalence estimates. Relationships among sample size, malformation prevalence, and the probability of determining difference from baseline (i.e., statistical power) are illustrated in Fig. 1.2. A sample size of 100 amphibians, for example, shows a significant ($\alpha = 0.05$) statistical comparison to the baseline level (> 5%) when the sampled malformation prevalence is 11% or greater, and a prevalence of less than 11% would require a larger sample size to be significantly above 5%. In contrast, if only 30 amphibians are sampled, the sampled malformation prevalence must be 17% or greater to be statistically different from 5%. The same statistical tests can also be used to look for differences in malformation prevalence over time or to make comparisons among sites. In such comparisons, however, the data need to be from the same species and life stage, and may require sample sizes larger than 100 if looking for small effect sizes.

For malformation prevalence data to be useful, they must be collected and analyzed at the relevant spatial scale, which is at the individual wetland, pond, or lake. Maintaining site-specific data is crucial to successfully discovering which sites have higher-than-baseline abnormality prevalence and identifying the cause(s) of the abnormalities at such sites. Datasets in which field observations from numerous sites have been combined together will fail to identify problematic sites and their causes. For example, if a regional survey sampling 100 frogs per wetland discovered one pond with 30% prevalence and nine with 1% but proceeded to combine all the data together, the overall prevalence would be 3.9%, which is close to the expected baseline. Thus, the one hotspot and the chance to screen potential causes at that site would be missed.

Independent of statistical power, malformation prevalence can be influenced by sampling bias, potentially leading to inaccurate estimates. For example, field researchers may catch malformed frogs more easily compared to normal frogs, thereby unwittingly inflating the prevalence estimate. Alternatively, malformed frogs might be selectively removed by natural predators prior to the sampling event; thus, the current population of malformed individuals would be an underestimate of the true prevalence. These challenges have caused some researchers to suggest that potential errors in estimating malformation prevalence render this statistic useless (e.g., Lannoo, 2008). However, malformation prevalence is the critical piece of data to determine whether a site has higher-than-expected numbers of malformations and, correspondingly, if there is in fact a problem at a wetland or within a region. Therefore, researchers can take solace in that many of these potential biases could cancel each other out, because some would lead to over estimates of prevalence while others would lead to underestimates. Sample bias can be reduced by visually identifying an amphibian to capture and following through with capturing that individual before repeating the process again.

II. DETERMINING THE CAUSES OF AMPHIBIAN ABNORMALITIES

Conclusively establishing that an agent (parasite, pesticide, predator, or other factor) is the proximate cause (etiologic agent) of observed abnormalities at a wetland necessitates conducting an experiment in which the hypothesized factor is experimentally removed from all or part of the wetland. Researchers have successfully conducted in-situ field studies to determine the major cause of malformations for *Ribeiroia* exposure (Kiesecker, 2002; See Dissertation Chapter 2), as well as abnormalities resulting from stickleback fish predators (Bowerman et al., 2010). However, this work often takes years to complete at a single wetland and is too time consuming and expensive to be conducted at the many sites with above-baseline abnormality prevalence. Further, simple exclosure or removal studies cannot be easily used to test for interactions among agents. Because of these limitations, I recommend adapting tools from disease ecology to best determine causation on a site-by-site basis.

Use of Multiple Lines of Evidence

The use of 'causal inference' is a valuable approach to investigate direct causes and indirect drivers of disease emergence (Plowright et al., 2008). Causal inference relies on using multiple tools (i.e., field correlations, long-term monitoring, causal diagrams, statistical modeling, dose-response relationships, nested field and laboratory experiments) to investigate complex interactions between ecological drivers and disease emergence. This approach is accomplished by using multiple lines of evidence to support causal relationships as opposed to experiments designed to test only a single hypothesis. Such research is best done through interdisciplinary cooperation, especially with an issue as complex as amphibian malformations, and should involve a combination of field and laboratory-based studies of developmental biology, herpetology, toxicology, physiology, and disease ecology. The adaptation of causal inference to determine the influence of a potential agent as the cause of malformations should include at minimum: 1) detection of the agent at an affected site at or above levels shown to induce malformations in laboratory settings, 2) experimental studies that demonstrate the candidate agent can cause similar types and frequencies of abnormalities in relevant amphibian species, and 3) an association between the presence and/or abundance of the agent in nature and the occurrence of such malformations.

Interpretation of Dose-response Relationships

The first step of determining causation is detecting the potential abnormality-inducing agent (whether chemical, fish, parasite, or other) at similar levels that have been shown to cause abnormalities or malformations in experimental studies. Such information may rely on dose-response relationships from laboratory studies or from field experiments (e.g., Johnson et al., 1999). It is important to consider, however, that dose response relationships for a single agent will vary depending on the amphibian species, as is the case for *Ribeiroia* infection (Johnson et al., 2010). Further, laboratory-based results do not always 'scale-up' to the ecosystem level due to the simplicity required in laboratory experiments versus the complexity found in nature. For example, pesticide exposure can sometimes weaken immune responses in frogs, increasing infection by trematode parasites (Kiesecker, 2002; Rohr et al., 2008a, b). In addition, field exposures to teratogens (agents that cause malformations) may occur at different times in larval development, especially if multiple species are present at the wetland. *Ribeiroia*, for example, only induces limb malformations during particular stages of limb development (Schotthoefer et al., 2003; Johnson et al. 2011). Thus, if the majority of a populations' parasite infection occurred in later stages, the site will appear below the typical dose-response curve.

Comparison of Malformation Compositions

Given that multiple factors cause amphibian abnormalities in nature, and it is not typically feasible to conduct intensive field experiments at the many wetlands with above-baseline levels of abnormalities, there is a desire to differentiate among causes using field-derived malformation data. Thus far, researchers have used the types of abnormalities observed to infer causative agents among sites, similar to classifying diagnostic signatures for human diseases. For instance, Sessions et al. (1999) provided evidence that the type of limb duplication observed (proximal-distal axis vs. anterior-posterior axis) could be used to differentiate between exposure to retinoids or mechanical perturbation, respectively. Such precise diagnostics, however, are often difficult to apply to amphibian abnormalities because a single agent can produce multiple classes or types of abnormalities (e.g., *Ribeiroia* produces both extra and missing limbs in larval amphibians), and a single malformation type can be produced by multiple agents. Partially missing limbs (hemimelia), for example, can be caused by aquatic predators (Ballengée and Sessions, 2009; Bowerman et al., 2010), UV-B exposure (Ankley et al., 2000), and parasites (Johnson et al. 1999, 2001a, 2006). Thus, the presence of an individual malformation type is unlikely to be diagnostic of the factor that caused them in nature.

Nevertheless, the relative proportion of malformation types can be used to help determine the etiology or cause of the malformations when a causative agent is known to be present, particularly when there are experimental data illustrating the malformation response resulting from specific factors. For example, predators generally cause partially missing hind limbs or missing feet (Ballengée and Sessions, 2009; Bowerman et al., 2010). Likewise, UV-B radiation caused predominantly missing limbs, but often in a bilaterally symmetric pattern (Ankley et al., 2000). In the case of *Ribeiroia* exposure, the types of malformations can vary among amphibian species. For example, Pacific Chorus Frogs exposed to *Ribeiroia* experimentally develop an average of 55% extra hind limbs and 20% missing limbs (Johnson et al., 1999). In Leopard Frogs (*L. pipiens*), the malformation response to *Ribeiroia* was also exclusive to hind limbs, but was mostly extra digits (25.6%) and extra hind limbs (22.2%) (Schotthoefer et al., 2003). In contrast, *Ribeiroia* exposure in Western Toads (*Anaxyrus boreas*) induced some fore limb malformations (8%), and among both *A. boreas* and American Toads (*A. americanus*) *Ribeiroia* caused predominantly skin webbings (34.4%), whereas extra limbs were less common (16%) (Johnson et al., 2001a; Johnson and Hartson, 2009).

The relative frequency of malformation types (malformation signature) is valuable data to establish causality at a site with above-baseline levels of malformations. When a sufficient number of malformed amphibians are detected at a wetland, generally 15-30 individuals, the species-specific malformation signature may be compared statistically to laboratory results or field experiments with specific causal agents (e.g., parasites, chemicals, etc.). Statistical comparisons provide a transparent and unbiased tool to determine if the types of malformations observed match a potential cause that is present at the wetland and is a substantial improvement from just comparing whether extra or missing limbs are found. Useful statistical tests for this comparison include quantitative similarity indices such as percent similarity or Bray-Curtis D (Boyle et al., 1990; Johnson et al., 2002). For example, malformation composition among *P. regilla* frogs at wetlands with *Ribeiroia* had a 70% similarity value when compared to results from experimental studies (Johnson et al., 2002). In contrast, similarities of < 21% were observed when comparing *Ribeiroia* induced malformations and abnormality composition among anurans at sites without *Ribeiroia* (Johnson et al., 2002).

Although similarity indices and other statistical tools could be promising approaches for helping to identify or potentially eliminate hypothesized causes, there are limitations to this approach. For example, background abnormalities (i.e., genetic, developmental) are present at all sites and could obscure this type of analysis. As discussed previously, malformation type may vary in response to dose and timing of exposure (Schotthoefer et al., 2003). Additionally, the approach requires species-specific response data for each agent and, unfortunately, laboratory-based malformation signatures for multiple species are not available for most malformation causes. Without such data, researchers may assume similar tendencies within genera or even family. Yet this needs to be done with caution as different genera within the same family have shown strong differences in response to *Ribeiroia* infection (Johnson and Hartson, 2009). In agreement with Ankley et al. (2004), I recommend that laboratory tests for dose-response or malformation models utilize affected native amphibian species and recommend against using *Xenopus laevis*, an amphibian native to Africa, considering that *Ribeiroia* infection and pesticides are known to have species-specific effects (Degitz et al., 2000).

III. METHODS TO SCREEN FOR TREMATODE (*RIBEIROIA ONDATRAE*) PRESENCE AND ABUNDANCE

As a detailed case example, I offer a description of how to find and identify one of the most well-studied causes of limb malformations: infection by the trematode *Ribeiroia ondatrae*. Unlike many factors implicated in amphibian malformations, *Ribeiroia* can be quickly assessed for presence and abundance using inexpensive tools available in most laboratories, making it an ideal candidate for a rapid screening procedure at sites with above-baseline malformations. If *Ribeiroia* metacercariae (the encysted stage of the parasite) are found in amphibian hosts at abundances known to induce malformations in laboratory studies, then relative malformation composition (malformation signature) for each affected species can be compared to the malformation response identified in laboratory studies and the role of the parasite as a causal agent can be evaluated. If, however, *Ribeiroia* is present only at very low infection intensities (e.g., 1–2 metacercariae cysts detected per frog) and the malformation signature differs substantially from laboratory studies, then it is probable that another factor is causing the majority of the malformations (see Kupferberg et al., 2009; Bowerman et al., 2010).

In this manner, the presence or absence of *Ribeiroia* infection at a given site can be extremely informative. However, adequate screening for *Ribeiroia* requires a background in the parasite's life history. *Ribeiroia* is a multi-host parasite, using aquatic snails as first intermediate hosts, amphibians as second intermediate hosts, and birds or mammals as definitive hosts (Johnson and McKenzie, 2008). Infected snail hosts produce cercariae, which are a free-swimming stage of the parasite infectious to larval amphibians. Because infection prevalence is generally much higher in amphibian hosts (50-100%) compared to snail hosts (1 to 5%) at the same sites, I suggest using amphibian hosts to screen for *Ribeiroia* presence and to use infection intensity in amphibians as a measure of the average parasite abundance (see below). Snail intermediate hosts can be useful for quantifying host-parasite dynamics but they require more time intensive field and laboratory methods. However, if the amphibian species under study is threatened, examination of snail hosts may provide a superior alternative.

Finding and Identifying *Ribeiroia* in Amphibians

Inspections for *Ribeiroia* should be conducted on the same species and life history stage as surveyed for malformation prevalence. Once again, metamorphic amphibians are the best indicator for several reasons: they are seasonally abundant; the removal of this life stage has reduced population impacts compared to adults; they are cumulative indicators of parasite exposure over the course of their larval periods; and they are very likely to be present at their natal pond. Larval anurans might be preferentially sampled if two wetlands are close and metamorphs may easily travel between sites or if studying larvae that take more than one season to develop, such as the Green Frog (*Lithobates clamitans*), or American Bullfrog (*L. catesbeianus*). When *Ribeiroia* is present at levels that can cause malformations, infection prevalence often approaches 50–90%, such that nearly every frog necropsied will be infected and parasite detectability is very high (Fig. 1.3a). However, when infection prevalence is extremely low, for instance in < 20% of the amphibians, a sample size of > 15 frogs is required to have a > 95% probability of detecting the parasite in at least one frog (Fig. 1.3b). For this reason, dissection of 10–15 frogs helps to limit the likelihood of missing *Ribeiroia* when it is present to less than 5% in most cases. *Ribeiroia* intensity (# cysts/infected individual) or abundance (# cysts/individuals dissected) has adequate 95% confidence limits for most statistical comparisons when 15 to 20 amphibians are dissected (Fig. 1.3c), but a researcher's optimal sample size will depend on the expected difference in infection abundance and variance within the specific population (Bush et al., 1997).

To document the occurrence and abundance of *Ribeiroia*, amphibians should be dissected following standardized parasitological procedures. The most reliable method of identifying *Ribeiroia* involves dissecting a recently euthanized host, identifying live parasites via microscopy, and viewing the esophageal diverticula of *Ribeiroia*, which is the diagnostic feature for this species, with a compound microscope (Fig. 1.4) (Beaver, 1939; Yamaguti, 1971; Schell, 1985; Stopper et al., 2002; Johnson et al., 2004; Sutherland 2005; Szuroczki and Richardson, 2009). *Ribeiroia* metacercariae are generally found just under the host skin and above the skeletal muscles around limb structures, tail resorption sites in anurans, and the lower mandible (Sutherland, 2005). Cysts are 300–350 μm in size, appear clear or brownish when melanized, and can be isolated using fine-tipped forceps (Johnson et al., 2004). Cysts can be identified as *Ribeiroia* or other species on a compound scope after breaking the cysts wall by gently tapping on the cover slip (Fig. 1.4). Detailed identification methods for *Ribeiroia* are described in other publications (Johnson et al., 2004; Sutherland, 2005; Szuroczki and Richardson, 2009).

The clearing and staining technique developed to visualize bones through skin and organs (e.g., Sessions and Ruth, 1990; Kiesecker, 2002) can be helpful in quantifying trematode parasite infection but will not always reliably allow for definitive identification of encysted parasites, of which there can be 10 or more species within a single amphibian host. Lentic amphibians are commonly infected with many species of digenetic trematode with cysts found under the skin such as *Alaria* spp., *Fibricola* spp., and *Manodistomum syntomentera* (Sutherland, 2005), yet thus far only *Ribeiroia* is known to cause limb malformations in North America (but see Rajakaruna et al., 2008). Moreover, examination of all cysts from multiple species in aggregate is likely to obscure relevant trends related to *Ribeiroia* because each parasite species utilizes different snail and definitive hosts.

Finding and Identifying *Ribeiroia* in Aquatic Snails

Compared to amphibians, determination of the presence of *Ribeiroia* in aquatic snail hosts is more difficult owing to low infection prevalence in first intermediate hosts. For example, at a seasonal pond in Mendocino County, California, a 1% *Ribeiroia* infection prevalence among rams horn (*Planorbella tenuis*) snails caused a 50% malformation prevalence among Pacific Chorus Frogs (*P. regilla*) (See Dissertation Chapter 2). Every single frog was infected (100% infection prevalence) with at least 36 metacercariae and an average infection intensity of 70 cysts. Detecting *Ribeiroia* in snail hosts is difficult and likely to produce false negatives (missing it when it is present) owing to the low infection prevalence compared to frogs. A random sample of 100 snails collected from this pond has a ~40% chance of failing to yield an infected host. If 200 snails are sampled, this false negative rate drops to 13.4%. A sample size of 300 snails is required to limit the false error rate to a level of 5%. This example illustrates why snails are less effective indicators of *Ribeiroia* presence compared to amphibian hosts.

Thus far, 12 species of snails worldwide and 7 in North America are known to support infection by *Ribeiroia*, all of which are within the family Planorbidae, a group commonly referred to as the 'rams horn' snails, and within three common genera *Helisoma*, *Planorbella*, or *Biomphalaria* (Fig. 1.5a; Johnson et al., 2004; Johnson and McKenzie, 2008). When snails are abundant, a quick search of the shoreline can often yield evidence of living snails or shells that can be identified to family or perhaps genus (Clarke, 1981; Burch, 1989; Dillon, 2000). However, exhaustive searching of snails along the shoreline and in the water can sometimes fail to detect the presence of snail hosts when present at low densities (Johnson et al., 2002). Therefore, an absence of the appropriate snail hosts from a single sample event should not be taken as proof of absence for these snail species nor for absence of *Ribeiroia*.

Quantifying infection prevalence among snail hosts is an important factor affecting *Ribeiroia* abundance and often requires intensive laboratory methods to estimate. The first step is to determine snail density at the wetland using replicated, fixed-area measurements within the littoral (shallow) zone of the lake, pond, or wetland. This can be done using a standard-sized dip net (net mesh 0.5–2 mm) or a trashcan with the bottom removed. All or a random subset of snails from these collections can then be screened for infection to find the number patent (cercariae-releasing) snails, followed by dissection of the remaining snails to determine the number of pre-patent or immature infections (Schell, 1985). Identification of patent infections is best accomplished by isolating individual snails into small containers (e.g., 50-ml vials or small cups) filled with filtered pond water or commercial spring water. Many trematodes emerge during the day but *Ribeiroia* is released at night, such that a full 24-hour cycle is necessary to estimate daily production per snail. Patent infection status of each snail can be assayed by looking for free-swimming cercariae which appear white against a dark background, a process that can be aided by using a strong overhead light source and a black backdrop. If cercariae are discovered in a vial, 3 to 4 can be pipetted onto a microscope slide and identified with a compound microscope using a larval identification key such as Schell (1985). *Ribeiroia* cercariae lack collar spines but possess esophageal diverticla (Fig. 1.5d; Stopper et al., 2002; Johnson et al., 2004; Szuroczki and Richardson, 2009). Staining of the cercariae with simple stains such as methylene blue can facilitate identification (see Szuroczki and Richardson, 2009).

Snails that do not 'shed' cercariae can be dissected by crushing the snails with pliers and using forceps to tease apart the gonad region (the end deepest inside the shell) to look for rediae, sporocysts, or immature cercariae, any of which can be used to document a pre-patent infection status (Fig. 1.5; Rohr et al., 2009). Although most cercariae in North America are not directly infectious to people, some can cause itching and irritation and researchers are advised to wear gloves and protective eyewear during dissections of snails or amphibians. With immature infections, it is rarely possible to determine if the parasite is in fact *Ribeiroia* or another morphologically similar parasite such as the common trematode *Echinostoma* spp. Molecular methods are needed for identification in these cases (Reinitz et al., 2007).

IV. CONCLUSIONS AND FUTURE RESEARCH

In this paper, I have presented the tools and information necessary to adequately design and conduct malformations surveys. Despite the growing body of knowledge regarding amphibian malformations and identified causes, many pressing questions remain. I highlight two pressing topics within the field of amphibian malformation study.

Identifying Important Causes of Malformations in Amphibian Populations

Although a number of malformation hotspot sites across the US have been associated with *Ribeiroia* infection, some wetlands with substantial numbers of malformations fail to support the trematode (Lannoo et al., 2003; Reeves et al., 2008). These sites are important places to discover the specific cause(s) of the malformations. Moreover, because the proximate cause of malformations often occurs in combination with other stressors, there is a need to examine additive or synergistic interactions between different factors. For example, exposure to *Ribeiroia* infection may occur alongside threats from chemical pollution, predators, or other pathogens, each of which have the potential to cause greater losses in amphibian populations (Koprivnikar et al., 2007; Rohr et al., 2008a, b). Kiesecker (2002), for example, found that experimental exposure to pesticides (Atrazine, Malathion, Esfenvalerate) reduced immune function that resulted in a three-fold increase in *Ribeiroia* infection in Wood Frog larvae (*Lithobates sylvatica*). Thiemann and Wassersug (2000) reported that the presence of predators significantly increased trematode infection in larval amphibians. *Ribeiroia* commonly occurs in ponds with dragonfly nymphs and fish predators (Ballengée and Sessions, 2009; Bowerman et al., 2010), highlighting that multiple agents can also act on the same amphibian species simultaneously.

Examining Conservation Implications Resulting from Malformations

Amphibian populations and species are in decline worldwide and understanding whether malformations have the potential to contribute to ongoing declines is an important research priority. Declines have been attributed to habitat loss, invasive species, and emerging diseases such as amphibian chytridiomycosis (reviewed in Stuart et al., 2004; Skerratt et al., 2007; Wake and Vredenburg, 2008). However, no study has directly examined whether malformations pose a threat to amphibian populations, and this absence of evidence should not be taken as evidence that there is no connection. Multiple lines of evidence suggest that malformations have the potential to contribute to amphibian declines in areas were they are widespread. First, malformations impair the ability of frogs to jump, swim, and obtain food, and malformed frogs in nature exhibit 22% lower survival than normal conspecifics (Goodman and Johnson, in press). Correspondingly, malformations are extremely rare in adult amphibians ($< 5\%$), even when abundant ($> 50\%$) in larval or metamorphic animals from the same wetland (Johnson et al., 1999; See Dissertation Chapter 2). Second, metamorphic amphibians with malformations may represent only a fraction of parasite-caused mortality with far more individuals dying as larvae, which is difficult to observe. Exposure to *Ribeiroia* is highly pathogenic and frequently causes substantial mortality in experimental studies (Johnson et al. 1999, 2001a, 2008; Stopper et al., 2002; Schotthoefer et al., 2003), and dead or dying tadpoles with hemorrhagic limb tissue characteristic of parasite exposure have frequently been observed at malformation hotspots. Thus, the total mortality as a consequence of *Ribeiroia* exposure, including direct death following infection and indirect losses associated with malformations, will be greater than the proportion of metamorphic frogs or toads that are malformed. Considering that species of amphibians declined or disappeared from Midwestern and western malformation hotpots (Hoppe, 2002; Vandenlangenberg et al., 2003), I, along with others (e.g., Sessions, 2003), suggest that malformed amphibians represent a valid conservation issue. In particular, malformations found in rare or endangered species or in populations already threatened by other factors such as habitat loss, invasive species, and *Bd* infection, represent the greatest concern.

ACKNOWLEDGMENTS

I thank V. Resh and T. Grantham for reviewing previous drafts of the manuscript and providing valuable insight. For use of data collected by the USFWS National Wildlife Refuge survey, I thank C. Lydick, S. Morey, F. Pinkney, S. Krest, M. Reeves, S. Millsap, K. Dickerson, J. Bettaso, J. Haas, R. Brinkley, L. Wellman, J. Hemming, K. Munney, K. Nguyen, G. Masson, and R. McWilliams. B. LaFonte assisted with photography. I acknowledge support from National Science Foundation Graduate Research Fellowship Program and the Environmental Protection Agency STAR Fellowship.

LITERATURE CITED

ANDERSON, M. E. 1977. Aspects of the Ecology of Two Sympatric Species of *Thamnophis* and Heavy Metal Accumulation within the Species. Unpubl. M.S. Thesis. University of Montana, Missoula.

ANKLEY, G. T., J. E. TIETGE, G. W. HOLCOMBE, D. L. DEFOE, S. A. DIAMOND, K. M. JENSEN, AND S. J. DEGITZ. 2000. Effects of laboratory ultraviolet radiation and natural sunlight on survival and development of *Rana pipiens*. Canadian Journal of Zoology 78:1092–1100.

ANKLEY, G. T., S. J. DEGITZ, S. A. DIAMOND, AND J. E. TIETGE. 2004. Assessment of environmental stressors potentially responsible for malformations in North American anuran amphibians. Ecotoxicology and Environmental Safety 58:7–16.

BACON, J. P., D. W. LINZEY, R. L. ROGERS, AND D. J. FORT. 2006. Deformities in cane toad (*Bufo marinus*) populations in Bermuda: Part I. frequencies and distribution of abnormalities. Applied Herpetology 3:39–65.

BALLENGÉE, B., AND S. K. SESSIONS. 2009. Explanation for missing limbs in deformed amphibians. Journal of Experimental Zoology Part B: Molecular and Developmental Evolution 312B:770–779.

BEAVER, P. C. 1939. The morphology and life history of *Psilostomum ondatrae* Price 1931 (Trematoda: Psilostomatidae). The Journal of Parasitology 25:383-393.

BLAUSTEIN, A. R., AND P. T. JOHNSON. 2003. The complexity of deformed amphibians. Frontiers in Ecology and the Environment 1:87–94.

BOHL, E. 1997. Limb deformities of amphibian larvae in Aufsess (Upper Franconia): Attempt to determine causes. Munich Contributions to Wastewater Fishery and River Biology 50:160–189.

BOWERMAN, J., P. T. J. JOHNSON, AND T. BOWERMAN. 2010. Sublethal predators and their injured prey: linking aquatic predators and severe limb abnormalities in amphibians. Ecology 91:242–251.

BORKIN, L. J., AND M. M. PIKULIK. 1986. The occurrence of polymely and polydactyl in natural populations of anurans of the USSR. Amphibia-Reptilia 7:205–216.

BOYLE, T. P., G. M. SMILLIE, J. C. ANDERSON, AND D. R. BEESON. 1990. A sensitivity analysis of 9 diversity and 7 similarity indexes. Research Journal of the Water Pollution Control Federation 62:749–762.

BRIDGES, C., E. LITTLE, D. GARDINER, J. PETTY, AND J. HUCKINS. 2004. Assessing the toxicity and teratogenicity of pond water in north-central Minnesota to amphibians. Environmental Science and Pollution Research 11:233–239.

BURCH, J. B. 1989. North American Freshwater Snails. Malacological Publications, Hamburg, Michigan.

BUSH, A. O., K. D. LAFFERTY, J. M. LOTZ, AND A. W. SHOSTAK. 1997. Parasitology meets ecology on its own terms: Margolis et al revisited. Journal of Parasitology 83:575–583.

CDC (CENTERS FOR DISEASE CONTROL AND PREVENTION). 2006. Improved national prevalence estimates for 18 selected major birth defects-United States, 1999–2001. MMWR Morbidity Mortality Weekly Reports 54:1301–1305.

CLARKE, A. H. 1981. The Freshwater Molluscs of Canada. National Museum of Natural Sciences, National Museums of Canada, Ottawa, Canada.

CONVERSE, K. A., J. MATTSSON, AND L. EATON-POOLE. 2000. Field surveys of Midwestern and Northeastern fish and wildlife service lands for the presence of abnormal frogs and toads. Journal of the Iowa Academy of Science 107:160–167.

DEGITZ, S. J., P. A. KOSIAN, E. A. MAKYNEN, K. M. JENSEN, AND G. T. ANKLEY. 2000. Stage- and species-specific developmental toxicity of all-trans retinoic acid in four native North American ranids and *Xenopus laevis*. Toxicological Sciences 57:264–274.

DILLON, R. T. 2000. The Ecology of Freshwater Molluscs. Cambridge University Press, Cambridge, United Kingdom.

DINGERKUS, G., AND L. D. UHLER. 1977. Enzyme clearing of Alcian Blue stained whole small vertebrates for demonstration of cartilage. Stain Technology 52:229–232.

DODD, C. K. 2010. Amphibian Ecology and Conservation: A Handbook of Techniques. Oxford University Press, Oxford, United Kingdom.

DUBOIS, A. 1979. Anomalies and mutations in natural populations of the *Rana* 'esculenta' complex (Amphibia, Anura). Mitteilungen aus dem Zoologischen Museum in Berlin 55:59–87.

EATON-POOLE, L., A. E. PINKNEY, D. E. GREEN, D. R. SUTHERLAND, AND K. J. BABBITT. 2003. Investigation of frog abnormalities on National Wildlife Refuges in the Northeast US. In G. Linder, S. K. Krest, D. W. Sparling, and E. Little (eds.), Multiple Stressor Effects in Relation to Declining Amphibian Populations, pp. 63–78. American Society for Testing Materials International, West Conshohocken, Pennsylvania.

EATON, B. R., S. EAVES, C. STEVENS, A. PUCHNIAK, AND C. A. PASZKOWSKI. 2004. Deformity levels in wild populations of the wood frog (*Rana sylvatica*) in three ecoregions of Western Canada. Journal of Herpetology 38:283–287.

GARDINER, D. M., AND D. M. HOPPE. 1999. Environmentally induced limb malformations in mink frogs (*Rana septentrionalis*). Journal of Experimental Zoology 284:207–216.

GILLILLAND, C. D., C. L. SUMMER, M. G. GILLILLAND, K. KANNAN, D. L. VILLENEUVE, K. K. COADY, P. MUZZALL, C. MEINE, AND J. P. GIESY. 2001. Organochlorine insecticides, polychlorinated biphenyls, and metals in water, sediment, and green frogs from southwestern Michigan. Chemosphere 44:327–339.

GOODMAN, B. A. AND P. T. J. JOHNSON. (in press). Disease and the extended phenotype: parasites control host performance and survival through induced changes in body plan. *PLoS ONE*

GOSNER, K.L. 1960. A simplified table for staging anuran larvae with notes on identification. Herpetologica 16:183–190.

GRAY, R. H. 2000. Morphological abnormalities in Illinois cricket frogs, *Acris crepitans*, 1968–71. Journal of the Iowa Academy of Science 107:92–95.

GREEN, D. E., M. J. GRAY, AND D. L. MILLER. 2010. Disease monitoring and biosecurity. In C. K. Dodd, Jr. (ed.), Amphibian Ecology and Conservation: A Handbook of Techniques, pp. 481–505. Oxford University Press, Oxford, United Kindgom.

GURUSHANKARA, H. P., S. V. KRISHNAMURTHY, AND V. VASUDEV. 2007. Morphological abnormalities in natural populations of common frogs inhabiting agroecosystems of central Western Ghats. Applied Herpetology 4:39–45.

HAYES, T. B., A. COLLINS, M. LEE, M. MENDOZA, N. NORIEGA, A. A. STUART, AND A. VONK. 2002. Hermaphroditic, demasculinized frogs after exposure to the herbicide atrazine at low ecologically relevant doses. Proceedings of the National Academy of Sciences of the United States of America 99:5476–5480.

HEBARD, W. B., AND R. B. BRUNSON. 1963. Hind limb anomalies of a western Montana population of the Pacific tree frog, *Hyla regilla* (Baird and Girard). Copeia 1963:570–572.

HELGEN, J., R. G. MCKINNELL, AND M. C. GERNES. 1998. Investigation of malformed northern leopard frogs in Minnesota. In M. J. Lannoo (ed.), Status and Conservation of Midwestern Amphibians, pp. 288–297. University of Iowa Press, Iowa City, Iowa.

HENLE, K. 1981. A unique case of malformations in a natural population of the green toad (*Bufo viridis*) and its meaning for environmental politics. British Herpetological Society Bulletin 4:48–49.

HEYER, R. W., M. A. DONNELLY, R. W. MCDIARMID, L. C. HAYEK, AND M. S. FOSTER. 1994. Measuring and Monitoring Biological Diversity: Standard Methods for Amphibians. Smithsonian Institute Press, Washington, DC.

HOPPE, D. M. 2000. History of Minnesota frog abnormalities: Do recent findings represent a new phenomenon? Journal of the Iowa Academy of Science 107:86–89.

HOPPE, D. M. 2002. Mortality and population declines associated with a Minneosta malformed frog site. In R. G. Mckinnell, and D. L. Carlson (eds.), Proceedings: Proceedings of the Sixth International Symposium of the Pathology of Reptiles and Amphibians, pp. 77–85.

HOPPE, D. M. 2005. Malformed frogs in Minnesota: history and interspecific differences. In M. J. Lannoo (ed.), Amphibian Declines: The Conservation Status of United States Species. pp. 103–108. University of California Press, Berkeley, California.

HUANG, D. J., Y. W. CHIU, C. M. CHEN, K. H. HUANG, AND S. Y. WANG. 2010. Prevalence of malformed frogs in Kaoping and Tungkang river basins of southern Taiwan. Journal of Environmental Biology 31:335–341.

JOHNSON, P. T. J., AND V. J. MCKENZIE. 2008. Effects of environmental change on helminth infections in amphibians: Exploring the emergence of *Ribeiroia* and *Echinostoma* infections in North America. Pp. 249–280. *In* B. Fried, and R. Toledo (Eds.), The Biology of Echinostomes: From the Molecule to the Community. Springer, New York, New York.

JOHNSON, P. T. J., AND R. B. HARTSON. 2009. All hosts are not equal: explaining differential patterns of malformations in an amphibian community. Journal of Animal Ecology 78:191–201.

JOHNSON, P. T. J., K. B. LUNDE, E. G. RITCHIE, AND A. E. LAUNER. 1999. The effect of trematode infection on amphibian limb development and survivorship. Science 284:802–804.

JOHNSON, P. T. J., K. B. LUNDE, R. W. HAIGHT, J. BOWERMAN, AND A. R. BLAUSTEIN. 2001a. *Ribeiroia ondatrae* (Trematoda : Digenea) infection induces severe limb malformations in western toads (*Bufo boreas*). Canadian Journal of Zoology 79:370–379.

JOHNSON, P. T. J., K. B. LUNDE, E. G. RITCHIE, J. K. REASER, AND A. E. LAUNER. 2001b. Morphological abnormality patterns in a California amphibian community. Herpetologica 57:336–352.

JOHNSON, P. T. J., K. B. LUNDE, E. M. THURMAN, E. G. RITCHIE, S. N. WRAY, D. R. SUTHERLAND, J. M. KAPFER, T. J. FREST, J. BOWERMAN, AND A. R. BLAUSTEIN. 2002. Parasite (*Ribeiroia ondatrae*) infection linked to amphibian malformations in the western United States. Ecological Monographs 72:151–168.

JOHNSON, P. T. J., K. B. LUNDE, D. A. ZELMER, AND J. K. WERNER. 2003. Limb deformities as an emerging parasitic disease in amphibians: Evidence from museum specimens and resurvey data. Conservation Biology 17:1724–1737.

JOHNSON, P. T. J., D. R. SUTHERLAND, J. M. KINSELLA, AND K. B. LUNDE. 2004. Review of the trematode genus *Ribeiroia* (Psilostomidae): Ecology, life history and pathogenesis with special emphasis on the amphibian malformation problem. Advances in Parasitology, Vol 57 57:191–253.

JOHNSON, P. T. J., M. K. REEVES, S. K. KREST, AND A. E. PINKNEY. 2010. A decade of deformities. Advances in our understanding of amphibian malformations and thier implications. Pp. 511–536. *In* Donald W. Sparling, Greg Linder, Christine A. Bishop, and S. K. Krest (Eds.), Ecotoxicology of Amphibians and Reptiles, 2nd ed. Soceity for Environmental Toxicology and and Contaminants (SETAC), Pensacoloa, Florida.

JOHNSON, P. T. J., E. KELLERMANNS, AND J. BOWERMAN. 2011. Critical windows of disease risk: amphibian pathology driven by developmental changes in host resistance and tolerance. Functional Ecology.

KAISER, J. 1999a. Frog declines: A trematode parasite causes some frog deformities. Science 284:731.

KAISER, J. 1999b. Deformed frogs: Link to parasites grows stronger. Science 286:2434.

KELLY, W. L., AND M. M. BRYDEN. 1983. A modified differential stain for cartilage and bone in whole mount preparations of mammalian fetuses and small vertebrates. Stain Technology 58:131–134.

KIESECKER, J. M. 2002. Synergism between trematode infection and pesticide exposure: A link to amphibian limb deformities in nature? Proceedings of the National Academy of Sciences of the United States of America 99:9900–9904.

KOPRIVNIKAR, J., M. R. FORBES, AND R. L. BAKER. 2007. Contaminant effects on host-parasite interactions: Atrazine, frogs, and trematodes. Environmental Toxicology and Chemistry 26:2166–2170.

KUPFERBERG, S. J., A. CATENAZZI, K. LUNDE, A. J. LIND, AND W. J. PALEN. 2009. Parasitic copepod (*Lernaea cyprinacea*) outbreaks in foothill yellow-legged frogs (*Rana boylii*) linked to unusually warm summers and amphibian malformations in Northern California. Copeia:529–537.

LANNOO, M. J. 2008. Malformed frogs: The Collapse of Aquatic Ecosystems. University of California Press, Berkeley, California.

LANNOO, M. J., D. R. SUTHERLAND, P. JONES, D. ROSENBERRY, R. W. KLAVER, D. M. HOPPE, P. T. J. JOHNSON, K. B. LUNDE, C. FACEMIRE, AND J. M. KAPFER. 2003. Multiple causes for the malformed frog phenomenon. In G. Linder, E. Little, S. Krest, and D. Sparling (eds.), Multiple Stressor effects in Relation to Declining Amphibian Populations, pp. 233–262. American Society for Testing and Materials International, West Conshoshocken, Pennsylvania.

LEVEY, R., N. SHAMBAUGH, D. J. FORT, AND J. ANDREWS. 2003. Investigations into the Causes of Amphibian Malformations in the Lake Champlain Basin of New England. Vermont Department of Environmental Conservation, Waterbury, Vermont.

MCCALLUM, M. L., AND S. E. TRAUTH. 2003. A forty-three year museum study of northern cricket frog (*Acris crepitans*) abnormalities in arkansas: Upward trends and distributions. Journal of Wildlife Diseases 39:522–528.

MERRILL, R. M. 2009. Introduction to Epidemiology, 5th ed. Jones and Bartlett Publishers, Sudbury, Massachusetts.

METEYER, C. U. 2000. Field guide to malformations of frogs and toads with radiographic interpretations. Biological Science Report, USGS/BRD/BSR-2000-0005. Available at http://www.nwhc.usgs.gov/publications/fact_sheets/pdfs/frog.pdf.

METEYER, C. U., I. K. LOEFFLER, J. F. FALLON, K. A. CONVERSE, E. GREEN, J. C. HELGEN, S. KERSTEN, R. LEVEY, L. EATON-POOLE, AND J. G. BURKHART. 2000. Hind limb malformations in free-living northern leopard frogs (*Rana pipiens*) from Maine, Minnesota, and Vermont suggest multiple etiologies. Teratology 62:151–171.

MEYER-ROCHOW, V. B., AND M. ASASHIMA. 1988. Naturally-occurring morphological abnormalities in wild populations of the Japanese newt *Cynops pyrrhogaster* (Salmandridae, Urodela, Amphibia). Zoologischer Anzeiger 221:70–80.

MILLER, J. D. 1975. Interspecific Food Relationships of Anurans in Northwestern Montana and Fluoride Accumulation in Amphibians and Reptiles in Northwestern Montana. Unpubl. M. S. Thesis. University of Montana, Polson.

MURPHY, T. D. 1965. High incidence of two parasitic infestation and two morphological abnormalities in a population of *Rana palustris* Le Conte. American Midland Naturalist 74:233-239.

NARCAM. 2010. North American Center for Amphibian Malformations. National Biological Information Infrastructure. Available at http://www.nbii.gov/portal/server.pt/community/amphibian_malformations/386.

OLSEN, A. R., AND D. V. PECK. 2008. Survey design and extent estimates for the Wadeable Streams Assessment. Journal of the North American Benthological Society 27:822–836.

OLSON, D. H., W. P. LEOARD, AND R. B. BURY (eds.). 1997. Sampling Amphibians in Lentic Habitats: Methods and Approaches for the Pacific Northwest. Society for Northwestern Vertebrate Biology, Olympia, Washington.

OUELLET, M. 2000. Amphibian deformities: Current state of knowledge. In D. W. Sparling, G. Linder, and C. A. Bishop (eds.), Ecotoxicology of Amphibians and Reptiles, pp. 617–661. Soceity for Environmental Toxicology and and Contaminants (SETAC), Pensacola, Florida.

OUELLET, M., J. BONIN, J. RODRIGUE, J. L. DESGRANGES, AND S. LAIR. 1997. Hindlimb deformities (ectromelia, ectrodactyly) in free-living anurans from agricultural habitats. Journal of Wildlife Diseases 33:95–104.

PIHA, H., M. PEKKONEN, AND J. MERILA. 2006. Morphological abnormalities in amphibians in agricultural habitats: A case study of the common frog *Rana temporaria*. Copeia:810–817.

PLOWRIGHT, R. K., S. H. SOKOLOW, M. E. GORMAN, P. DASZAK, AND J. E. FOLEY. 2008. Causal inference in disease ecology: investigating ecological drivers of disease emergence. Frontiers in Ecology and the Environment 6:420–429.

RAJAKARUNA, R. S., P. PIYATISSA, U. A. JAYAWARDENA, A. N. NAVARATNE, AND P. H. AMERASINGHE. 2008. Trematode infection induced malformations in the common hourglass treefrogs. Journal of Zoology 275:89–95.

REEVES, M. K., C. L. DOLPH, H. ZIMMER, R. S. TJEERDEMA, AND K. A. TRUST. 2008. Road proximity increases risk of skeletal abnormalities in wood frogs from National Wildlife Refuges in Alaska. Environmental Health Perspectives 116:1009–1014.

REEVES, M. K., P. JENSEN, C. L. DOLPH, M. HOLYOAK, AND K. A. TRUST. 2010. Multiple stressors and the cause of amphibian abnormalities. Ecological Monographs 80:423–440.

REINITZ, D. M., T. P. YOSHINO, AND R. A. COLE. 2007. A *Ribeiroia* spp. (Class: Trematoda)--Specific PCR-based diagnostic. Journal of Parasitology 93:1234–1238.

ROHR, J. R., T. R. RAFFEL, S. K. SESSIONS, AND P. J. HUDSON. 2008a. Understanding the net effects of pesticides on amphibian trematode infections. Ecological Applications 18:1743–1753.

ROHR, J. R., A. M. SCHOTTHOEFER, T. R. RAFFEL, H. J. CARRICK, N. HALSTEAD, J. T. HOVERMAN, C. M. JOHNSON, L. B. JOHNSON, C. LIESKE, M. D. PIWONI, P. K. SCHOFF, AND V. R. BEASLEY. 2008b. Agrochemicals increase trematode infections in a declining amphibian species. Nature 455:1235–1239.

ROHR, J., T. RAFFEL, AND S. K. SESSIONS. 2009. Digenetic trematodes and their relationship to amphibian declines and deformities. In H. Heatwole, and J. W. Wilkinson (eds.), Amphibian Biology vol. 8. Amphibian Decline: Diseases, Parasites, Maladies, and Pollution, pp. 3067–3088. Surrey Beatty & Sons, Chipping Norton, NSW, Australia.

RORABAUGH, J. C. 2005. *Rana pipiens* Schreber, 1782 Northern leopard frog. In M. J. Lannoo (ed.), Amphibian Declines: The Conservation Status of United States Species, pp. 570–577. University of California Press, Berkeley, California.

RORABAUGH, J. C., AND M. J. LANNOO. 2005. *Pseudacris regilla* (Baird and Girard, 1852[b]) Pacific treefrog. In M. J. Lannoo (ed.), Amphibian Declines: The Conservation Status of United States Species, pp. 478–484. University of California Press, Berkeley, California.

ROSTAND, J. 1949. Sur diverses anomalies relevées dans une population de crapauds (*Bufo bufo*). Comptes Rendus Des Seances De La Societe De Biologie Et De Ses Filiales 143:758–760.

SCHELL, S. C. 1985. Handbook of Trematodes of North America North of Mexico. University Press of Idaho, Moscow, Idaho.

SCHOFF, P. K., C. M. JOHNSON, A. M. SCHOTTHOEFER, J. E. MURPHY, C. LIESKE, R. A. COLE, L. B. JOHNSON, AND V. R. BEASLEY. 2003. Prevalence of skeletal and eye malformations in frogs from north-central United States: Estimations based on collections from randomly selected sites. Journal of Wildlife Diseases 39:510–521.

SCHOTTHOEFER, A. M., A. V. KOEHLER, C. U. METEYER, AND R. A. COLE. 2003. Influence of *Ribeiroia ondatrae* (Trematoda: Digenea) infection on limb development and survival of northern leopard frogs (*Rana pipiens*): effects of host stage and parasite-exposure level. Canadian Journal of Zoology 81:1144–1153.

SESSIONS, S. K. 2003. What is causing deformed amphibians? In R. D. Semlitsch (ed.), Amphibian Conservation, pp. 168-186. Smithsonian Books, Washington, DC.

SESSIONS, S. K., AND S. B. RUTH. 1990. Explanation for naturally-occuring supernumerary limbs in amphibians. Journal of Experimental Zoology 254:38–47.

SESSIONS, S. K., R. A. FRANSSEN, AND V. L. HORNER. 1999. Morphological clues from multilegged frogs: Are retinoids to blame? Science 284:800–802.

SKERRATT, L. F., L. BERGER, R. SPEARE, S. CASHINS, K. R. MCDONALD, A. D. PHILLOTT, H. B. HINES, AND N. KENYON. 2007. Spread of chytridiomycosis has caused the rapid global decline and extinction of frogs. Ecohealth 4:125–134.

SPOLYARICH, N., R. V. HYNE, S. P. WILSON, C. G. PALMER, AND M. BYRNE. 2011. Morphological abnormalities in frogs from a rice-growing region in NSW, Australia,

with investigations into pesticide exposure. Environmental Monitoring and Assessment 173:397–407.
SOUDER, W. 2000. A Plague of Frogs: The Horrifying True Story. University of Minnesota Press, Minneapolis, Minnesota.
SPEARE, R., L. BERGER, L. F. SKERRATT, R. ALFORD, D. MENDEZ, S. CASHINS, N. KENYON, K. HAUSELBERGER, AND J. ROWLEY. 2004. Hygiene protocol for handling amphibains in field studies. James Cook Univerity, Quensland, Australia. Available at http://www.jcu.edu.au/school/phtm/PHTM/frogs/field-hygiene.pdf.
STUART, S. N., J. S. CHANSON, N. A. COX, B. E. YOUNG, A. S. L. RODRIGUES, D. L. FISCHMAN, AND R. W. WALLER. 2004. Status and trends of amphibian declines and extinctions worldwide. Science 306:1783–1786.
SUTHERLAND, D. 2005. Parasites of North American frogs. In M. J. Lannoo (ed.), Amphibian Declines: The Conservation Status of United States Species, pp. 109–123. University of California Press, Berkeley, California.
SZUROCZKI, D., AND J. M. L. RICHARDSON. 2009. The role of trematode parasites in larval anuran communities: an aquatic ecologist's guide to the major players. Oecologia 161:371–385.
TAYLOR, B., D. SKELLY, L. K. DEMARCHIS, M. D. SLADE, D. GALUSHA, AND P. M. RABINOWITZ. 2005. Proximity to pollution sources and risk of amphibian limb malformation. Environmental Health Perspectives 113:1497–1501.
TYLER, M. J. 1998. Australian Frogs: A Natural History. Cornell University Press, Ithaca, New York.
THIEMANN, G. W., AND R. J. WASSERSUG. 2000. Patterns and consequences of behavioural responses to predators and parasites in *Rana* tadpoles. Biological Journal of the Linnean Society 71:513–528.
USFWS (UNITED STATES FISH AND WILDLIFE SERVICE). 2008. Standard operating procedures for abnormal amphibian surveys: Abrnormality slassifcation SOP. Annapolis, Maryland. http://www.jcu.edu.au/school/phtm/PHTM/frogs/field-hygiene.pdf.
USFWS (UNITED STATES FISH AND WILDLIFE SERVICE). 2011. The National Abnormal Amphibian Monitoring Program Ten Year Summary Report (2000-2009) Final Report. U.S. Fish and Wildlife Service Technical Report.
VAN GELDER, J. J., AND H. STRIJBOSCH. 1995. Adult common toads (*Bufo bufo*) with mutilated legs. Alytes 13:105–108.
VANDENLANGENBERG, S. M., J. T. CANFIELD, AND J. A. MAGNER. 2003. A regional survey of malformed frogs in Minnesota (USA) (Minnesota malformed frogs). Environmental Monitoring and Assessment 82:45–61.
VEITH, M., AND B. VIERTEL. 1993. Damaged hindlimbs of common toads (*Bufo bufo*): Analysis of potential causes. Salamandra 29:184–199.
WAKE, D. B., AND V. T. VREDENBURG. 2008. Are we in the midst of the sixth mass extinction? A view from the world of amphibians. Proceedings of the National Academy of Sciences of the United States of America 105:11466–11473.
WOITKEWITSCH, A. A. 1959. Natürliche Mehrfachbildungen an Froschextremitäten. Gustav Fischer Verlag, Jena, Germany.
YAMAGUTI, S. 1971. Synopsis of Digenetic Trematodes of Vertebrates. Vol I. Keigaku Publishing Co., Tokyo, Japan.
ZAR, J. H. 1999. Biostatistical Analysis, 4th ed. Prentice Hall, Upper Saddle River, New Jersey.

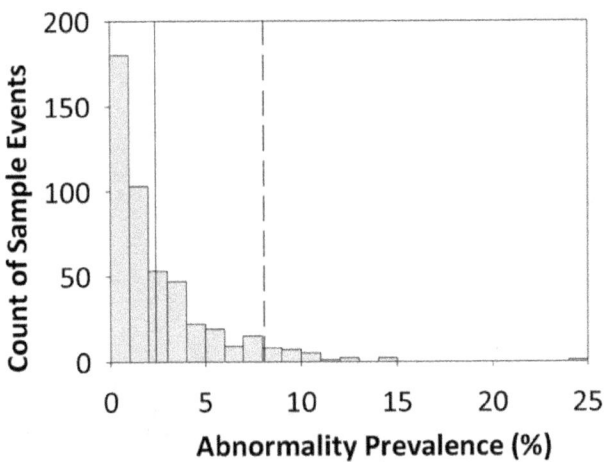

Figure 1.1. Histogram of abnormality prevalence among 672 wetlands, 37 amphibian species and 45 US states. Mean prevalence was 3.3% (solid line) and ranged from 0 to 24% at specific wetlands. The upper 95th percentile of the distribution was 8.1% (dashed line), suggesting populations with > 10% can be considered 'hotspots' when used in conjunction with statistics. Data were collected by USFWS personnel from National Wildlife Refuges from 2000–2009 according to standardized protocols (USFWS, 2008, 2011). The analysis includes wetlands at which ≥50 metamorphic anurans were sampled. Abnormality types included in the analysis were skeletal (limb) malformations and skeletal (limb) abnormalities of unclear etiology; other abnormality types such as eye and surficial abnormalities, visible disease, and recent injury were excluded (see USFWS protocol for further explanation of these classification systems).

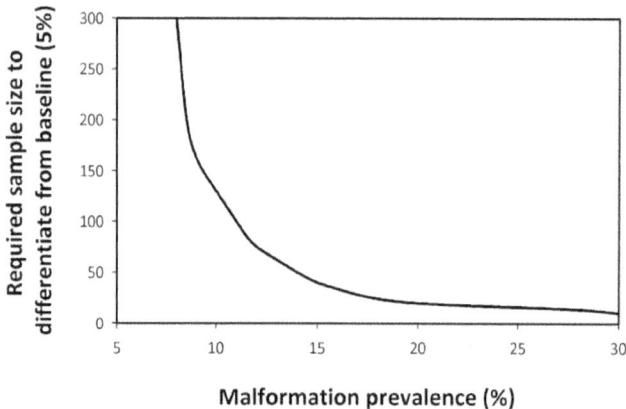

Figure 1.2. Effects of amphibian sample size on a researcher's ability to reject the null hypothesis that an observed malformation frequency is within the 'expected' baseline level of malformations (i.e., < 5%) using a simple two-way Chi-squared test ($\alpha = 0.05$). With a sample size of 100 examined frogs, the observed malformation frequency must exceed ~12% to be statistically distinguishable from 5%, for example. Individual statistical comparisons can be made by calculating 95% confidence intervals ($\alpha = 0.05$) of the prevalence estimate with statistical software packages such as JMP, STATA, or various web sites with binomial calculators, and determining if the interval overlaps the expected baseline (e.g., 5%).

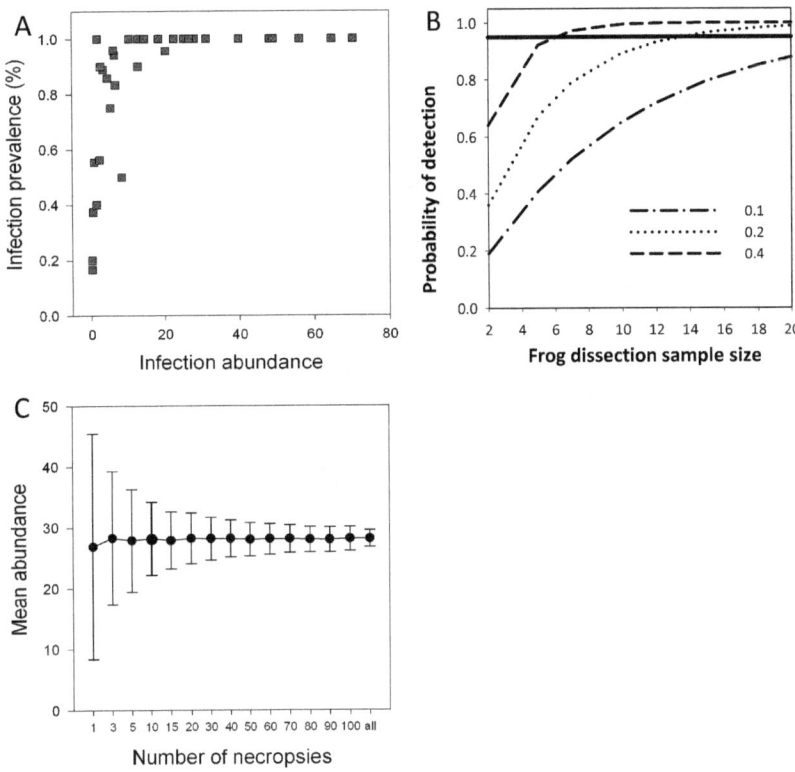

Figure 1.3. (A) Relationship between *Ribeiroia* infection prevalence (% of infected frogs) and abundance (number of metacercariae per frog) in Pacific Chorus Frogs from California (2004–2007). Prevalence increases rapidly with infection abundance, such that most frogs are infected at all but the lowest abundances of *Ribeiroia*. (B) Probability of detecting *Ribeiroia* in metamorphic frogs at 10, 20, and 40% infection prevalence in frogs. A sample size of 15 dissected frogs has a 96% probability of detecting *Ribeiroia* when it occurs at 20% (0.2) infection prevalence, which was the lowest prevalence observed in field-collected samples from Fig. 1.3a. The solid horizontal line represents a 95% probability of detection, a desired level of statistical power. (C) Relationship between the number of necropsied frogs and the estimate of *Ribeiroia* abundance. Error bars represent the standard deviation of the estimate following 1000 resampling events. The "true" estimate of the mean was derived from 168 necropsies. Sample sizes of 10-15 frogs will generally have adequate error to make powerful statistical comparisons between populations.

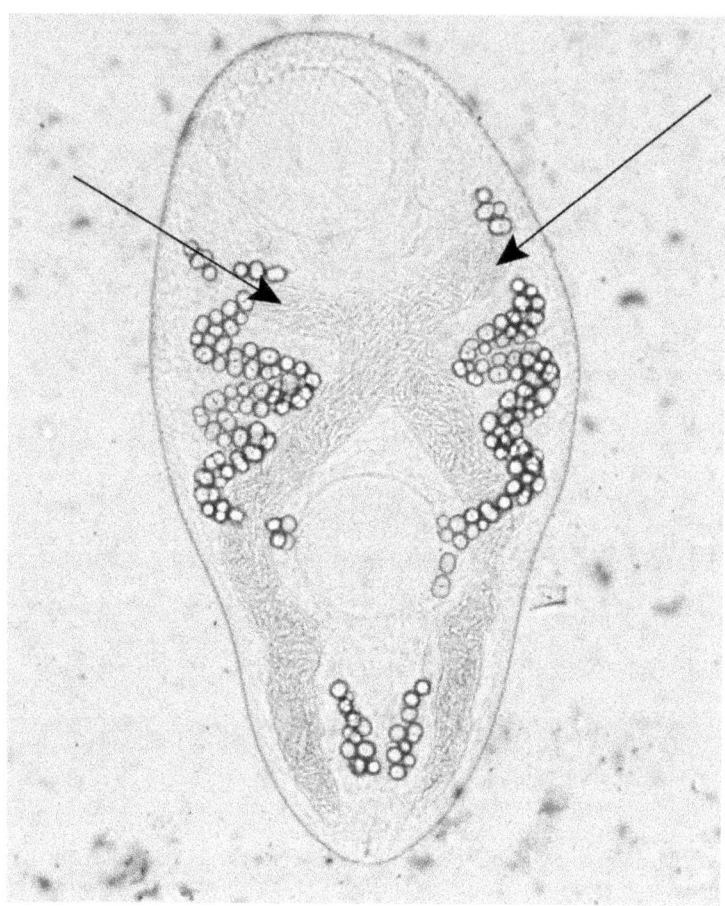

Figure 1.4. Photograph of *Ribeiroia ondatrae* excysted metacercariae (opened cyst) isolated from an amphibian host. Esophageal diverticula noted with two arrows. Oral sucker (acetabulum) is located at the top of the image, and ventral sucker is towards the bottom.

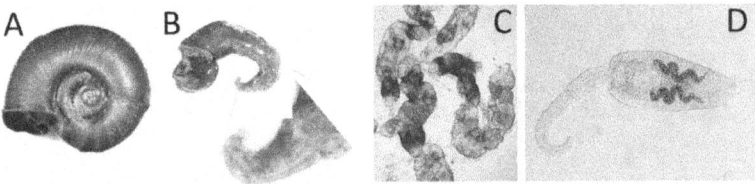

Figure 1.5. (A) Rams horn snail (*Helisoma* sp.) in the family Planorbidae, which is the only family of freshwater snails known to host *Ribeiroia*. (B) *Ribeiroia*-infected rams horn snail, with inset of gonad tissue illustrating rediae that produce free-living cercariae infectious to amphibians. (C) *Ribeiroia* rediae under a compound microscope, which illustrates how partial and fully mature cercariae can be seen inside rediae during snail dissections. (D) *Ribeiroia* cercaria taken from a compound microscope. Photo credit: Bryan LaFonte.

Table 1.1. Summary of recent multi-site field surveys and museum studies of ambient abnormality prevalence. These surveys can be used to calculated a baseline or expected abnormality prevalence. Field surveys specifically investigating malformation hotspots or intentionally disturbed sites were not included in this table unless reference site data were provided.

Author(s)	Country	Region	Study year(s)	Species	Abnormality Prevalence	Sample size	Site level data	Source
McCallum and Trauth, 2003	USA	Arkansas	1957-2000	*Acris crepitans*	7.1%	1,464	0 to 25%	Museum
Gray, 2000	USA	Illinois	1968-1971	*Acris crepitans*	0.4%	9,987	not provided	Field
Gillilland et al., 2001	USA	Michigan	1998	*Lithobates clamitans**	0.3%	1,445	0 to 2.7%	Field
Converse et al., 2000	USA	Midwest, Northeast	1997	*Lithobates pipiens, L. clamitans**	1.9%	8,899	0.4 to 15.6%	Field
Hoppe, 2000	USA	Minnesota	1996-1997	*Lithobates pipiens*	2.3%	2,548	0-3.7%	Field
Vandenlangenberg et al., 2003***	USA	Minnesota	1997-1999	*Lithobates pipiens*	4.3%	1,127	0 to 7%	Field
Hoppe, 2000	USA	Minnesota	1958-1963	*Lithobates pipiens*	0.7%	2,433	n/a	Museum
Schoff et al., 2003	USA	North Central US	1998-2000	*Lithobates pipiens**	1.6%	2,605	0.8 to 8.8%	Field
Levey et al., 2003***	USA	Vermont	1997-2001	*Lithobates pipiens***	3.4%	1,723	0 to 4.5%	Field
Taylor et al., 2005	USA	Vermont	2002	*Lithobates pipiens**	1.6%	5,264	0 to 10.2%	Field
Johnson et al., 2002***	USA	Western US	1999	*Pseudacris regilla*	2.4%	1,722	0 to 10%	Field
Johnson and Lunde, 2005	USA	Western US	pre 1990	*Pseudacris regilla*	0.9%	658	n/a	Museum
Johnson and Lunde, 2005	USA	Western US	pre 1990	*Pseudacris regilla*	1.7%	1,328	n/a	Museum
Spolyarich et al., 2011	Australia	New South Whales	2005-2007	*Limnodynastes tasmaniensis, L. fletcheri, Litoria ranformis*	7.0%	1,209	not provided	Field
Eaton et al., 2004	Canada	Western Canada	1995-2002	*Lithobates sylvaticus*	0.6%	13,235	not provided	Field
Piha et al. 2006	Finland	South Finland	2002	*Rana temporaria*	1.0%	4,115	not provided	Field
Rostand, 1949 by Ouellet, 2000	France	France	not provided	*Bufo bufo*	1.0%	44,000	n/a	Field
Meyer-Rochow and Asashima, 1988	Japan	Japan	1981-1985	*Cynops pyrrhogaster*	4.8%	13,815	4.2-5.1%	Field
Huang et al., 2010	Taiwan	Taiwan	2006-2007	*Rana limnocharis, R. rugulosa*	2.2%	10,944	not provided	Field

*focal species of study, but additional species were surveyed
**metamorphic frogs only
***Summary of reference site data as defined by the authors.

CHAPTER 2

**BEYOND LABORATORY EXPERIMENTS:
USING AN ECOSYSTEM-LEVEL MANIPULATION TO UNDERSTAND HOST-PARASITE DYNAMICS**

Beyond laboratory experiments:
Using an ecosystem-level manipulation to understand host-parasite dynamics

Abstract

An understanding of the causes and consequences of host-parasite interactions under ecologically relevant conditions remains a fundamental challenge in disease ecology. Under natural conditions, numerous biotic and abiotic factors can mediate both the type and magnitude of interactions between hosts and parasites. Here, I investigated interactions between the virulent trematode *Ribeiroia* ondatrae, which is an important cause of amphibian malformations across the United States, and its amphibian hosts using a hierarchical approach involving comparative field surveys, in situ pond exclosures, and a whole-ecosystem manipulation of parasite infection. Specifically, I evaluated temporal and spatial variability in the linkage between *Ribeiroia* infection and amphibian malformations through regional sampling of 17 wetlands in northern California alongside multi-year (2006-2010) monitoring of a known malformation hotspot (Hog Lake) in Mendocino county. To understand the causal relationship between infection and pathology at relevant ecological scales, I divided Hog Lake into two nearly identical (1600 m^2) sections using a barrier impermeable to *Ribeiroia* and amphibians. In spring 2009, 517 *Ribeiroia* infected snails were added to one side of the pond (addition treatment) while the other side remained at ambient *Ribeiroia* levels (control treatment). Concurrently, replicated cages (0.5 m^3) with 25 Pacific chorus frog (*Pseudacris regilla*) larvae that varied in mesh size to either allow or prevent parasite entry were installed on each side of the pond (n=8 cages per pond treatment). Results of this multi-tiered approach provide strong evidence of the causal linkage between infection and malformations while offering additional insights about the influence of experimental venue on effect size. Among years and regional wetlands, *Ribeiroia* infection was a strong predictor of malformation frequency in *P. regilla* frogs. Correspondingly, the addition of infected snails to Hog Lake caused sharp increases in *Ribeiroia* infection and severe malformations in all stages of *P. regilla* (but not in California newts, *Taricha torosa*). However, this effect was present only during the manipulation year (not pre- or post-manipulation). Moreover, I observed a significant interaction between cage treatment and pond manipulation, such that caged larvae showed increased infection and malformations only in coarse-mesh cages on the manipulated side of Hog Lake. Comparisons of the dose-response relationships from previous laboratory work and the two spatial scales of this study (cages and whole-pond) indicated that small-scale experiments exhibit amplified effects relative to results from larger spatial extents. This suggests that additional factors at the individual (e.g., immunity, behavior, and mortality) and community (dilution effect, predation on parasites) levels can moderate the relationship between infection and host response. Taken together, these data provide compelling evidence regarding not only the causal relationship between parasite infection and amphibian malformations but also emphasizing the importance of ecological relevant manipulations in understanding species interactions.

Key words: *Ribeiroia*, disease ecology, ecosystem manipulation, abnormalities, malformations

INTRODUCTION

Worldwide, emerging infectious diseases continue to have significant ecological, economic, and public health effects (Daszak et al., 2000; Patz et al., 2005; W.H.O., 2004). The causes of disease emergence frequently involve interactions between local or regional environmental factors and forms of anthropogenic change, including climate change, land use shifts, and pollution (Daszak et al., 2000; Dobson and Foufopoulos, 2001; Jones et al., 2008). Importantly, disease effects are not limited to the host species, but can extend to other community members though food web interactions, altered ecosystem services, or changes in habitat availability (Daszak et al., 1999; Lessios et al., 1984; Oldroyd, 1999). Broader examination of host-parasite dynamics within an ecological framework can facilitate identification of emergence factors, determine the direct and indirect effects of disease on ecological communities, and model these dynamics across spatial and temporal scales (Jones et al., 2008; Lafferty et al., 2006; Smith et al., 2007).

A fundamental challenge in disease ecology is developing an understanding of the causes and consequences of host-parasite interactions under ecologically relevant conditions. Experimental models in ecology typically rely on simplification to determine the effect and relative importance of potential explanatory variables. Although controlled microcosm experiments can identify important species interactions, large-scale experiments can produce contrasting or novel results (Schindler, 1998; Tilman, 1997; Vredenburg, 2004). Thus, field-based experiments, including large-scale manipulations, are needed to test whether laboratory results can be "scaled-up" to the ecosystem scale (Carpenter, 1999; Carpenter et al., 1995). Although ecologists often perform ecosystem manipulations, such undertakings are comparatively rare in disease ecology (but see: Hudson et al., 1998; Suzan et al., 2009; Swei et al., 2011; Tsao et al., 2004). Examples in both aquatic and disease ecology have shown that results from simplified experiments may not always scale up, and there have been calls to increase the use of field experiments (Kiesecker, 2002). An understanding of the disease dynamics at large spatial scales is particularly important for multi-host parasites that affect several trophic levels (Lafferty and Kuris, 1999). Owing to the complexity of pathogen-host-environment interactions, however, studies of disease dynamics at appropriately sized spatial scales are often correlative. Confirmation of these associative relationships using experiments that manipulate disease drivers under ecologically relevant conditions can be highly informative, sometimes yielding results that differed from simple laboratory experiments (Bruno et al., 2003; Hudson et al., 1998; Tsao et al., 2004).

In the past decade, amphibians with severe malformations have been reported in wetlands across the United States and Canada (Johnson and Lunde, 2005; Ouellet, 2000). Most often, these reports describe frogs with missing, extra, or malformed limbs (Johnson et al., 2010). Although there are many causes on a national scale, laboratory and field studies indicate that the trematode parasite *Ribeiroia ondatrae* is an important driver of such malformations, particularly in the western USA (Blaustein and Johnson, 2003). Typical of many trematodes, *R. ondatrae* has a complex life cycle that involves snail, amphibian, and bird hosts (Johnson et al., 2004). In laboratory studies, *Ribeiroia ondatrae* (hereafter "*Ribeiroia*") increased mortality and induced limb deformities in six amphibian species (Johnson et al., 1999, 2001a, 2006, 2008; Kiesecker, 2002; Schotthoefer et al., 2003; Stopper et al., 2002). However, few studies have examined *Ribeiroia*-malformation dynamics using field experiments (e.g., Kiesecker, 2002) and none have conducted ecosystem manipulations of this system to explore its causal relationships.

This study uses an ecosystem manipulation to explore parasite-host dynamics under conditions that allow for important co-factors to affect these dynamics. Under natural conditions, numerous biotic and abiotic factors can mediate the strength – or alter the direction – of interactions between hosts and parasites (e.g., Marcogliese and Pietrock, 2011; Thieltges et al., 2008). In laboratory studies with parasites, amphibian hosts are typically raised individually in small containers (1-2 L), fed artificial food, and exposed to single or pulsed doses of parasites with no opportunity to escape (e.g., Johnson et al., 1999, 2001a). Clearly these conditions do not reflect the actual pond environment in which larval amphibians live, where they have ample space to avoid infection through behavior, and various additional factors (e.g., physical and biological environment) that can alter transmission patterns (Johnson et al., 2008; Taylor et al., 2004). For example, the presence of predators can reduce larval activity, thereby increasing infection risk (Thiemann and Wassersug, 2000), or predators can actively reduce parasites through direct consumption (Orlofske et al., in submission; Schotthoefer et al., 2007). A "dilution effect" caused by presence of species that are less susceptible to infection (incompetent hosts) can also reduce infection levels in other host species (Dobson et al., 2006; Johnson et al., 2008; Keesing et al., 2006). Collectively, these factors illustrate the complexity of parasite transmission patterns in natural environments and underscore the difficulties in translating the results of simplified laboratory studies to disease dynamics within real ecosystems.

In the current study, I used a multi-scale, multi-year study design to examine how host-parasite interactions within the *Ribeiroia*-snail-amphibian model vary spatially and temporally. The first objective was to document if *Ribeiroia* was a significant cause of limb malformations in amphibians from 17 wetlands in northern California use these data to contextualize experimental results. The second objective was to experimentally test the influence of *Ribeiroia* infection on amphibian malformations and mortality within field settings by increasing parasite levels at the ecosystem scale, and to examine how experimental scale (venue) affect parasite-host dynamics. The third objective was to highlight the conservation implications of parasite infection on amphibian hosts by evaluating patterns of malformations and infection over time and among amphibian life history stages. Given ongoing declines in amphibian populations worldwide and the added emphasis on infectious diseases as a conservation threat (Collins and Crump, 2009; Stuart et al., 2004), critical assessments of the impact of parasites on host populations under natural conditions are an increasingly important management priority.

METHODS

Study Site

I selected Hog Lake (Lat: 39.0316, Long: -121.0788) as the location to study broad ecological mediators of parasite infection. Because the wetland supports two native amphibian species, Pacific chorus frog (*P. regilla*) and California newt (*Taricha torosa*), yet only one snail species (*Helisoma trivolvis*), a known *Ribeiroia* host (Johnson et al. 2004), it is a tractable site for ecological research and manipulation. The pond's intermediate size (3200 m^2) and low depth (maximum of 1 m) further facilitated the collection of data on snails and larval amphibians as well as the installation of mesh enclosures. Hog Lake is located within the University of California Hopland Research and Extension Center, which is a 2,145 hectare property located in Mendocino County, California, directly east of the town of Hopland. The area receives an average rainfall of 94 cm (range: 34-191 cm) and supports an oak woodland and annual grasses vegetation, and a variety of natural wetlands (sag ponds, seasonal ponds, and vernal pools) and created ponds (Regents of the University of California, 2008).

Overall Study Design

I used a multi-tiered field experiment to determine the effects of *Ribeiroia* infection on host populations at varying ecological scales. Specifically, I implemented a large-scale manipulation that divided the wetland into two comparable experimental units and added *Ribeiroia*-infected snails to one side while leaving the other as an unmanipulated control treatment. I compared survivorship and malformation prevalence between the two pond treatments both before (2008) and after (2009) the manipulation according to a basic Before-After-Control-Impact (BACI) sample design (Smith, 2006). Additional experimental approaches were used because of the unreplicated nature of the large-scale manipulation. For example, size, growth, and survival are variables that cannot be reliably calculated from field measures. Therefore, I also conducted a replicated enclosure study within each side of Hog Lake.

The enclosure experiment was designed to be complementary to the ecosystem manipulation by specifically quantifying survivorship, malformation response, developmental rate, and health (i.e. mass) for hosts. Enclosures containing Pacific chorus frog (*Pseudacris regilla*) larvae either allowed or prevented parasite cercariae entry as a function of mesh size (see below). Additionally, by conducting a simultaneous large-scale experiment and a nested enclosure study, I could compare results across experimental spatial scales.

Long-term Monitoring and Regional Field Surveys

Prior to conducting the experiment, background data were collected from Hog Lake and a series of additional ponds within northern California to inform the study design and determine which amphibian species exhibited malformations. I sampled metamorphic *P. regilla* from Hog Lake and inspected them for limb abnormalities in the field (Johnson et al., 2001b). Frogs were collected by hand and stored in a cooler until inspection. The majority of frogs were released back into the pond after inspection while a random subset of approximately 10 normal and 10 abnormal frogs were necropsied to quantify *Ribeiroia* infection (Sutherland, 2005). To determine malformation frequencies in the California newt (*T. torosa*) from Hog Lake, I sampled larval newts on 11 July 2006, 22 May, 8 and 23 June in 2007, 18 May and 2 June in 2008, and 21 July 2009. Newt larvae were sampled in the late spring and early summer because, by this time, the limbs have developed fully and *T. torosa* remain concentrated within the pond prior to metamorphosis, which helps to collect adequate sample sizes (See Dissertation Chapter 1).

Newts were captured with a 1200-μm D-frame dip net and inspected for malformations in the laboratory using a dissection scope (Johnson et al., 2001b). During each sampling event, I attempted to collect at least 100 amphibians to minimize sampling error and maximize statistical power. When multiple sampling events were conducted in a given year, the total number of examined and malformed animals were summed over the season to derive an annual seasonal total. In 2009, data from the control (unmanipulated) side of the pond were used to reflect ambient malformation and *Ribeiroia* levels.

I monitored the rams horn snail *H. trivolvis* (Planorbidae) population at Hog Lake in from 2006 to 2008 to determine the mean density of snails infected with *Ribeiroia* and document the life history of the snail and parasite in the pond. Snails were sampled using either a) 12, 1-m pulls with a 1200-μm D-frame dip net in the littoral zone (total sampled area 3.7 m^2) or b) 16, depth-stratified 1-m^2 quadrats that were swept with a 1200-μm D-frame dip net (total sampled area 16 m^2). Either all or a random subset of snails were 'shed' to look for patent infections (i.e., those releasing cercariae, see Chapter 1 for methods) or necropsied to determine whether the snails were infected with *Ribeiroia* but had prepatent (immature) infections. During the dry season (summer/fall) when Hog Lake had no surface water, continuous soil moisture readings were collected in 2008 to quantify the soil moisture dynamics and to determine how this variable may affect survivorship during aestivation. Four soil moisture probes (EC-5) were installed around the pond just after it dried completely on July 27, 2008 and data were recorded until the first storm of the season on September 19, 2008. The data were recorded continuously every 4 hours using a EM-50 data logger (http://www.decagon.com/). In 2009, soil moisture data were collected with the same methods from August 6, 2009 September 2, 2009, and recording started slightly after the pond dried on July 20 2009.

Finally, I surveyed ponds across Northern California (Lassen, Mendocino, Sonoma, Alameda, Contra Costa, Santa Clara, and San Mateo Counties) to identify wetlands with and without *Ribeiroia* to explore the parasite dose-malformation response relationship at Hog Lake in a broader spatial context. Between 2006 and 2009, I sampled 14 ponds with *Ribeiroia* and 3 without, and often sampling sites over multiple years (n= 42 site*years). Pacific chorus frogs (*P. regilla*) were used as an indicator species for these surveys because they are common in many pond habitats, often locally abundant, and frequently exhibit a strong malformation response to infection (see Dissertation Chapter 1). I used least-squares regression to document the statistical relationship between malformation frequency (arcsin-square-root transformed) and *Ribeiroia* infection intensity (ln(x+1) transformed) variables and to draw conclusions regarding *Ribeiroia* as a general cause of malformations at these sites.

Hog Lake: Ecosystem Manipulation

In December 2007, prior to the pond filling, I divided Hog Lake into two, comparably-sized wetlands approximately 1600 m^2 each, using a 60 m x 1.8 m Ethylene Propylene Diene Monomer (EPDM) pond liner with 1 mm thickness (Fig. 2.1a). Eight 100 cm^2 sections were removed from the liner and replaced with 35 μm Nitex bolt cloth to allow exchange of water (but not tadpoles, snails, or parasite cercariae) between the two sides. I then randomly assigned the west side of the pond to the *Ribeiroia* addition treatment while the east side remained as a control with ambient (unmanipulated) levels of *Ribeiroia* infected snails. The split-pond design is superior to manipulating two different ponds because of the difficulties in finding ponds with similar water chemistry, hydrology, and ecological conditions. This design follows methods similar to those used in large-scale lake manipulations (e.g., Brezonik et al., 1986) and allows for side-by-side comparisons of the two treatments. Furthermore, because *Ribeiroia* abundance and malformations exhibit strong interannual variability (see Results), the split-plot design helps to reduce confounding effects of individual wetland variability. Parasite addition was chosen as the optimal study design as opposed to parasite removal because removing parasites generally requires the removal of all snails, which adds a confounding effect by simultaneously eliminating an important pond herbivore and potential competitor of *P. regilla*.

In 2008, prior to any manipulations of either pond side, I collected baseline data on the malformation prevalence in *P. regilla* larvae and frogs as well as *T. torosa* larvae, which serve as a temporal comparison for the experiment. During May – June, bi-weekly visits were made to the pond to sample these populations, although not all life stages were present at every sample period. *P. regilla* and *T. torosa* larvae were collected using fixed area netsweeps and randomized netsweeps with a D-frame dip net (1200 μm). Metamorphic frogs were inspected for malformation in the field and released, except for a subset that was dissected to determine *Ribeiroia* parasite loads. All larvae were preserved and returned to the laboratory for inspection using a stereo-dissection microscope. Gosner (1960) stage, a system to note developmental stage of anuran larvae, was recorded for all *P. regilla* and a subset of ~30 from each pond treatment were dissected to determine *Ribeiroia* parasite load. *T. torosa* were measured size as an indicator of condition.

For the *Ribeiroia* manipulation in 2009, I added 517 *Ribeiroia*-infected snails to the west side of the pond (*Ribeiroia* addition) while leaving the east side as an unmanipulated control (Fig. 2.1b). Infected snails were added in four batches as laboratory infections matured starting 25 April ending 2 June 2009. Approximately 60% of the infected snails added were allowed to move freely through the pond while the remaining 40% were isolated within enclosures (45 cm diameter and 50 cm high, 2 mm mesh size). Snail enclosures were used to estimate survivorship over the study and to prevent accidental trampling during the bi-weekly sampling events that occurred throughout the summer. Snails in cages were fed boiled lettuce every two weeks to enhance the available food supply. Infected snails were either collected from Bart's Pond, which is also located on the Hopland Research and Extension Center property (n = 79), or infected in the laboratory (n = 438) using parasite eggs from a colony of *H. trivolvis* snails originally from Hog Lake. To experimentally infect snails, they were exposed to *Ribeiroia* eggs obtained from surrogate definitive hosts (*Rattus rattus*) (for methods see Johnson et al., 2007; Paull and Johnson, 2011). Ten weeks following exposure, I confirmed whether snails were infected by shedding snails to confirm active cercariae release and visually counted the cercarial production over a 24 hr period to determine cercariae production. Based on the 2006-2007 data from Hog Pond, a density of 0.25 infected snails m^{-2} incurred a mean *Ribeiroia* intensity of 25-70 metacercariae per frog with a malformation prevalence of 40-60%. I therefore estimated that adding > 400 infected snails into half the pond (1600 m^2) would yield the target density of infected snails at 0.25 m^{-2} (see results). The addition of 400 snails would be a negligible increase to the overall *H. trivolvis* density or biomass, as the total spring population of snails in Hog Pond ranges from 30,000 to 60,000 (i.e., added snails represent <0.001% of the population).

In 2009, larval and metamorphic (recently emerged) *P. regilla* were sampled twice a month between May 15 and July 9, when larvae were developed enough to view possible limb malformations. Collection of data for both larval and metamorphic *P. regilla* allowed comparisons of infection and malformations between treatments and life history stages. In addition, *Ribeiroia* infection intensity in larval animals provides information on the parasite accumulation as a function of sample date. *P. regilla* larvae and frogs and *T. torosa* larvae were collected and analyzed according to the same protocols used in 2008.

To determine whether water quality varied between the two treatments, I measured surface water temperature (°C) and specific conductance (conductivity calibrated to 25°C) using a YSI MP 556 meter, and pH using Oakton pHTstr 3. Turbidity (NTU) was measured with a HACH 2100P turbidity meter. Additional water samples were collected within the littoral area on each sampling event for analysis of heavy metals and nutrients. Water samples for total Chromium and total Lead were stored at 5°C until testing by the UC Davis DANR Laboratory. Water samples for total dissolved nitrogen (TDN) and total dissolved phosphorus (TDP) were frozen within 8 hrs of collection, then thawed and filtered using glass fiber filters (Whatman GF/D 2.7 μm) prior to analysis (Cukjati and Seibold, 2010). Continuous temperature data were recorded using a Hobo UA-001-64 pendant logger (http://www.onsetcomp.com/) positioned at the benthos of each treatment at an initial depth of 0.8 m below the water surface when the pond was full. The logger recorded temperature every 30 minutes between May 1 and July 17 2009.

Hog Lake: Cage Experiment

To complement the large-scale manipulation, I conducted an enclosure experiment nested within both sides of Hog Lake (Fig. 2.1b). The study involved two different enclosure treatments: one that prevented (35 µm mesh) and one that permitted (500 µm mesh) entry of *Ribeiroia* cercariae from the surrounding habitat. This experimental design is similar to that of Kiesecker (2002) but involved finer mesh to exclude trematode cercariae. This finer 35µm mesh size was selected for this study because pilot tests with 53 µm and 75 µm mesh cages allow passage of parasites. Enclosures were 0.5 x 0.5 x 1 m in size (1 m^3), closed on the bottom to prevent predator entry (e.g., Odonata, Hirudinea), and closed on the top to prevent vertebrate predation (Fig. 2.2). On each pond side, eight cages were installed: 4 that allowed parasite entry and 4 that prohibited parasite entry. On 25 June 2009 cages were checked to confirm that no predators were in the cages. In early spring, *P. regilla* egg masses were removed from the pond and raised in a parasite-free environment until they reached susceptible developmental stage between Gosner stage 26-28 (Johnson et al., 2011). Each cage was stocked with 25 larvae on 25 June 2009. To ensure adequate food supplies, 50 g of frozen spinach was added to each cage once a week for the duration of the study. The study was terminated 21 days later, at which time the following data were collected on each surviving individual: Gosner stage, mass (blot dried weight), malformation presence (and description if present), and *Ribeiroia* infection intensity (number of metacercariae cysts per larvae).

Comparison of Host Pathology Across Spatial Scales

Comparisons across spatial scales involved a comparison of slope (representing the dose-response relationship) between parasites recovered from *P. regilla* and malformation prevalence in that population. I predicted that *P. regilla* frogs outside of enclosures (e.g., free-living individuals) would have lower malformations response because severely malformed larvae will not survive up to metamorphosis. I predicted that caged animals would have a higher response if the stress from being in the field (e.g., exposed to cues of predators or poor water quality) would reduce immune response or alter behaviors that could increase infections.

Comparison of Malformations Between Amphibian Life Stages

To document whether severe limb malformations might increase mortality of metamorphic frogs, a result that could lead to population-level impacts, I compared metamorphic amphibians emerging from the pond (summer) with adult amphibians returning to breed (late winter) at two ponds between 2006 and 2009. Hog Lake and Hidden Pond were selected for this comparison because each supported high levels of *Ribeiroia* infection and malformations in one or more years of sampling. Hidden Pond is a stockpond located in Santa Clara County (lat: 37.08898, long: -121.73965). At both sites, ≥ 50 adult *P. regilla* were sampled in winter (December-January) while ≥ 100 metamorphic frogs were sampled in early summer (May-July). Malformation inspection and enumeration procedures were described previously. The 95% binomial confidence limit was determined for each sample event to compare the difference between the adult malformation prevalence and the metamorphic population the preceding year.

Statistical Analyses
To analyze data from the Hog Lake manipulation study, I used Generalized Linear Mixed Models (GLMM) because they (1) allow for non-normally distributed response variables, such as malformation presence and parasite count data, and (2) facilitate the nesting of samples by time or space (see Bolker et al., 2009; Zuur et al., 2009). Specifically, I sought to compare changes in response variables as a function of pond manipulation (*Ribeiroia* addition vs. control), time period (premanipulation year [2008], manipulation year [2009], and post-manipulation year [2010, if sampled]), and their interaction. I was particularly interested in the presence of an interaction, which would suggest that parasite addition had an effect but only during the manipulation year. The primary response variables were malformations (present or absent in an individual) and *Ribeiroia* infection intensity (number of metacercariae per individual). I analyzed these responses for larval and metamorphic *P. regilla* as well as larval *T. torosa*, although sample sizes and sampling frequency varied by species and life history stage. When there were multiple sampling dates within a year, as was often the case for larval animals, individual amphibians were nested by date. Julian date was considered a random effect because I wanted to account for potential seasonal variation in malformation and parasite levels so this did not influence the fixed effects (e.g., time period, pond manipulation, and their interaction). Analyses were performed using the lmer function within the lme4 package in the statistical program R (R Development Core Team, 2011). For metamorphic *P. regilla*, I included data on malformations and infection from 2008-2010, whereas for larvae I included multiple sampling events per year for 2008 and 2009. Larval newts were sampled for malformations in 2008 and 2009 but no dissection data were collected.

For the cage study within Hog Lake, I analyzed the data in two ways. Because animals within fine-mesh cages that prevented parasite entry had no infection and no malformations, it was not possible to use the GLMM approach above while incorporating cage treatment (i.e., the fine-mesh cages had no variance in the response variable of interest). Thus, I used the summary data for each cage (averaged among animals) and standard general linear model approaches. The primary response variables of interest were survival (proportion of animals recovered at the end of the study relative to the number stocked, arcsin-square-root transformed), malformations (proportion of surviving animals with 1 or more malformations, arcsin-square-root transformed), *Ribeiroia* infection (average number of metacercariae among animals surviving the study period), and host stage/mass (average mass and Gosner stage of animals surviving the study, log_{10}-transformed). For comparative purposes, I also used the GLMM approach to analyze *Ribeiroia* infection and malformations among animals from the coarse mesh treatment only, with pond side (manipulated vs. control) as a fixed effect and cage identity as a random effect.

RESULTS

Long-term Monitoring and Regional Field Surveys
Long-term monitoring data at Hog Lake prior to and after the experiment show extremely high variation in *Ribeiroia* infection and *P. regilla* malformations (Fig. 2.3a). For example, in July of 2006, 48.6% (n=257 total examined) of emerging *P. regilla* exhibited one or more limb malformations, with *Ribeiroia* abundance averaging 22.6 metacercariae per frog. In 2007, malformation frequency in *P. regilla* metamorphs increased slightly to 55.4% (n=115 total examined), whereas mean infection abundance quadrupled to 70.4 metacercariae. Following a

severe drought in 2008, malformation prevalence fell to 5.5% (n=419 total examined), with a corresponding decrease in mean infection intensity to 1.5 metacercariae per frog. Malformation prevalence continued to be low (2.5%) in 2009 for the control treatment (n=198 total examined) and low again (2.4%) in 2010 for the entire pond (n=211 total examined). Similarly, *Ribeiroia* infection levels remained low in 2009 on the control side (4.8 metacercariae per frog), and 2010 across the whole pond (0.2 metacercariae per frog). The composition of malformations observed in *P. regilla* in 2006 and 2007 involved hind limb abnormalities, of which a large proportion were extra limbs or digits, malformed feet or limbs, and very few missing or partially missing limbs or digits.

Malformation levels in the California newt *T. torosa* remained relatively low throughout the study period, and demonstrated slight variation over time which was not association with *Ribeiroia* infection levels as indicated from *P. regilla* dissections (Fig. 2.3b). For example, in 2006 3.6% of 21 larvae exhibited limb abnormalities. Malformation prevalence increased in 2007 when 4.8% of 173 larvae exhibited limb abnormalities, mostly missing digits or partially missing limbs. In 2008, malformation prevalence decreased to 4.9% of the 203 newts inspected. The types of malformations were mostly missing limbs or digits (64%). Only 29% involved extra limbs or projections near limbs. A majority of abnormalities were confined to the hind limbs (68%) as opposed to the forelimbs (30%) and only one eye abnormality (2%).

Over the three years of monitoring, snail (*H. trivolvis*) populations fluctuated drastically both within and among years. *Helisoma trivolvis* reproduced in March and April and snails quickly increased in abundance as egg masses hatched in April and May (Fig. 2.4). The population level is highest after hatching is complete, and then declines until the pond dries out. The new cohort's individuals grow rapidly in the warm water that provides an ample algae/diatom supply for food. Although Hog Lake did not have surface water for about 6 months a year, the deep clay soils retained a significant amount of moisture, allowing for snails to aestivate. In 2008, the average soil moisture during the time the pond was dry was 19.5% VWC but the average minimum moisture was 13.7% (volumetric water content) VWC recorded just before the first rain of the season which occurred early for this area on 9/16/2008. In 2009, average soil moisture during the time the pond was dry was 14.0% VWC but the average minimum moisture was 11.1% VWC. During the dry season (summer/fall) snails aestivate in the moist clay soils of the pond, which maintain a soil moisture of > 10%. An abrupt difference in population size was noted between the last sample of the wet season and the first sample of the next wet season (e.g., from 138,000 ± 6,747 snails in June 2007 to 65,000 ± 9,375 in winter 2008) (Fig. 2.4).

Ribeiroia was found at a very low prevalence in *H. trivolvis* snails despite the high parasite loads observed in frogs during 2006 and 2007 (Table 2.1). In 2006, one snail out of 113 examined (0.9%) was infected with *Ribeiroia*, and in 2007 three snails out of 802 examined (0.4%) were infected. In 2008, no snails were infected despite examination of 1116 snails over the spring season. Based on infection prevalence and density data from 2006 and 2007, a density of 0.25 infected snails m^{-2} was correlated to a mean *Ribeiroia* intensity of 25-70 metacercariae per frog, which produced a malformation prevalence of 45-55% in frogs (Table 2.1). Therefore, 0.25 infected snails m^{-2} was selected as a target infection rate for the parasite addition, which corresponded to 400 infected snail for the 1600 m^2 treatment.

Malformations in *P. regilla* at wetlands with *Ribeiroia* ranged from 4 to 60% and showed a functional relationship to infection intensity ($R^2 = 0.62$, $p < 0.0001$; Fig. 2.5). Alternatively, in five ponds without *Ribeiroia* that were monitored over the same time, *P. regilla* exhibited a low frequency (<5%) of predominantly minor abnormalities (e.g., missing digits, partially missing limbs).

Hog Lake: Pond Experiment

The addition of infected snails to Hog Lake resulted in a successful ecosystem scale manipulation of parasite levels. A total of 517 *Ribeiroia*-infected *H. trivolvis* were added to the western half (1600 m^2) of Hog Lake in May and June of 2009. According to shedding data, the 438 lab infected snails were producing an average of 34 cercariae per night. In contrast, wild infected *H. trivolvis* from Bart's Pond (n = 79), another pond at the Hopland Research and Extension Center, were producing an average of 91 cercariae per night. The four week survivorship of caged snails was ~50% for the laboratory-raised snails and ~80% for the wild-infected snails. Overall shedding data from the snails prior to addition indicated that snails were producing approximately 15,000 cercariae produced on the addition treatment per night throughout the study based on snail survivorship data and the expectation that snails continued to produce comparable numbers of cercariae. Based on the estimated number of *P. regilla* larvae on the addition side (~19,000 using information from quadrats) and assuming an average larval period of 40 days following snail additions, these figures would translate to a maximum infection load of 16 cysts per larvae (((15,000 cercariae per night x *P. regilla* larval period of 40 days) / 19,000 *P. regilla*) x 50% cercarial success rate in finding a host).

Results of the ecosystem manipulation showed that the *Ribeiroia* parasite addition increased parasite infection intensity in both *P. regilla* larvae and metamorphic frogs, which coincided with an increase in severe limb malformations in both life stages (Fig. 2.6). Prior to the manipulation in 2008, *P. regilla* larvae from the control treatment had a 6.3% (n = 287) malformation prevalence and low *Ribeiroia* load (1.9 cysts per larvae) compared to a 2.5% (n=200) malformation prevalence and a low *Ribeiroia* load (1.1 cysts per larvae) on the addition treatment before parasites were added. After adding parasites in 2009, *Ribeiroia* levels increased seven-fold among *P. regilla* larvae from the treatment group but decreased on the control side compared to the previous year (Fig. 2.6a). In 2009, 1.7% (n = 349) of larvae were malformed on the control side and *Ribeiroia* infection loads were very low (0.06 cysts per larvae), compared to a higher malformation prevalence 7.8% (n = 293) and an increased parasite load (7.5 cysts per larvae) on the addition side (Fig. 2.6a). Based on the statistical analysis for larval data, which only included examinations of animals in 2008 and 2009 (i.e., no animals examined in 2010 post-manipulation), the results support the observed trends. Responses in both infection and malformation risk revealed a significant interaction between treatment and year (GLMM infection: treatment*period $z = -6.08$, $p < 0.0001$; GLMM malformations: treatment*period $z = -3.61$, $p < 0.005$). The effect of treatment was significant and positive only in 2009 (infection $z = 8.73$, $p < 0.0001$; malformations $z = 3.24$, $p < 0.005$).

Similarly, *P. regilla* metamorphic frogs following the addition of *Ribeiroia* had significantly higher infection levels and significantly greater prevalence of limb malformations (Fig. 2.6b). On the addition side malformation prevalence increased from 4.9% (n = 163) to 7.9% (n = 265) and the infection load increased from 0.8 to 7.6 cysts per frog. Concurrently the malformation response in frogs from the control treatment decreased from 6.3% (n = 144) to 2.5% (n=198), even though *Ribeiroia* infection showed an increase in parasite load from 2.1 to 4.8 cysts per frog. Based on the statistical analysis, pond treatment interacted significantly with study period to determine malformation risk in metamorphosing *P. regilla* (GLM, treatment*period $z = -2.046$, $p < 0.05$). Re-analyzing the data after separating it by study period (pre-, during- and post-manipulation), I found that the *Ribeiroia* addition treatment led to an increase in malformations only during the manipulation in 2009 (GLM, treatment $z = 2.369, p = 0.02$). Indeed, while malformation frequency varied substantially among years, it was generally similar between the treatment and control side in years other than 2009 (Fig. 2.3). Correspondingly, patterns of *Ribeiroia* infection in metamorphosing frogs exhibited a similar interaction between treatment and period (GLMM, treatment*period $z = -2.19, p = 0.028$), such that infection increased in the treatment side only during the manipulation year (2009 treatment effect $z = 3.22, p = 0.001$). During the pre-manipulation year *Ribeiroia* infection was slightly greater on the reference side (2008 $z = -2.51, p = 0.0121$), whereas during the post-manipulation year infection was equivalent between the two sides (2010 $z = -0.18, p = 0.85$). Notably the prediction of 22 cysts per larvae was not achieved with the addition.

In contrast, the parasite manipulation did not affect *T. torosa* malformation prevalence or infection levels. Malformation prevalence in *T. torosa* did increase in from 1.7% (n=58) in 2008 to 9.4% (n = 106) in 2009. In contrast, malformation prevalence of *T. torosa* from the control treatment was 6.3% (n = 144) in 2008 and decreased slightly to 5.9% (n = 51) in 2009. The *Ribeiroia* infection data from 2009 did not show a significant difference between the addition (1.6 cysts per larvae) and the control (2.9 cysts per larvae) treatments ($t = -1.6, p = 0.12$). According to the GLMM analysis, malformations in newts showed no increase with pond treatment or any interactions with time period (all tests $p > 0.05$). Water chemistry as well as amphibian and snail density data at the pond were fairly similar but showed some minor differences throughout the during 2009 (Table 2.2).

Hog Lake: Cage Experiment

Results from the cage-study conducted within Hog Lake in 2009 further bolstered findings from the whole pond results and provided additional insights. The cage experiment confirmed that the addition of *Ribeiroia* was responsible for the increase in infection levels in *P. regilla* larvae, and that larvae exposed to *Ribeiroia* developed a wide range of severe limb malformations (Fig. 2.7, Table 2.3). No parasites were recovered from *P. regilla* larvae raised within fine-mesh cages, supporting the effectiveness of the manipulation. In support of the link between *Ribeiroia* and malformations, only one abnormality (2%) was observed in animals from the fine-mesh cages. In contrast, 63% of larvae recovered from the coarse-mesh cages from the addition side exhibited malformations, and all animals were infected with *Ribeiroia* metacercariae (Fig. 2.7). Similar to the whole pond results, *Ribeiroia* levels from larvae from coarse cages from the control treatment were very low (.02 cysts per individual) and correspondingly no malformed animals were observed. Cage treatment (fine vs. coarse) and pond treatment (*Ribeiroia* addition vs. control) interacted significantly to influence infection and malformation risk (Malformations ANOVA, $F_{3,11} = 28.73$, pond*cage $p < 0.0001$; *Ribeiroia* infection ANOVA, $F_{3,11} = 583.85$, pond*cage $p < 0.0001$). While pond treatment had no effect on animals within the fine mesh cages (all $p > 0.3$), larvae in the coarse mesh cages showed significant increases in infection and malformations on the *Ribeiroia* addition side of Hog Lake Malformations: cage effect, $F_{1,5}=62.79, p = 0.0005$; *Ribeiroia* infection: cage effect, $F_{1,5}=605.26, p < 0.0001$). Fine-mesh cages tended to increase host mass ($F_{3,10} = 3.18$, p < 0.005) and neither cages nor pond treatment altered developmental stage ($F_{3,11} = 0.944$). Neither pond treatment or interaction of pond treatment and cage treatment were significant (all, $p > 0.05$). Survival, which averaged 30% among cages, was not affected by cage treatment or pond manipulation ($p > 0.5$). Generalized linear mixed effects models using only the data from the coarse-mesh cages provided comparable results.

Water chemistry within the cages showed some significant differences between treatments (Table 2.4). Conductivity was higher on the control side compared to the addition side, which led to a significant difference between the addition coarse and control coarse cages (F = 9.8, p = 0.001). Temperatures were slightly higher in the control coarse compared to the Addition fine treatments (F = 4.1, p = 0.032). Dissolved oxygen did vary among individual cages but no significant differences were observed between treatments (F = 0.4, p = 0.7).

Comparison of Host Pathology Across Spatial Scales

The dose-response curve from the three spatial scales [laboratory (0.001 m^3); mesocosm (0.5 m^3); and ecosystem scale (800 m^3)] show significant differences resulting from the complex interactions operating at each venue (Fig. 2.8). For example, comparable levels of *Ribeiroia* infection were recorded in the addition coarse cages and the wild larvae, but the malformation prevalence in the cages (63%) was 8 times higher than wild larvae (7.8%). On the control pond treatment the *Ribeiroia* infection levels were low but similar, yet the wild larvae had slightly higher malformation prevalence (1.7%) compared to the caged larvae (0%). A statistical comparison of the dose response (e.g. slope) relationship among laboratory results (0.001 m^3), field cage results (0.5 m^3) and field results (1000-10,000 m^3) revealed that the dose-response for cage and laboratory results were not different, but the dose-response for field was significantly lower than the other two ($F_{3,63}$ = 47.51, p <0.001).

Comparison of Malformations Between Amphibian Life Stages

Repeated, multi-year comparisons of *Ribeiroia* infection loads and malformation patterns in metamorphosing and adult frogs at two independent ponds show that limb malformations generally result in mortality (Fig. 2.9). Even following years in which malformations were common (>50%) in metamorphic frogs, adult frogs consistently exhibited a low level (<5%) of minor abnormalities, including missing digits and partially missing limbs.

DISCUSSION

By combining whole-pond manipulations, long-term monitoring, and *in situ* cage experiments, this study provides compelling evidence that *Ribeiroia* infection is a major cause of amphibian malformations. The experiment at Hog Lake, which represents one of the rare examples of an ecosystem manipulation of parasite infection, showed that large-scale manipulations of trematode populations are feasible. The study also demonstrated that dose-response effects of parasite exposure vary depending on experimental venue (e.g., field monitoring vs. laboratory experiment) which bolsters the claim that ecological co-factors are important to assess in predicting realistic outcomes from small-scale studies. Lastly, this paper demonstrated that animals with severe limb malformations caused by parasite infection are unlikely to return as breeding adults, which has important implications for conservation.

Long-term Monitoring and Regional Field Surveys

Ribeiroia was the major cause of severe limb malformations observed in *P. regilla* at Hog Lake and appears a significant cause of malformations at many wetlands in Northern California. The observed patterns during the long-term monitoring at Hog Lake illustrate both the remarkable interannual and species level variability in host-parasite dynamics. For example

P. regilla malformation prevalence was high (50%) for 2006 and 2007 and then rapidly decreased to near baseline levels (5%) for the following three years. The decrease in malformation prevalence was associated with a sharp decline in *Ribeiroia* infection intensity, which represents one piece of data supporting the hypothesis that *Ribeiroia* was the natural cause of malformations for this species. These natural fluctuations in *Ribeiroia* levels may have been a results of precipitation differences, or to changes in definitive host activity at the pond. Additional supporting evidence that *Ribeiroia* was the cause of malformations of *P. regilla* at Hog Lake was the match between the types and relative proportions of malformation observed in this species with the malformation composition observed in laboratory infections with *Ribeiroia*, and the parasite loads in wild amphibians were similar to levels required to induce malformations in laboratory settings (Johnson et al., 1999). Use of multiple lines of evidence is a recommended technique to establish causation at malformation hotspots (See Dissertation Chapter 1).

Among the regional wetland sites, the relationship between *Ribeiroia* infection intensity and malformation response supports the hypothesis that the majority of malformations observed at other sites were caused by *Ribeiroia*. The composition of malformations at sites with *Ribeiroia* was similar to malformation compositions observed in laboratory settings and other field sites with *Ribeiroia* (Johnson et al., 1999, 2002). These findings suggest that malformations are widespread in this region, and associate strongly with the presence and abundance of *Ribeiroia*. The prevalence and types of abnormalities at *Ribeiroia* negative sites was <5%, similar to baseline abnormality levels identified from museum collections (Hoppe, 2000; Johnson and Lunde, 2005).

In contrast, malformation prevalence in *T. torosa* was more consistent over time and the observed variance was not associated with *Ribeiroia* infection levels. In 2009, I did not observe a significant difference in *Ribeiroia* infection in newts, despite the addition of over 500 *Ribeiroia* infected snails. Furthermore, malformation composition observed across all years did not match malformations recorded in laboratory studies, nor were infection levels in wild animals similar to those that induced limb malformations in controlled settings (Johnson et al., in submission). For example, laboratory experiments have shown that *T. torosa* is relatively tolerant to the effects of parasitism compared to *P. regilla*, and infection exposure levels of 40 are required to produce a malformation prevalence higher than baseline (>5%) (Johnson et al., in submission). Therefore, the low infection levels observed in Hog Lake (average of 2 cysts per individual) and the mismatch between the malformation composition observed in wild newts compared to laboratory studies are evidence that *Ribeiroia* is not responsible for a majority of the malformations in this species at Hog Lake. Potential causes of these abnormalities include cannibalism (Elliott et al., 1993) and predation by invertebrates (Ballengée and Sessions, 2009; Bowerman et al., 2010)

Hog Lake: Pond Experiment

This study was the first to manipulate *Ribeiroia* levels at the ecosystem scale to document amphibian host-responses (e.g., limb malformations, mortality). A number of laboratory studies have been conducted to demonstrate that *Ribeiroia* can cause malformations in multiple amphibians, including frogs, toads and newts (see Dissertation Chapter 1; Johnson et al., 2010), but only one study has attempted to change infection levels using field experiments (Kiesecker, 2002). Novelties in this study design build on this past research by manipulating pond *Ribeiroia* levels levels, examining effects of *Ribeiroia* on multiple species and multiple life stages, and definitively identifying *Ribeiroia* cysts via dissection, which is the only way to confirm the correct species of trematode in natural ponds (see Dissertation Chapter 1). Research on ecological interactions need to be tested at the ecosystems scale because experiments in simplified settings often fail to produce predicted results at the ecosystem scale (see Carpenter, 1999; Carpenter et al., 1995; Skelly, 2002; Skelly and Kiesecker, 2001). More studies are needed in disease ecology literature at spatial and temporal scales relevant to the multi-host life histories of many parasites. However, these studies are difficult to conduct because of the large scale and may lack of replication, yet they are valuable because results can counter expectations (e.g., Swei et al., 2011).

The addition of over 500 infected snails, which were estimated to collectively produce up to ~15,000 *Ribeiroia* cercariae per night, was a significant ecosystem manipulation that increased the prevalence of amphibians with limb malformations at Hog Lake. Two life stages of *P. regilla*, larvae and metamorphic frogs, both had 3-6 more *Ribeiroia* cysts per individual on the addition side and this was correlated with 2-4 fold increase in limb malformations prevalence. This result confirms results from laboratory experiments and field-based correlations that *Ribeiroia* can induce a wide array of limb malformations in *P. regilla* (Johnson et al., 1999, 2002). In contrast, *T. torosa* at Hog Lake did not show an increase in malformation response, indicating that this species is less susceptible to *Ribeiroia* pathology. Cumulatively, these whole pond results confirm previous laboratory experiments about the species-specific pathology differences between these two amphibian hosts (Johnson et al., in submission).

The difference in expected parasite load based on modeling compared to the observed infection levels offers important insight regarding how successful cercariae can locate hosts in natural environments. I predicted parasite loads of 16 cysts per frog on the addition treatment, yet this was three times greater than the observation of 7.5 cysts per larvae. Although estimates of cercariae production over time and mortality rates of snail have uncertainty affecting the parasite budget of the *Ribeiroia* addition, the direction and magnitude of the over-prediction indicate two potential ecological factors might be involved. First, predation on the cercariae by newts (*T. torosa*), damselflies (Lestidae, Coenagrionidae), and clam shrimp (*Cyzicus* sp.), all of which are abundant in Hog Lake, could have reduced the number of cercariae by 50% based on laboratory studies (Orlofske et al., in submission). Second, the dilution/decoy effect provided by *T. torosa* could have also reduced infection loads in *P. regilla* by absorbing a large number of cercariae (Dobson et al., 2006; Johnson et al., 2008; Keesing et al., 2006).

Hog Lake: Cage Experiment

The cage results validated the unreplicated design results from the ecosystem manipulation showing that the addition of *Ribeiroia* to half of Hog Lake was the cause of the increased malformation prevalence in *P. regilla* larvae and frogs. The cage results showed an even stronger effect of the parasite addition, with a mean malformation prevalence of 63% in the coarse cages on the addition treatment whereas no malformations were observed in the fine cage on the addition treatment. Although one malformed animal was observed in the fine cage from the control pond treatment, the skin projection originating from the tail was probably related to the systemic swelling (edema) that this tadpole was experiencing because it did not originate from the limb bud like *Ribeiroia* malformations. Thus, the fine cage mesh and structure were successful in preventing any trematodes from entering the cages and was finer mesh compared to the only other study designed to exclude *Ribeiroia* in field settings (Kiesecker, 2002). The malformation prevalence in *P. regilla* caged animals was much greater than the mean prevalence of approximately 10% observed in a cage enclosure study of wood frogs (*Lithobates sylvaticus*) in Pennsylvania. Infection levels in that study were not reported but this difference could be related to parasite load and host tolerance. Laboratory infections have shown that *L. sylvaticus* have a lower malformation response compared to *P. regilla* (Johnson et al., in submission).

Contrary to our prediction, parasite exposure did not increase mortality in the caged larvae, nor was it associated with differences in size or developmental stage. These null results are likely affected by the lower than expected parasite load in the addition pond treatment. For example, based on a previous laboratory study with *P. regilla*, I would expect an 11% reduction in survivorship for a parasite dose comparable to infection levels, which would require a substantially larger sample size to detect a significant difference.

The comparison between malformations in the caged larvae compared to free-living larvae and frogs offer insight into causes of limb malformations that are not related to *Ribeiroia*. No caged animals exhibited abnormalities involving missing digits, which did occur in wild *P. regilla* larvae and frogs at low levels. This observation supports the theory that this malformation type is not cause by *Ribeiroia* but by a pond predator (Ballengée and Sessions, 2009; Bowerman et al., 2010). Possible pond predators in this system are *T. torosa*, damselfly, and dragonfly larvae. I did commonly observe predacious diving beetle (Dytiscidae) larvae attacking *P. regilla* larvae in the field but this type of predation was almost always lethal and did not involve the hind limbs.

Comparison of Dose-response Effect Across Spatial Scales

The *Ribeiroia* dose-response effect (i.e., sublethal pathology) showed significant variability across spatial scales. The two small scale experimental venues (field cages and laboratory microcosms) showed similar and stronger dose response relationships compared to frogs which were free living as tadpoles in Hog Lake (Fig. 2.7). The lack of difference between the caged larvae compared to laboratory-raised animals suggests that the lab environment was a good predictor for field results when predation on larvae is prevented. In the field, these larvae were exposed to cues from dragonfly, damselfly, beetle, and leach predators which could have affected behavior of larvae resulting in different infection levels (Taylor et al., 2004; Thiemann and Wassersug, 2000) or predator effluent could alter immune response resulting in increased infections (Belden and Kiesecker, 2005; Rohr et al., 2008). Yet, my results suggest that these factors did not have a strong effect in this study. Because the wetland is isolated from anthropogenic disturbance and there is no active land use within 3 km, poor water quality such as presence of pesticides (Kiesecker, 2002) or heavy metals (Reeves et al., 2010) are not suspected to act in combination with *Ribeiroia* infection. The weaker dose-response relationship observed in *P. regilla* frogs could result: a) from lower survivorship of malformed larvae and malformed metamorphs compared to their normal counterparts (Johnson and Lunde, 2005), or b) because the laboratory dose was concentrated during a precise window of critical development when *P. regilla* is most sensitive compared to infection across the entire larval lifespan in wild-frogs (Johnson et al., 2011). This study was not designed to identify which precise ecological factors are most important but rather to document the direction and magnitude of difference in pathology based on experimental venue. These results support other studies in aquatic ecology showing that experimental scale or venue can alter results based on the level of ecological realism in the experiment (Carpenter, 1996; Carpenter et al., 1995; Skelly, 2002; Skelly and Kiesecker, 2001).

Conservation Implications of *Ribeiroia* Infection

Amphibians are suffering global declines because of a number of factors including habitat loss, invasive species, exploitation, pesticide exposure, and disease (e.g., Berger et al.,

1998; Collins and Storfer, 2003; Hayes et al., 2002; Stuart et al., 2004)., In general, *Ribeiroia* infection is not considered a potential factor in regions where it is abundant, yet data from this study suggest that this parasite can cause significant mortality within a single population. These findings strongly suggest that malformed frogs fail to reach sexual maturity, given that *P. regilla* generally takes 1-2 years to reach reproductive maturity (Rorabaugh and Lannoo, 2005). At two independent ponds, malformation prevalence in adult frogs was consistently low (2-6%) in spite of an extremely high (30-55%) malformation prevalence in the previous cohorts juvenile frogs. This pattern indicates that most malformed frogs die before reproducing. These results extend previous findings on this topic (Johnson et al., 1999) with data from multiple ponds. Because previous laboratory studies found that direct exposure to *Ribeiroia* cercariae caused up to 60% mortality in tadpoles at realistic parasite doses (Johnson et al., 1999, in submission), the cumulative effect on infection both life stages at Hog Lake could have removed approximately 75% of frogs at infection levels observed in 2006 and 2007. Although sites in this study only had a mean malformation prevalence of 19%, the constant loss of such large proportion of the population to a single cause could have significant population effects. These results have implications for declining amphibian populations, such as the California red-legged frog (*Rana draytonii*) and the Oregon spotted frog (*Rana pretiosa*) (Johnson and Lunde, 2005).

H. trivolvis Life History and Parasite Dynamics

The *Ribeiroia* infection pattern in snails demonstrated that the parasite needs to re-infect this system annually to maintain a stable population. Infection data in the two size classes support the hypothesis that *Ribeiroia* miracidia hatch from eggs deposited by birds and infect the current year's cohort in April and May. Because this infection takes approximately two months before cercariae are produced, these snails aestivate as infected individuals. It is not until the next year that surviving infected snails release cercariae as waters warm the next spring (April-June). The laboratory procedure for infecting snails with *Ribeiroia* eggs showed that egg development takes an average of three weeks before they hatch into free swimming miracidia and are able to infect snails and that infected snails take between 7-10 weeks to mature, somewhat longer than previous reports for this species (Johnson et al., 2004).

The precipitous decline in amphibian malformations and infection observed between 2007 and 2008 may be partially related to a weather-mediated reduction in the snail host population. Both 2005 and 2006 were wet years (> 60th percentile annual rainfall), whereas 2007 and 2008 were extremely dry years (< 30th percentile annual rainfall); thus, between summer 2007 and winter 2008, Hog Lake was dry for six months as opposed to the typical four months, which could cause substantial increases in mortality of aestivating snails. Snail population dynamics alone do not explain the difference in parasite levels. I hypothesized that the definitive host in the region, which is probably some species of bird (Johnson et al., 2004), either no longer was *Ribeiroia* infected or stopped visiting the pond after 2007. Although bird observations were made at Hog Lake during every visit, the only recorded bird hosts observed were mallards and a great egret, and no clear trends of these birds were observed over time.

Conclusions

The large-scale manipulation was designed to examine amphibian responses to infection at the ecosystem scale. However, because of logistical and financial constraints, manipulating multiple ponds was beyond the scope of this study. To avoid pseudoreplication issues (Hurlbert, 1984), I nested a replicated enclosure study within the larger ecosystem manipulation experiment. The use of GLMM was able to address the strong interannual variance observed in Hog Lake but still detect differences the year of the manipulation. This hierarchical study design was sufficient to conclude the effects of parasite differences and corresponding amphibian malformations were due the ecosystem manipulation.

ACKNOWLEDGMENTS

I thank P Johnson for reviewing this manuscript and for assisting with statistical analyses, A Merenlender for assistance with the study design, K Fraiola, S Poor, T McWilliams for assistance installing the divider, B. Keiffer, S Feirer for logistical support, J Ball for help with the cage experiment, I Buller, B LaFonte, E Kellermanns, M Aghaee with dissection of amphibians, and M Aghaee, M Baragona, C Castanon, A Cuneo, J Dugan, C Dunn, L Gomez, K He, S Ly, M, McKillop, M Miranda, S Osman, K Thi, J Wang, J Xin for assistance in the field or with snail dissections. This work was funded with assistance from a University of California Berkeley Committee on Research Faculty Research Grant, and I was supported by the National Science Foundation Graduate Research Fellowship Program and EPA STAR Fellowship Program.

LITERATURE CITED

BALLENGÉE, B., AND S. K. SESSIONS. 2009. Explanation for missing limbs in deformed amphibians. Journal of Experimental Zoology Part B: Molecular and Developmental Evolution 312B:770-779.

BELDEN, L. K., AND J. M. KIESECKER. 2005. Glucocorticosteroid hormone treatment of larval treefrogs increases infection by *Alaria* sp trematode cercariae. Journal of Parasitology 91:686-688.

BERGER, L., R. SPEARE, P. DASZAK, D. E. GREEN, A. A. CUNNINGHAM, C. L. GOGGIN, R. SLOCOMBE, M. A. RAGAN, A. D. HYATT, K. R. MCDONALD, H. B. HINES, K. R. LIPS, G. MARANTELLI, AND H. PARKES. 1998. Chytridiomycosis causes amphibian mortality associated with population declines in the rain forests of Australia and Central America. Proceedings of the National Academy of Sciences of the United States of America 95:9031-9036.

BLAUSTEIN, A. R., AND P. T. JOHNSON. 2003. The complexity of deformed amphibians. Frontiers in Ecology and the Environment 1:87-94.

BOLKER, B. M., M. E. BROOKS, C. J. CLARK, S. W. GEANGE, J. R. POULSEN, M. H. H. STEVENS, AND J.-S. S. WHITE. 2009. Generalized linear mixed models: a practical guide for ecology and evolution. Trends in Ecology & Evolution 24:127-135.

BOWERMAN, J., P. T. J. JOHNSON, AND T. BOWERMAN. 2010. Sublethal predators and their injured prey: Linking aquatic predators and severe limb abnormalities in amphibians. Ecology 91:242-251.

BREZONIK, P. L., L. A. BAKER, J. R. EATON, T. M. FROST, P. GARRISON, T. K. KRATZ, J. J. MAGNUSON, W. J. ROSE, B. K. SHEPHARD, W. A. SWENSON, C. J. WATRAS, AND K. E. WEBSTER. 1986. Experimental acidification of Little Rock Lake, Wisconsin. Water Air and Soil Pollution 31:115-121.

BRUNO, J. F., L. E. PETES, C. D. HARVELL, AND A. HETTINGER. 2003. Nutrient enrichment can increase the severity of coral diseases. Ecology Letters 6:1056-1061.

CARPENTER, S. R. 1996. Microcosm experiments have limited relevance for community and ecosystem ecology. Ecology 77:677-680.

CARPENTER, S. R. 1999. Microcosm experiments have limited relevance for community and ecosystem ecology: Reply. Ecology 80:1085-1088.

CARPENTER, S. R., S. W. CHISHOLM, C. J. KREBS, D. W. SCHINDLER, AND R. F. WRIGHT. 1995. Ecosystem Experiments. Science 269:324-327.

COLLINS, J. P., AND M. L. CRUMP. 2009. Extinction in our Times: Global Amphibian Decline. Oxford University Press, Inc, New York, NY.

COLLINS, J. P., AND A. STORFER. 2003. Global amphibian declines: sorting the hypotheses. Diversity and Distributions 9:89-98.

CUKJATI, J., AND C. SEIBOLD. 2010. Kiowa Environmental Chemistry Laboratory Procedure Manual. Mountain Research Station & Institute of Arctic and Alpine Research, University of Colorado Boulder. http://snobear.colorado.edu/Kiowa/Kiowaref/procedure.html.

DASZAK, P., L. BERGER, A. A. CUNNINGHAM, A. D. HYATT, D. E. GREEN, AND R. SPEARE. 1999. Emerging infectious diseases and amphibian population declines. Emerging Infectious Diseases 5:735-748.

DASZAK, P., A. A. CUNNINGHAM, AND A. D. HYATT. 2000. Wildlife ecology - Emerging infectious diseases of wildlife - Threats to biodiversity and human health. Science 287:443-449.

DOBSON, A., I. CATTADORI, R. D. HOLT, R. S. OSTFELD, F. KEESING, K. KRICHBAUM, J. R. ROHR, S. E. PERKINS, AND P. J. HUDSON. 2006. Sacred Cows and Sympathetic Squirrels: The Importance of Biological Diversity to Human Health. Plos Medicine 3:714-718.

DOBSON, A., AND J. FOUFOPOULOS. 2001. Emerging infectious pathogens of wildlife. Philosophical Transactions of the Royal Society of London Series B-Biological Sciences 356:1001-1012.

ELLIOTT, S. A., L. B. KATS, AND J. A. BREEDING. 1993. The use of conspecific chemical cues for cannibal avoidance in California newts (*Taricha torosa*). Ethology 95:186-192.

GOSNER, K. L. 1960. A simplified table for staging anuran embryos and larvae with notes on identification. Herpetologica 16:183-190.

HAYES, T. B., A. COLLINS, M. LEE, M. MENDOZA, N. NORIEGA, A. A. STUART, AND A. VONK. 2002. Hermaphroditic, demasculinized frogs after exposure to the herbicide atrazine at low ecologically relevant doses. Proceedings of the National Academy of Sciences of the United States of America 99:5476-5480.

HOPPE, D. M. 2000. History of Minnesota frog abnormalities: Do recent findings represent a new phenomenon? Journal of the Iowa Academy of Science 107:86-89.

HUDSON, P. J., A. P. DOBSON, AND D. NEWBORN. 1998. Prevention of population cycles by parasite removal. Science 282:2256-2258.

HURLBERT, S. H. 1984. Pseudoreplication and the design of ecological field experiments. Ecological Monographs 54:187-211.

JOHNSON, P. T. J., J. M. CHASE, K. L. DOSCH, R. B. HARTSON, J. A. GROSS, D. J. LARSON, D. R. SUTHERLAND, AND S. R. CARPENTER. 2007. Aquatic eutrophication promotes pathogenic infection in amphibians. Proceedings of the National Academy of Sciences of the United States of America 104:15781-15786.

JOHNSON, P. T. J., R. B. HARTSON, D. J. LARSON, AND D. R. SUTHERLAND. 2008. Diversity and disease: community structure drives parasite transmission and host fitness. Ecology Letters 11:1017-1026.

JOHNSON, P. T. J., E. KELLERMANNS, AND J. BOWERMAN. 2011. Critical windows of disease risk: Amphibian pathology driven by developmental changes in host resistance and tolerance. Functional Ecology 25:726-734.

JOHNSON, P. T. J., AND K. B. LUNDE. 2005. Parasite infection and limb malformations: a growing problem in amphibian conservation. Pp. 124-138. *In* M. J. Lannoo (Ed.), Amphibian Declines: The Conservation Status of United States Species. University of California Press, Berkeley, CA.

JOHNSON, P. T. J., K. B. LUNDE, R. W. HAIGHT, J. BOWERMAN, AND A. R. BLAUSTEIN. 2001a. *Ribeiroia ondatrae* (Trematoda : Digenea) infection induces severe limb malformations in western toads (*Bufo boreas*). Canadian Journal of Zoology 79:370-379.

JOHNSON, P. T. J., K. B. LUNDE, E. G. RITCHIE, AND A. E. LAUNER. 1999. The effect of trematode infection on amphibian limb development and survivorship. Science 284:802-804.

JOHNSON, P. T. J., K. B. LUNDE, E. G. RITCHIE, J. K. REASER, AND A. E. LAUNER. 2001b. Morphological abnormality patterns in a California amphibian community. Herpetologica 57:336-352.

JOHNSON, P. T. J., K. B. LUNDE, E. M. THURMAN, E. G. RITCHIE, S. N. WRAY, D. R. SUTHERLAND, J. M. KAPFER, T. J. FREST, J. BOWERMAN, AND A. R. BLAUSTEIN. 2002. Parasite (*Ribeiroia ondatrae*) infection linked to amphibian malformations in the western United States. Ecological Monographs 72:151-168.

JOHNSON, P. T. J., E. R. PREU, D. R. SUTHERLAND, J. M. ROMANSIC, B. HAN, AND A. R. BLAUSTEIN. 2006. Adding infection to injury: Synergistic effects of predation and parasitism on amphibian malformations. Ecology 87:2227-2235.

JOHNSON, P. T. J., M. K. REEVES, S. K. KREST, AND A. E. PINKNEY. 2010. A decade of deformities. Advances in our understanding of amphibian malformations and thier implications. Pp. 511-536. *In* Donald W. Sparling, Greg Linder, Christine A. Bishop, and S. K. Krest (Eds.), Ecotoxicology of Amphibians and Reptiles, Second Edition. Soceity for Environmental Toxicology and and Contaminants (SETAC), Pensacoloa, Florida, USA.

JOHNSON, P. T. J., J. R. ROHR, J. T. HOVERMAN, E. KELLERMANNS, J. BOWERMAN, AND K. B. LUNDE. in submission. Living fast and dying of infection: Host life history explains interspecific variation in disease risk. Ecology Letters.

JOHNSON, P. T. J., D. R. SUTHERLAND, J. M. KINSELLA, AND K. B. LUNDE. 2004. Review of the trematode genus *Ribeiroia* (Psilostomidae): Ecology, life history and pathogenesis with special emphasis on the amphibian malformation problem. Advances in Parasitology, Vol 57 57:191-253.

JONES, K. E., N. G. PATEL, M. A. LEVY, A. STOREYGARD, D. BALK, J. L. GITTLEMAN, AND P. DASZAK. 2008. Global trends in emerging infectious diseases. Nature 451:990-U994.

KEESING, F., R. D. HOLT, AND R. S. OSTFELD. 2006. Effects of species diversity on disease risk. Ecology Letters 9:485-498.

KIESECKER, J. M. 2002. Synergism between trematode infection and pesticide exposure: A link to amphibian limb deformities in nature? Proceedings of the National Academy of Sciences of the United States of America 99:9900-9904.

LAFFERTY, K. D., A. P. DOBSON, AND A. M. KURIS. 2006. Parasites dominate food web links. Proceedings of the National Academy of Sciences of the United States of America 103:11211-11216.

LAFFERTY, K. D., AND A. M. KURIS. 1999. How environmental stress affects the impacts of parasites. Limnology and Oceanography 44:925-931.

LESSIOS, H. A., D. R. ROBERTSON, AND J. D. CUBIT. 1984. Spread of Diadema Mass Mortality through the Caribbean. Science 226:335-337.

MARCOGLIESE, D. J., AND M. PIETROCK. 2011. Combined effects of parasites and contaminants on animal health: parasites do matter. Trends in Parasitology 27:123-130.

OLDROYD, B. P. 1999. Coevolution while you wait: *Varroa jacobsoni*, a new parasite of western honeybees. Trends in Ecology & Evolution 14:312-315.

ORLOFSKE, S. A., R. JADIN, D. L. PRESTON, AND P. T. J. JOHNSON. in submission. Parasite transmission in complex communities: Predators and alternative hosts alter pathogenic infections in amphibians. Ecology.

OUELLET, M. 2000. Amphibian deformities: Current state of knowledge. Pp. 617-661. *In* D. W. Sparling, G. Linder, and C. A. Bishop (Eds.), Ecotoxicology of Amphibians and Reptiles.

Soceity for Environmental Toxicology and and Contaminants (SETAC), Pensacola, Florida, USA.
PATZ, J. A., D. CAMPBELL-LENDRUM, T. HOLLOWAY, AND J. A. FOLEY. 2005. Impact of regional climate change on human health. Nature 438:310-317.
PAULL, S. H., AND P. T. J. JOHNSON. 2011. High temperature enhances host pathology in a snail-trematode system: possible consequences of climate change for the emergence of disease. Freshwater Biology 56:767-778.
R DEVELOPMENT CORE TEAM. 2011. R: A Language and Environment for Statistical Computing. R Foundation for Statistical Computing, Vienna, Austria. http://www.R-project.org.
REEVES, M. K., P. JENSEN, C. L. DOLPH, M. HOLYOAK, AND K. A. TRUST. 2010. Multiple stressors and the cause of amphibian abnormalities. Ecological Monographs 80:423-440.
REGENTS OF THE UNIVERSITY OF CALIFORNIA. 2008. Hopland Research and Extension Center. University of California, Agriculture and Natural Resources, Hopland, CA. http://ucanr.org/sites/hopland/.
ROHR, J. R., A. M. SCHOTTHOEFER, T. R. RAFFEL, H. J. CARRICK, N. HALSTEAD, J. T. HOVERMAN, C. M. JOHNSON, L. B. JOHNSON, C. LIESKE, M. D. PIWONI, P. K. SCHOFF, AND V. R. BEASLEY. 2008. Agrochemicals increase trematode infections in a declining amphibian species. Nature 455:1235-1239.
RORABAUGH, J. C., AND M. J. LANNOO. 2005. *Pseudacris regilla* (Baird and Girard, 1852[b]) Pacific treefrog. Pp. 478-484. *In* M. J. Lannoo (Ed.), Amphibian Declines: The Conservation Status of United States Species. University of California Press, Berkeley, CA.
SCHINDLER, D. W. 1998. Replication versus realism: The need for ecosystem-scale experiments. Ecosystems 1:323-334.
SCHOTTHOEFER, A. M., A. V. KOEHLER, C. U. METEYER, AND R. A. COLE. 2003. Influence of *Ribeiroia ondatrae* (Trematoda: Digenea) infection on limb development and survival of northern leopard frogs (*Rana pipiens*): effects of host stage and parasite-exposure level. Canadian Journal of Zoology 81:1144-1153.
SCHOTTHOEFER, A. M., K. M. LABAK, AND V. R. BEASLEY. 2007. *Ribeiroia ondatrae* cercariae are consumed by aquatic invertebrate predators. Journal of Parasitology 93:1240-1243.
SKELLY, D. K. 2002. Experimental venue and estimation of interaction strength. Ecology 83:2097-2101.
SKELLY, D. K., AND J. M. KIESECKER. 2001. Venue and outcome in ecological experiments: manipulations of larval anurans. Oikos 94:198-208.
SMITH, E. P. 2006. BACI Design. Pp. 141-148. *In* A. H. El-Shaarawi, and W. W. Piegorsch (Eds.), Encyclopedia of Environmetrics. John Wiley & Sons, Ltd, Chichester, UK.
SMITH, K. F., D. F. SAX, S. D. GAINES, V. GUERNIER, AND J. F. GUEGAN. 2007. Globalization of human infectious disease. Ecology 88:1903-1910.
STOPPER, G. F., L. HECKER, R. A. FRANSSEN, AND S. K. SESSIONS. 2002. How trematodes cause limb deformities in amphibians. Journal of Experimental Zoology 294:252-263.
STUART, S. N., J. S. CHANSON, N. A. COX, B. E. YOUNG, A. S. L. RODRIGUES, D. L. FISCHMAN, AND R. W. WALLER. 2004. Status and trends of amphibian declines and extinctions worldwide. Science 306:1783-1786.
SUTHERLAND, D. 2005. Parasites of North American frogs. Pp. 109-123. *In* M. J. Lannoo (Ed.), Amphibian declines: the conservation status of United States species. University of California Press, Berkeley, CA.

SUZAN, G., E. MARCE, J. T. GIERMAKOWSKI, J. N. MILLS, G. CEBALLOS, R. S. OSTFELD, B. ARMIEN, J. M. PASCALE, AND T. L. YATES. 2009. Experimental Evidence for Reduced Rodent Diversity Causing Increased Hantavirus Prevalence. Plos One 4.

SWEI, A., R. S. OSTFELD, R. S. LANE, AND C. J. BRIGGS. 2011. Impact of the experimental removal of lizards on Lyme disease risk. Proceedings of the Royal Society B-Biological Sciences 278:2970-2978.

TAYLOR, C. N., K. L. OSEEN, AND R. J. WASSERSUG. 2004. On the behavioural response of *Rana* and *Bufo* tadpoles to echinostomatoid cercariae: implications to synergistic factors influencing trematode infections in anurans. Canadian Journal of Zoology 82:701-706.

THIELTGES, D. W., K. T. JENSEN, AND R. POULIN. 2008. The role of biotic factors in the transmission of free-living endohelminth stages. Parasitology 135:407-426.

THIEMANN, G. W., AND R. J. WASSERSUG. 2000. Patterns and consequences of behavioural responses to predators and parasites in *Rana* tadpoles. Biological Journal of the Linnean Society 71:513-528.

TILMAN, D. 1997. Community invasibility, recruitment limitation, and grassland biodiversity. Ecology 78:81-92.

TSAO, J. I., J. T. WOOTTON, J. BUNIKIS, M. G. LUNA, D. FISH, AND A. G. BARBOUR. 2004. An ecological approach to preventing human infection: Vaccinating wild mouse reservoirs intervenes in the Lyme disease cycle. Proceedings of the National Academy of Sciences of the United States of America 101:18159-18164.

VREDENBURG, V. T. 2004. Reversing introduced species effects: experimental removal of introduced fish leads to rapid recovery of a declining frog. Proceedings of the National Academy of Sciences of the United States of America 101:7646-7650.

W.H.O. 2004. The World Health Report 2004: Changing History. . World Health Organization.

ZUUR, A. F., E. N. IENO, N. WALKER, A. A. SAVELIEV, AND G. M. SMITH. 2009. Mixed Effects Models and Extensions in Ecology with R (Statistics for Biology and Health). Springer, New York, NY.

2.1. A) Photograph of Hog Lake following installation of the pond divider in December 2007. B) Photograph of Hog Lake following installation of the cage experiment in June 20009 with notes to illustrate the pond level manipulation of *Ribeiroia* parasite levels.

Figure 2.2. Example of 0.5 m x 0.5 m x 1 m 35µm "fine" mesh cage that is parasite impermeable (left) and 500µm "coarse" mesh that is parasite permeable (right).

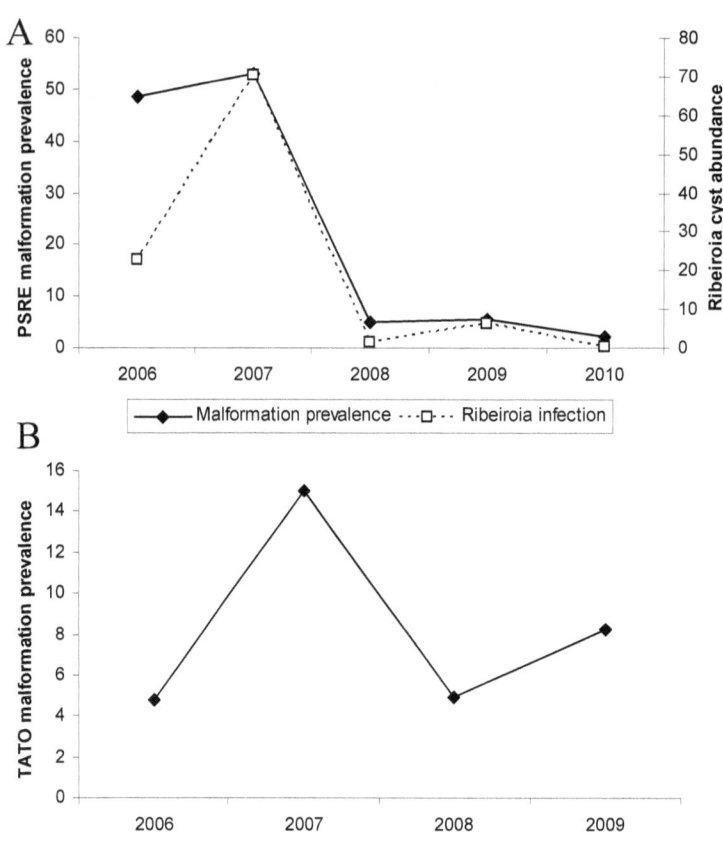

Figure 2.3. A) Long-term malformation prevalence and *Ribeiroia* infection data from Pacific chorus frog *Psuedacris regilla* (PSRE) at Hog Lake. B) Long-term malformation prevalence and *Ribeiroia* infection data from California newt *Taricha torosa* (TATO) at Hog Lake.

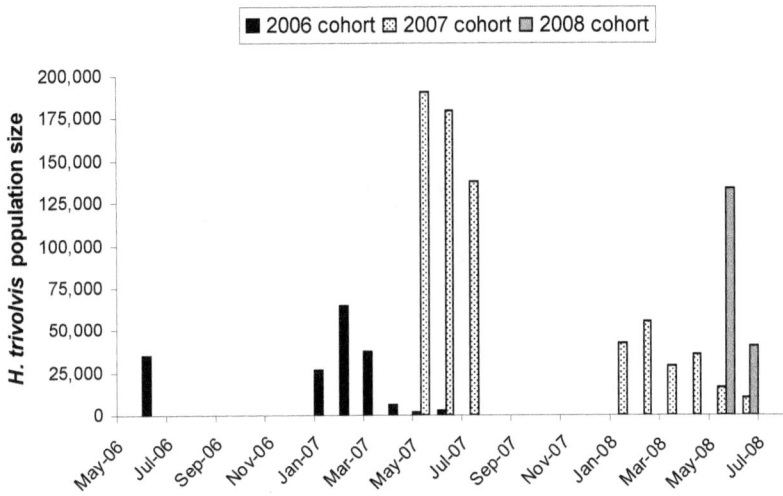

Figure 2.4. Seasonal and interannual population dynamics in the snail *Helisoma trivolvis* (Planorbidae) at Hog Lake from 2006 to 2008.

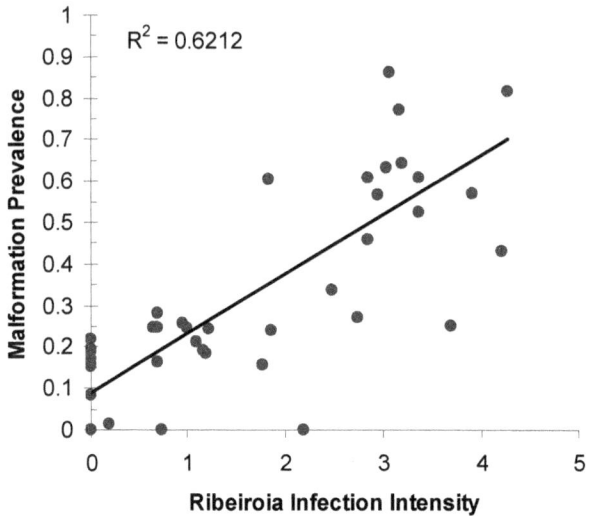

Figure 2.5. Relationship between *Ribeiroia* metacercariae cyst infection intensity (natural log transformed) and malformation prevalence (arcsin-square-root transformed) among Pacific chorus frogs (*P. regilla*) at ponds in Northern California. Ponds sampled on different years were treated as independent for this analysis.

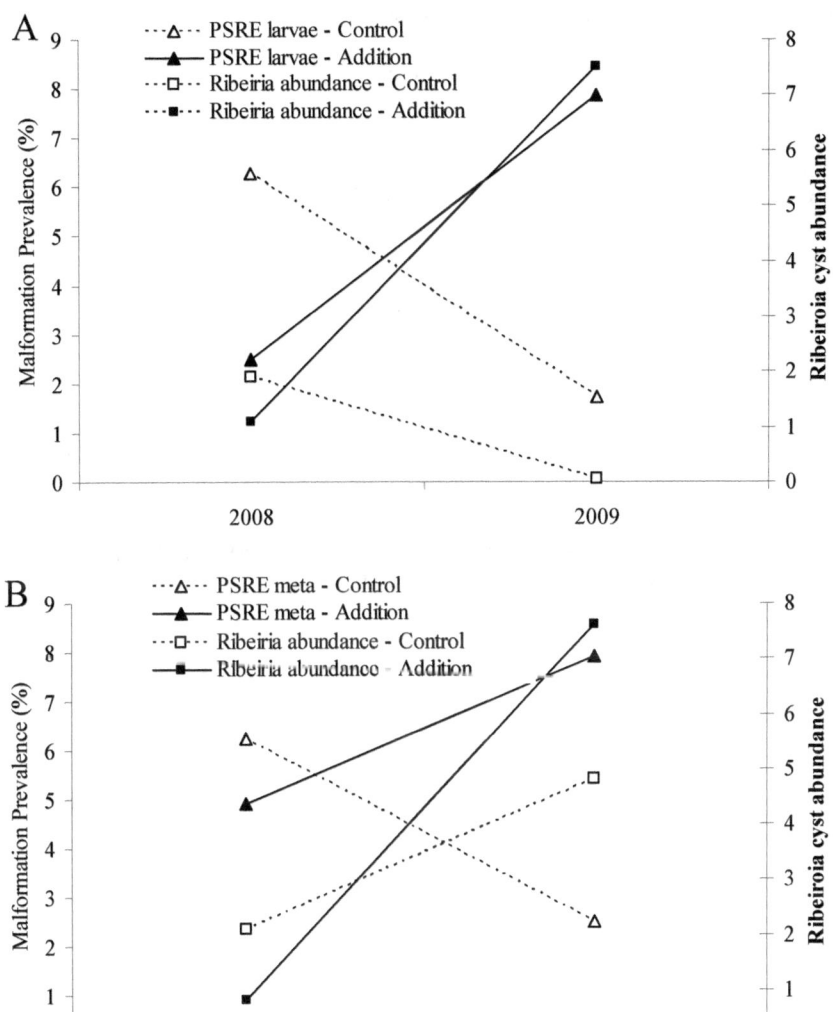

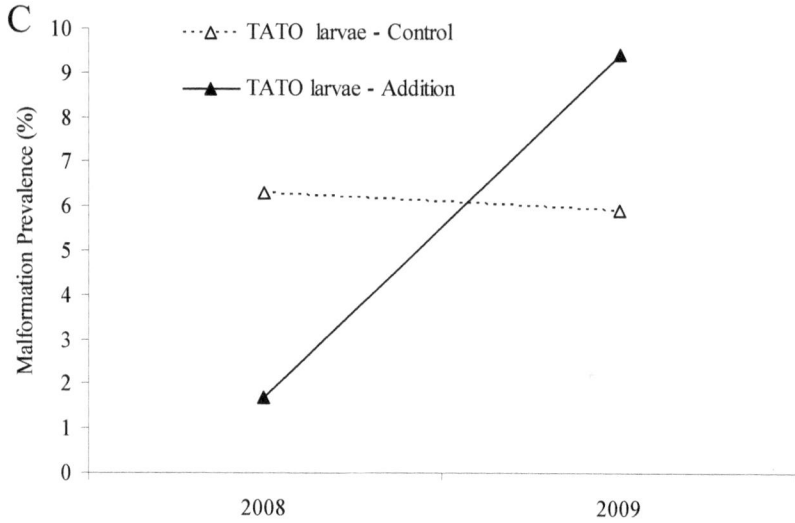

Figure 2.6. Effects of *Ribeiroia* parasite addition on *P. regilla* (PSRE) larvae (A), *P. regilla* metamorphic frogs (B), and *Taricha torosa* (TATO) larvae (C).

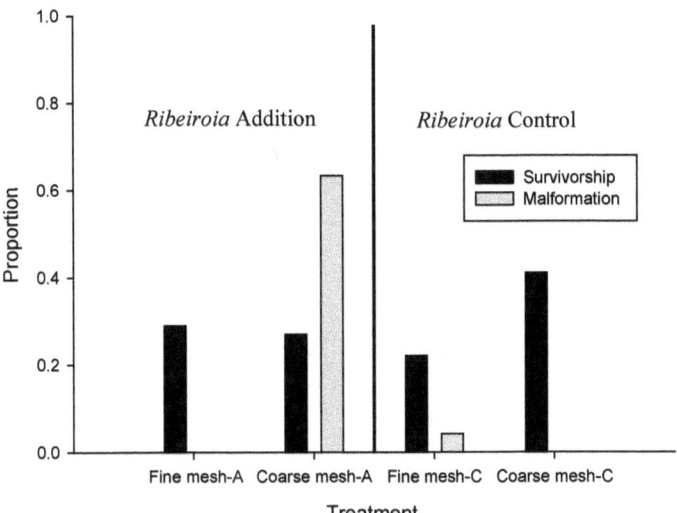

Figure 2.7. Results from cage study within Hog Lake. "Addition" refers to the half-pond treatment of adding *Ribeiroia* infected snails while "Control" refers to the control half-pond that reflects ambient *Ribeiroia* levels. "Fine mesh" refers to the cage mesh of 35 μm which prevents trematodes from entering the cages and "Coarse mesh" refers to 500 μm mesh which will allow parasites to enter.

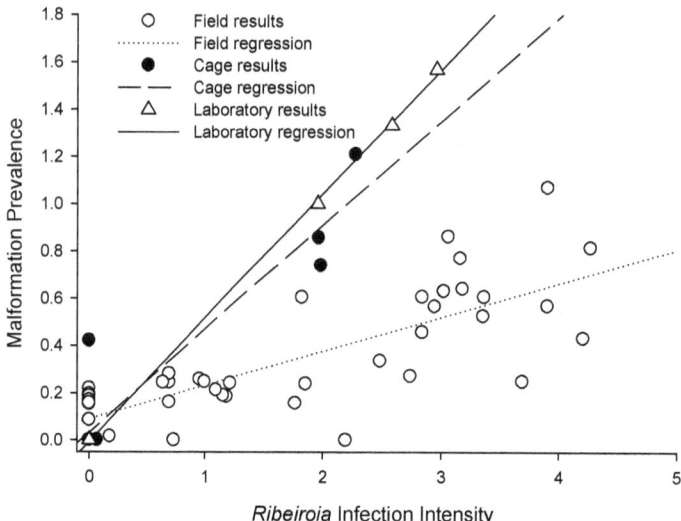

Figure 2.8. Comparison of the dose response effect of *Ribeiroia* on malformation response in *P. regilla* at various spatial scales. Cage results from animals in the Hog Lake cage experiment in 2009 (n=7). Field *P. regilla* frogs from sites across Northern California (n = 42). Laboratory results from Johnson et al. (1999).

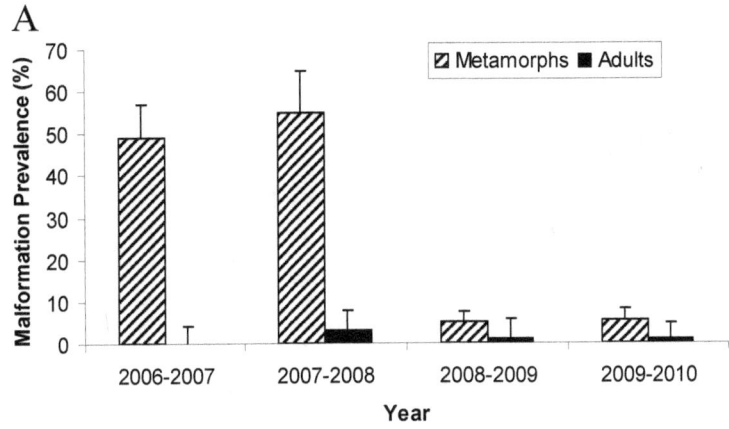

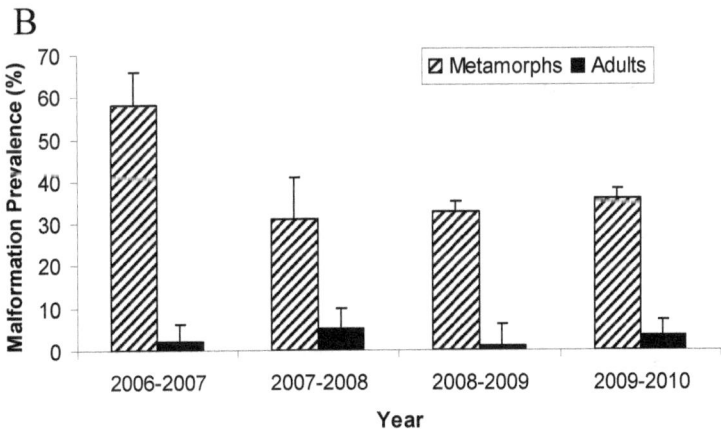

Figure 2.9. Malformation prevalence comparing malformation prevalence of *P. regilla* metamorphic frogs and adult frogs during the following year at Hog Lake (A) and Hidden Pond (B) over four consecutive years.

Table 2.1. Parasite results from *H. trivolvis* snail dissections 2006-2008.

Sample date	Snails shed or dissected	*Ribeiroia* infection prevalence	No. infected snails /m²	Wetland size (m²)	No. infected snails in wetland	*P. regilla* infection rate (for year)	*P. regilla* malformation rate (for year)
7/11/2006	113	0.9%	0.27	700	191	22.6	48.6%
5/21/2007	392	0.5%	0.55	1500	825	70.4	55.4%
6/08/2007	525	0.2%	0.06	1159	72	70.4	55.4%
6/23/2007	158	0	0	500	0	70.4	55.4%
5/18/2008	342	0	0	n/a	0	1.5	5.5%
6/03/2008	510	0	0	n/a	0	1.5	5.5%
6/16/2008	314	0	0	n/a	0	1.5	5.5%

Table 2.2. Mean parameters measured between May and July 2009 at Hog Lake.

Parameter	Control Treatment	Addition Treatment
Water Chemistry		
Turbidity (NTU)	1.6	2.7
Temperature loggers* (°C)	21.8	21.7
Specific Conductance (uS/cm)	154.5	131.6
Dissolved Oxygen (% sat)	146.6	141.0
Dissolved Oxygen (mg/L)	12.1	11.6
pH	8.5	8.8
Total nitrogen (mg/l)	0.887	0.883
Total phosphorus (mg/l)	0.044	0.030
Dissolved organic carbon mg C/L	16.0	15.5
Chromium (mg/L)	0.0004	0.0011
Lead (mg/L)	0.0027	0.0023
Biological Variables		
Planorbid density 2008 (#/m^2)	1.4	0.3
Planorbid density 2009 (#/m^2)	59.0	30
PSRE density (#/m^2)	17.4	13.1
TATO density (#/m^2)	2.3	1.2

* 5/1-7/16 continuous collection every 30 minutes

Table 2.3. Results from nested enclosure study within the Hog Lake in 2009. Pond Treatment refers to *Ribeiroia* addition or control.

Cage number	Cage mesh (μm)	Cage treatment	Hog Lake treatment	Initial sample size	% Survival	% Malformed	*Ribeiroia* cyst load	Weight (g)	Gosner stage
1	35	fine	addition	25	40	0	0	0.633	39
4	35	fine	addition	25	20	0	0	0.601	39
6	35	fine	addition	25	24	0	0	0.708	39
7	35	fine	addition	25	32	0	0	0.747	39
2	500	coarse	addition	25	0	n/a	n/a	n/a	n/a
3	500	coarse	addition	25	28	57.1	6.1	0.496	37
5	500	coarse	addition	25	48	45.5	6.3	0.488	39
8	500	coarse	addition	25	32	87.5	8.8	0.525	38
9	35	fine	control	25	4	0	0	n/a	35
12	35	fine	control	25	20	0	0	0.672	40
14	35	fine	control	25	36	0	0	0.588	39
15	35	fine	control	25	28	16.7	0	0.495	38
10	500	coarse	control	25	56	0	0.1	0.570	39
11	500	coarse	control	25	28	0	0	0.529	38
13	500	coarse	control	25	40	0	0	0.482	39
16	500	coarse	control	25	40	0	0	0.533	39

Table 2.4. Water chemistry conditions on 16 June 2009 within the cage and pond treatments with standard deviation in parenthesis.

Cage treatment	Hog Lake treatment	Specific conductance ($\mu s/cm^2$)	Temperature °C	Dissolved oxygen (%)
fine	addition	184 (5)	23.2 (0.4)	171 (25)
coarse	addition	181 (7)	24.0 (1.0)	170 (54)
fine	control	193 (2)	23.9 (0.9)	181 (14)
coarse	control	195 (1)	25.3 (1.0)	196 (16)

CHAPTER 3

MACROINVERTEBRATE AND AMPHIBIAN ASSEMBLAGES IN STORMWATER PONDS, STOCKPONDS, AND NATURAL PONDS IN NORTHERN CALIFORNIA: THE CONSERVATION VALUE OF CREATED WETLANDS

Macroinvertebrate and amphibian assemblages in stormwater ponds, stockponds, and natural ponds in Northern California: The conservation value of created wetlands

Abstract

Created ponds and wetlands are common features found across urban and agricultural landscapes but little is known about what aquatic species are supported by these habitats and how these habitats may enhance the conservation of aquatic biodiversity. To answer these questions, I sampled the aquatic macroinvertebrate (e.g., insects, snails, crustaceans, and worms) and amphibian assemblage, along with landscape, habitat, and water chemistry variables at natural ponds (n=15) and two types of created ponds, stormwater ponds (n=18) and stockponds (n=16). Based on NMS ordination, the macroinvertebrate community in stormwater ponds was significantly different from those in natural ponds, whereas stockponds supported a macroinvertebrate assemblage that was more similar to natural ponds. Overall, landscape variables (i.e., percent urban and natural, number of ponds within 1 km, and elevation) were the most associated with differences in macroinvertebrate community structure, but specific conductance and percent littoral vegetation were also important co-factors. Native amphibian species richness was highest at stockponds, closely followed by natural ponds, and lowest in stormwater ponds. Native amphibian species richness was positively associated with percent natural land within a 1 km buffer of the ponds, and negatively associated with specific conductance and number of invasive predators (i.e., non-native fish and crayfish, and bullfrogs). Macroinvertebrate taxa richness was positively associated with annual average precipitation, pond surface area, and elevation. Management activities significantly altered the faunal composition at these sites. Among the 31 rural ponds, cattle grazing was associated with increased amphibian species richness, and had moderate association with changes in the community assemblage. Among the 13 perennial ponds, the introduction of invasive fish, whether for vector control (*Gambusia affinis*) or sport fishing (Centrarchidae), was associated with a small shift in macroinvertebrate community structure, mostly reducing taxa that live in the open water column. Ponds with invasive fish were also more likely to support the invasive American bullfrog (*Lithobates catesbeianus*). This study demonstrates the significant conservation value of stockponds within this region and discusses ways to optimally manage both stormwater ponds and stockponds to enhance wildlife resources.

Key words: stressor identification, cattle grazing, introduced fish, wetland, biomonitoring, invasive species, farm pond

INTRODUCTION

Inland freshwater wetlands are physically, chemically, and biologically diverse habitats found throughout the world (Mitsch and Gosselink, 2000). However, they experience severe anthropogenic stress related to water extraction and dams, as well as land conversion to agricultural and urban areas (Baron et al., 2002). A large proportion of historical freshwater wetlands across the world have been drained or destroyed and remaining habitats are extremely threatened (Brinson and Malvarez, 2002).

California has lost over 90% of its natural wetlands (Dahl, 1990), but a large number of artificial wetlands have been created with unknown ecological values or consequences. For example, stockponds, sometimes called farm ponds or cattle ponds, are created as a water source for sheep and cattle and are abundant in the foothills of California's mediterranean climate regions. Additionally, many urban ponds have been created to control flooding or stormwater runoff. Combined, these created ponds comprise an estimated 99% of the 23,000 acres of depressional wetland in the San Francisco Bay Area (http://www.sfei.org/BAARI), yet are poorly studied.

Created wetlands are "novel" ecosystems. Studies on these systems are increasing as ecologists recognize the important role that created or anthropogenically modified habitats can have on biological resources (Hobbs et al., 2006). The creation of novel aquatic habitats can lead to unintended consequences such as providing habitat for invasive species such as the American bullfrog (*Lithobates catesbeianus*) or for mosquitoes, which at minimum are pestiferous but also can serve as vectors for diseases (Knight et al., 2003; O'Geen et al., 2010). Another concern is that wetland organisms could bioaccumulate heavy metals, pesticides, or toxins, bringing these harmful elements into the aquatic food chain (Helfield and Diamond, 1997; Pascoe et al., 1996). A less known consequence is that created eutrophic wetlands might increase aquatic parasites such as trematodes, thereby increasing the prevalence of amphibian malformations (Johnson et al., 2007).

In contrast to potential ecological and human health risks, created wetland habitats can fulfill some functions of natural wetlands including supporting native species and serving as a conservation resource, especially in areas where natural wetlands have been destroyed. Wetland loss is particularly widespread in the San Francisco Bay area where a majority of natural wetlands have been drained to mosquito control or converted to agricultural or urban areas (National Resouces Agency, 2010).

A number of created aquatic habitats including rice fields, farm ponds, stormwater ponds, and golf course ponds have been shown to provide habitat for aquatic birds, fish, amphibians, and insects (e.g., Colding et al., 2009; Elphick and Oring, 1998; Fasola and Ruiz, 1996; Knutson et al., 2004; Ostergaard et al., 2008; Scher and Thiery, 2005; Simon et al., 2009). Despite this emerging interest in created wetlands, however, no studies in California have investigated the fauna found in stockponds or stormwater ponds, or examined environmental variables that may promote native species diversity in created wetlands.

Management of natural and created ponds as well as their surrounding landscape can have significant effects on aquatic communities. For example, a wide body of literature indicates that introduced fish to naturally fishless and created ponds can have negative effects on macroinvertebrate and amphibian populations (Diehl, 1992; Hecnar and McLoskey, 1997; Knapp et al., 2005; Knapp et al., 2001; Knutson et al., 2004; Lawler et al., 1999; Leyse et al., 2004; Morin, 1984; Schilling et al., 2009; van Kleef et al., 2008; Venturelli and Tonn, 2005;

Vredenburg, 2004). Cattle grazing is another managed activity around wetlands that is generally perceived to negatively impact amphibian and invertebrate populations (e.g., Jansen and Healey, 2003; Knutson et al., 2004), and grazing is particularly common around wetlands, vernal pools, and ponds in Northern California.

In order to understand how amphibians and macroinvertebrates use created wetlands in northern California, I sampled natural ponds, stormwater ponds, and stockponds, recording landscape, habitat, and water chemistry variables at each site. The objectives of this research were to: 1) compare the community composition of macroinvertebrates and amphibians among stormwater ponds, stockponds, and natural ponds; 2) investigate the relative importance of various water chemistry, habitat, and landscape factors controlling community composition and species richness; and 3) examine how management activities of cattle grazing and invasive fish stocking can influence amphibian and macroinvertebrate communities.

METHODS

Site Selection

The sampling region of this study encompassed nine counties within the North Coast and Central Valley of California (Fig. 3.1). This region of California experiences a mediterranean climate, characterized by wet, cold winters followed by dry, warm summers, with large annual precipitation differences between years. Average annual rainfall also varies spatially within the region, ranging from 35 cm in the valleys of the region to 135 cm in the mountainous areas (Gilliam, 2002).

A total of 49 sites were selected by targeted sampling, with a focus on capturing a similar number of stormwater ponds, stockponds, and natural ponds throughout the region. Stormwater ponds, constructed from terrestrial areas in order to retain and treat urban runoff and store water during flood events, were identified in urban areas through discussions with personnel of clean water programs, mosquito and vector control agencies, and flood control districts.

Stockponds are artificial ponds created to provide a water source to cattle, sheep or other livestock and were classified as such based on reports from the property manager or by looking for a berm, dike, or dam located on one side of the pond. Not all stockponds are currently used by cattle even though they may have initially been built for that purpose. The stockpond class also included a small number of ponds build in rural areas as a fishpond, reservoir, or for aesthetics. Stockponds were typically built just below a natural spring or in the upper portions of a headwater stream that only has flowing water during and a few days after storm events.

Natural ponds included perennial sag ponds, seasonal depressional wetlands, and vernal pools, and were confirmed as natural based on information from land managers. Among all ponds, the term perennial is used to describe ponds that have surface water year-round, whereas seasonal ponds typically start to fill in the first large storm of the season (October to December) and dry out between May and September. Natural sites mostly occurred within regional parks, reserves, and private properties with low urban development and without active agriculture on the property.

The landscape surrounding natural ponds and stockponds was typically composed of oak woodlands, chaparral shrubs, and exotic annual grasses. These habitats were hydrologically isolated (i.e., not riparian or connected via a floodplain) freshwater systems with salinities below

6 ppt. Site selection focused on small wetlands, generally 0.1 - 2 hectares in size. Ponds were sampled in 2007 (n = 5), 2008 (n = 3), 2009 (n = 33), and 2010 (n = 8).

In order to limit the effects of seasonality (i.e., intra-annual variability), sampling was restricted to a specific index period, as is recommended for aquatic macroinvertebrate biomonitoring protocols in streams and wetlands (Barbour et al., 1999; Trigal et al., 2006). Sample dates of the main study were restricted to late spring and early summer (May 5 – July 12), at which time most macroinvertebrates captured would be large enough to identify but most taxa would not have already emerged.

Macroinvertebrate Sampling and Laboratory Methods

Freshwater wetlands were sampled to determine the composition of the overall aquatic macroinvertebrate community, which included all crustaceans greater than 500 µm, mollusks, and insects. Following results described elsewhere in this dissertation (Dissertation Chapter 4), macroinvertebrates were sampled using 20 active netsweeps with a 500-µm D-frame dipnet by the same person (KBL). Each sweep involved a 1 m long pull that sampled organisms through the water surface, limnetic zone, and benthic zone, thereby collecting neuston, nekton/zooplankton, and benthos respectively. In total, the 20 sweeps sampled 6.1 m^2 of pond area, collected at various depths throughout the wadeable littoral zone.

Macroinvertebrates were collected using a novel, standardized multi-habitat sampling approach. I sampled different microhabitats present in lentic habitats in proportion to their relative abundance because taxonomic groups show strong affinities to vegetation and sediment structure (e.g., Garcia-Criado and Trigal, 2005; Trigal et al., 2006).

Sampling was focused throughout the wadeable littoral zone because that area was accessible by wading and contains the majority of species found in lentic habitats (Garcia-Criado and Trigal, 2005; Trigal et al., 2006). The sampling area was classified into four habitat types prior to sampling: emergent vegetation (e.g., *Typha* spp., *Scirpus* spp., *Eleocaris* spp.), submerged vegetation (e.g., *Ceratophyllum* spp., *Myriophyllum* spp., *Potamogeton* spp.), floating vegetation (e.g., *Lemna* spp., *Azola* spp., algae), and open areas (absence of vegetation). The 20 sweeps were stratified according to percent occupied by the four sample types. For example, if 30% of the littoral zone was occupied with emergent vegetation, then 6 of the 20 sweeps (30%) were taken from that habitat class. For wetlands that were extremely small (< 0.03 ha) and where 20 independent sweeps could not be taken, a composite sample based on only 10 total sweeps was taken.

In the field, composite macroinvertebrate samples were double-elutriated to reduce the amount of aquatic vegetation and organic debris in the sample. Macroinvertebrates were preserved with 95% ethanol in the field for a final concentration of 70% and returned to the laboratory.

In the laboratory, macroinvertebrate samples were randomly subsampled to a fixed count of 500 organisms and identified to genera. Subsampling was accomplished using a custom-made 30.5 x 35.5 cm Caton-type tray (Dissertation Chapter 4). At least 3 out of 42 total 5 x 5-cm sections were sampled and then each of those was randomly subsampled using a 5-cm square Petri dish divided into 16 subsections. Sorted individuals were identified to SAFIT Standard taxonomic effort (STE) Level I (Richards and Rogers, 2006) with additional resolution for Chironomidae (subfamily), Oligochaeta (order/family), Hirudinea (genus), Copepoda (genus), Cladocera (genus), and Ostracoda (order/family) by EcoAnalysts Inc. Obligate terrestrial

Coleoptera as well as all pupal and adult Diptera were excluded. To test for quality assurance three samples were selected for a replicate susbsample and identification.

Environmental and Stressor Variables

To determine how water quality, local physical habitat, landscape, and human- altered biotic variables affect the macroinvertebrate assemblage, a number of variables were collected in the field or obtained using geographic information systems (GIS). In the field temperature (°C) and specific conductance (conductivity calibrated to 25°C) were measured using a YSI MP 556 meter, and pH using Oakton pHTstr 3. Turbidity (NTU) was measured with a HACH 2100P turbidity meter.

Water samples were collected with a single grab sample within the littoral area of each wetland. Water samples for total chromium and total lead were stored at 5°C until testing by the UC Davis DANR Laboratory. Water samples for total dissolved nitrogen (TDN), and total dissolved phosphorous (TDP) were frozen within 8 hrs of collection, then thawed and filtered using glass fiber filter (Whatman GF/D 2.7 µm) prior to analysis (Cukjati and Seibold, 2010). The TDN:TDP ratio was calculated as a stoichiometric atomic ratio to evaluate N or P limitation in the systems (Guildford and Hecky, 2000). A metric for nutrient enrichment was calculated based on the stoichiometric quantities of primary production that could be created from the TDN:TDP assuming a 16:1 molar ratio.

The number of invasive predators metric was calculated using field observations and reports from landowners or managers regarding the presence of (1) introduced Centrarchidae (e.g., *Micropterus* spp., *Lepomis* spp.), (2) Western mosquitofish (*Gambusia affinis*), (3) predatory bullfrogs (i.e., *Rana catesbeiana*), or (4) invasive crayfish (i.e., *Pacifastacus leniusculus, Procambarus clarikii*). Native fish such as the Sacramento perch (*Archoplites interruptus*) or the three-spined stickleback (*Gasterosteus aculeatus*) were not counted in the invasive metric even if they were introduced to the pond because they are native to the region. Each invasive predator received a score of 1 for presence or 0 for absence. Therefore, the total score for invasive predators could range from 0 to 4. Also a binary metric based on the presence of any invasive centrarchrid or *G. affinis* was created to test for explicit effect of fish management.

Landscape variables were calculated with ESRI ArcInfo v9.2 or Google Earth (ESRI, 2005; Google Inc., 2009). The effects of landscape variables were assessed at a 1-km radius surrounding the center point of the wetland. The proportion of urbanization within these zones (percent urban) and proportion natural (percent natural) was calculated from the National Land Cover Dataset 2001 dataset (Homer et al., 2004). The NLCD categories of low (code 22), medium (code 23), and high (code 24) intensity developed were collapsed into a single urban category. Pond size (surface area) was determined using Google Earth Professional and the most currently available imagery during the wet season (December-May).

To assess the importance of connectivity to other aquatic habitats two variables were calculated: (1) the influence of proximate streams measured the stream length from the National Hydrography Dataset (U.S. Geological Survey and U.S. Environmental Protection Agency, 1999) within each 1-km buffer zone; and (2) the importance of lentic habitats measured the number of natural or artificial wetlands, ponds, and reservoirs within the 1-km buffer that were visible in Google Earth imagery obtained during the wet season. Buffers of 1 km in Google Earth were calculated around the midpoint of the wetland using the GE-Path 1.4.4 extension (Sgrillo, 2009).

The mean value and standard error for landscape, habitat, and water chemistry variables were calculated for all continuous data. For binary response variables, data were represented as percent of ponds with the given variable present.

Species Composition, Diversity, and Abundance: Macroinvertebrates

To determine if the macroinvertebrate assemblage showed distinct differences between stormwater ponds, stockponds, and natural ponds, assemblage data were compared using ordination, multi-response permutation procedures (MRPP), analysis of variance (ANOVA), and t-tests. Nonmetric multidimensional scaling (NMS) ordination was performed on 49 sites based on Sørenson/ Bray Curtis distance measures in PC-ORD (McCune and Mefford, 2006). NMS Ordination criteria were two axis, 250 runs with real data, 300 runs with randomized data, a stability criterion of < 0.001, 10 iterations to evaluate stability, and a maximum number of iterations of 250. Raw relative abundance data was natural log transformed (ln (x + 1)) prior to analysis. To limit the noise from rare taxa, taxa that occurred at only one site were excluded if less than 10 individuals out of the 500 were identified (Van Sickle et al., 2007). Continuous explanatory variables were shown in ordination space if it was strongly associated with a given axis based on the squared correlation coefficient (R^2) greater than 0.2. Non-normally distributed explanatory variables were either natural log (ln (x)) or arcsine square root transformed (arcsine($\sqrt{x}$)). Indicator species analysis in PC-ORD (McCune and Mefford, 2006) was used to identify particular taxa that were statistically more common and abundant within a particular group based on an indicator value > 20 and p < 0.05 (McCune and Grace, 2002). Pond type was treated as a categorical variable and compared using MRPP in PC-ORD (McCune and Grace 2002). MRPP is analogous to a nonparametric MANOVA and looks to minimize total variability in the data by assigning sites to groups. In general, statistically significant A statistics resulting from ecological data are often < 0.1 although this number can range from 0 (no grouping effect) to 1 (each group is composed of identical sites) (McCune and Grace, 2002). Tests for differences among groups with continuous explanatory variables used ANOVA or t-test. Comparisons of two continuous variables involved ordinary least squares regression.

A general linear model was used to predict macroinvertebrate taxa richness in JMP (JMP, 2010). A total of 21 variables were screened for potential inclusion in this model. Bayesian information criterion (BIC) was used in testing various models to find the most parsimonious model and identify the most relevant explanatory variables.

Species Composition and Diversity: Amphibian Assemblage

Amphibian presence or absence of larvae was evaluated at each site using observations from the same 20 netsweeps used for macroinvertebrates. Metamorphic (i.e., those that emerged that summer) and adult life stages were sampled visually by inspecting a survey zone 2 m in either direction of the water line (Olson et al., 1997). Additionally, American bullfrogs (*L. catesbeianus*) or Pacific chorus frogs (*Pseudacris regilla*) were identified by breeding calls. If any life stage of any species was observed, that species was recorded as present. The native amphibian species richness metric was calculated from these data and bullfrog presence was incorporated into the invasive predator metric.

A general linear model was used to predict native amphibian species richness (JMP, 2010). A total of 17 variables were screened for potential inclusion in this model. Bayesian information criterion (BIC) was used in testing various models to find the most parsimonious model and identify the most relevant explanatory variables.

Management Effects on Pond Communities: Grazing

To determine if grazing was associated with differences in macroinvertebrate community composition, the analysis was limited to 31 rural (non-stormwater) sites to remove urban impacts from the analysis. Reports of grazing history were taken from landowners and property managers regarding whether cattle or livestock had access to graze around and within the pond for at least two weeks during that season. This information was incorporated in a binary variable of grazed or not-grazed. A pond was considered not-grazed if no cattle were in the watershed or cattle were excluded by a fence surrounding the entire pond with a buffer of at least 3 m. Grazing intensity was not recorded for this study.

NMS ordination was performed on 31 sites based on Sørenson/ Bray Curtis distance measures in PC-ORD (McCune and Mefford, 2006). NMS Ordination criteria were two axis, 250 runs with real data, 300 runs with randomized data, a stability criterion of < 0.001, 10 iterations to evaluate stability, and a maximum number of iterations of 250. Raw relative abundance data was natural log transformed (ln (x + 1)) prior to analysis. To limit the noise from rare taxa, taxa that occurred at only one site were excluded if less than 10 individuals out of the 500 were identified (Van Sickle et al., 2007). Continuous explanatory variables were shown in ordination space if it was strongly associated with a given axis based on the squared correlation coefficient (R^2) threshold of 0.25. Non-normally distributed explanatory variables were either natural log transformed or arcsine square root transformed (for proportions). Indicator species analysis in PC-ORD (McCune and Mefford, 2006) was used to identify particular taxa that were statistically more common and abundant within a particular group based on an indicator value > 20 and p < 0.10 (McCune and Grace, 2002). The 16 non-grazed ponds were compared to the 15 grazed ponds using MRPP in PC-ORD (McCune and Grace, 2002). In JMP, a t-test was used to examine how grazing affected macroinvertebrate richness, biomass, nutrient levels, and nutrient ratios, and chi-squared tests to examine if grazing was associated with the presence of invasive bullfrogs (JMP, 2010).

Management effects on Pond Communities: Invasive Fish Stocking

To determine how the introduction of invasive fish affected macroinvertebrate community composition, the analysis was limited to non-urban perennial stockponds or natural ponds (n=13). Criteria to classify invasive fish were described previously. The data from the NMS ordination of the 49 sites was used for the MRPP analysis of only the 13 perennial ponds comparing the 6 fishless ponds and the 7 ponds with invasive fish using PC-ORD (McCune and Grace, 2002). Indicator species analysis in PC-ORD (McCune and Mefford, 2006) was used to identify particular taxa that were statistically more common and abundant within a particular group based on an indicator value > 20 and p value < 0.05 (McCune and Grace, 2002). I used t-tests to examine how fish presence affected macroinvertebrate richness and biomass as well as native amphibian species richness. A Chi-squared test was used to determine if the presence of the invasive American bullfrog was associated with the presence of invasive fish.

RESULTS

Stormwater ponds, stockponds, and natural ponds varied in their water chemistry, physical habitat, and landscape variables (Table 3.1). For example, stormwater ponds tended to be larger, perennial, and to occur at lower elevations with less average rainfall than natural ponds or stockponds. Natural ponds tended to the smaller, shallower, and to occur in a landscape with more surrounding ponds. Natural ponds were more likely to be seasonal, i.e., the ponds dry out sometime between May and September each year. In terms of potential stressor variables, stormwater ponds were surrounded by more urban land and had the most invasive predators, highest specific conductance, and highest molar productivity. Stockponds were similar to natural ponds except for having the lowest turbidity levels and slightly more invasive predators.

Species Composition, Diversity, and Abundance: Macroinvertebrates

A diverse and abundant macroinvertebrate complex was identified across all pond types. In total, 157 macroinvertebrate taxa were identified at 49 ponds. On average, each pond supported 19.6 taxa and richness ranged from 6 to 36 taxa per site. The most common taxa overall were the water flea *Simocephalus*, chironomid midges (subfamilies Chironominae and Orthocladiinae), and damselflies (Coenagrionidae). The most abundant taxa overall was *Simocephalus*, which was present in 26% of the overall samples. In general, crustaceans (zooplankton) were more abundant than insects, snails, or worms (Table 3.2).

Macroinvertebrate taxa richness was partially predicted by three environmental variables (annual average precipitation, pond surface area, and elevation), which together explained 37.9 % of the variation in the data ($F = 9.2, p < 0.001$). Although macroinvertebrate diversity and richness differed slightly between pond types, there were no significant differences between them. There also were no significant differences in taxonomic richness between the three pond classes ($p = 0.67$; Table 3.3). Taxonomic richness showed a positive but weak relationship with wetland size ($p = 0.1$) and was not correlated with percent of the wetland classified as littoral ($p = 0.5$).

Macroinvertebrate density varied substantially between the 49 ponds, but these differences were not associated water chemistry or pond class. Macroinvertebrate density ranged from 47 to 10,781 individuals/m^2 (median = 2071). Although total macroinvertebrate density differed slightly between pond types (Table 3.3), these differences were not significant ($p = 0.7$). Macroinvertebrate density was also not significantly associated with changes in TDN, TDP, Redfield Ratio (molar TDN:TDP), or molar productivity ($p > 0.7$).

The composition of macroinvertebrate assemblages observed at the three pond types showed distinct differences. For example, the NMS ordination identified significant clustering of taxa between stormwater ponds, stockponds, and natural ponds (Fig. 3.2; MRPP: $A = 0.16; p < 0.00001$). According to indicator species analysis, water boatmen (*Corisella* sp., *Cenocorixa* sp., *Trichocorixa* sp.), oligochaete worms (Lumbriculidae and Culicidae), chironomid midges (Orthocladiinae), and springtails (Isotomidae) were unique to stormwater ponds. Stormwater ponds also supported a few taxa that were specifically more common and abundant in rural artificial habitats. In contrast, stockponds were more likely to support planorbid snails (*Helisoma* sp.), mayflies (*Callibaetis* sp.), damselflies (Libellulidae, Coenagrionidae), beetles (*Haliplus* sp.), water fleas (*Macrocyclops* sp.), and chironomid midges (Tanypodiinae). Lastly, natural ponds favored a different type of planorbid snail (*Mentus* sp.), water fleas (*Moina* sp.), clam shrimps (*Lynceus brachyurus*), copepods (*Letpodiaptomus* sp.), and phantom midges (*Chaoborus* sp.). The most common taxa found at each of these pond classes was similar to the most common taxa overall (Table 3.4).

Overall, landscape variables (i.e., elevation, percent natural, percent urban, number of ponds within 1 km) were the most common continuous explanatory variables in the NMS ordination of 49 sites (Fig. 3.2). Specific conductance was associated with sites on the right side of the ordination, which were stormwater ponds. The percent of littoral pond vegetation was a significant variable in the model and tended toward stockponds and natural ponds. Sample date was an important factor in the ordination, suggesting that the order of pond sampling or natural phenology could be affecting composition. Lastly, native amphibian richness was strongly associated with axis 1 and showed an increase among stockponds. Therefore, most water chemistry (e.g., nutrients, heavy metals) and pond structure (e.g., mean depth, size, and percent littoral) variables were not associated with biological differences in this model.

Rare taxa that are adapted to annual pond desiccation were encountered at seasonal ponds. For example, one species of fairy shrimp (*Linderiella occidentalis*) was identified from a natural, seasonal pond. Likewise, two genera of clam shrimp (i.e., *Cyzicus* sp., *Lynceus* sp.) were identified in four samples, three of which were natural ponds and the fourth was a seasonal stockpond. Fingernail clams (Sphaeriidae), also a rare taxa, were observed at five sites, two stockponds and three natural ponds.

Mosquitoes (Culicidae) were uncommon in all pond types, and were detected at only 9 out of 49 ponds (18%). In general, average abundance when present was 6 individuals /m^2 (range 1 – 150). Although stormwater ponds are the habitat types most likely to produce vectors that can transmit diseases between humans because of their proximity to large population centers, only 3 of the 18 stormwater ponds supported a detectable mosquito population. Further, no significant differences in mosquito density were observed between the three pond classes ($p = 0.4$, Table 3.3).

Species Composition and Diversity: Amphibians

Amphibian presence and diversity varied according to pond class (Table 3.5). Amphibian species richness was highest in the stockponds, whereas richness in both natural and stockponds was significantly greater than stormwater ponds ($p < 0.0001$). Of the 7 native pond breeding amphibian species in this region, 6 were encountered in this study (Table 3.5). In general the ponds supported a median of 1 species, with individual sites supporting 0 to 4 native species. The Pacific chorus frog (*P. regilla*) was the most common amphibian (67% of sites), followed by the California newt (*Taricha torosa*) at 41% of sites, western toad (*Bufo boreas*) at 16% of sites, California red-legged frog (*Rana draytonii*) at 8% of sites, the California tiger salamander (*Ambystoma californiense*) at 4% of sites, and the western spadefoot toad (*Spea hamondii*) at 2% of sites (Table 3.5). The rough skinned newt (*Taricha granulosa*) was not sampled in this study although it can be found in this region in natural and created ponds (Kuchta, 2005, P. Johnnson unpubl. data). The most common amphibian at stormwater ponds was *P. regilla*, and both *P. regilla* and *T. torosa* were common at stockponds and natural ponds. The invasive American bullfrog (*R. catesbeiana*), which is native to the midwestern US (Stebbins, 2003), was encountered at 27% of sites. Of the 14 bullfrog occurrences, only two were in natural ponds while 4 were observed in stormwater ponds and 8 in stockponds. Bullfrogs were rarely observed in seasonal ponds which dry once a year, and the two observations seasonal ponds were of adults as opposed to the larval (i.e., tadpole) life stage that would indicate successful reproduction.

Amphibian species richness was largely predicted by three environmental variables. A stepwise general linear regression model screening 17 potential explanatory variables related to basic water quality (pH, specific conductivity, and turbidity), landscape variables (number of ponds, percent urban, and percent natural within in 1 km), heavy metals (chromium, copper), nutrients (Redfield ratio, molar productivity), vegetation (percent vegetation in littoral and whole pond), and pond structure (pond size, hydrology, number of invasive predators, percent littoral, and littoral slope). The model with the lowest BIC included three variables which explained 43.6% of the variance in amphibian species richness ($F = 13.0, p < 0.001$). The order of importance in the model was percent natural, specific conductance, and number of invasive predators. Number of invasive predators and specific conductance were negatively correlated with richness, while percent of natural area within a 1-km buffer of the pond was positively correlated with richness.

Management Effects on Pond Communities: Cattle grazing

Pond grazing by livestock was associated with significant differences in both the macroinvertebrate and amphibian communities. For example, the NMS ordination of the 31 rural ponds showed a mild difference in community composition between the grazed ponds (n = 15) and non-grazed ponds (n = 16), a difference confirmed by MRPP analyses ($A = 0.047, p < 0.025$; Fig. 3.3). Indicator species analysis identified five taxa unique to non-grazed ponds: water fleas (*Simocephalus* sp., *Ceriodaphnia* sp.), water mites (Acari), damselflies (*Lestes* sp.), and calanoid copepods (*Acanthocyclops* sp.). In contrast, no taxa were identified as unique in grazed ponds. The difference in taxonomic richness between grazed (23) and non-grazed (16) ponds trended toward significance ($t = -1.7, p = 0.1$); however, grazing showed no association with differences in macroinvertebrate abundance ($t = 0.04, p = 0.97$). Grazing was not associated with increased nutrient levels as measured by TDN, TDP, the Redfield ratio, or the productivity score ($p > 0.2$), but grazed ponds did have significantly higher turbidity ($t = 3.1, p < 0.005$). MRPP of rural ponds identified a strong and significant difference between perennial and seasonal ponds ($A = 0.11, p < 0.001$).

Grazing was positively associated with native amphibian species richness. Among the same 31 rural ponds, grazed ponds had a mean amphibian diversity of 2.6 compared to 1.6 at non-grazed ponds ($t = 2.2, p = 0.035$). Grazing showed no significant association with invasive bullfrog presence ($\chi^2 = 0.08, p = 0.78$).

Management Effects on Pond Communities: Invasive Fish

The introduction of non-native sunfish (Centrarchidae) for sport fishing or vector control (*Gambusia affinis*) was associated with differences in macroinvertebrate community structure. Macroinvertebrate community composition at ponds with non-native fish (n=6) and ponds without (n=7) were visibly distinct according to the NMS (Fig. 3.4). Although the MRPP group analysis found a moderate A statistic for this difference, the statistical probability was greater than 0.05 ($A = 0.07, p = 0.08$). According to the indictor species analysis, ponds without invasive fish had more cladocerans (*Simocephalus* sp), backswimmers (Notonectidae), and water mites (Acari), all three of which commonly use open water. In contrast, the ponds with invasive fish had a greater number of tanypodine midges, which generally reside in sediment. Although macroinvertebrate density was 50% less in ponds with invasive fish, this difference was not statistically significant ($t = -1.15, p = 0.27$). Macroinvertebrate richness in ponds with fish (20.7) was not significantly different in ponds without (23.3) ($t = -0.65, p = 0.52$).

The amphibian community showed negative associations to introduced invasive fish within the 13 non-urban perennial ponds. In terms of diversity, a small difference in native amphibian richness was observed between ponds with fish (2.2) and those without (1.6), yet this difference was not statistically significant ($t = -0.9$, $p = 0.37$). In contrast, the invasive American bullfrog was significantly more common at ponds with invasive fish than those without ($\chi^2 = 6.2$, $p < 0.013$). Of the seven perennial non-urban ponds with bullfrogs, six supported invasive fish, which included both invasive sunfish and mosquitofish at four ponds and just mosquitofish at two.

DISCUSSION

This study examined the macroinvertebrate and amphibian communities found in two types of created ponds (stormwater ponds and stockponds) and compared these findings to natural ponds. In general this study identified a wide array of lentic taxa by sampling among pond vegetation, along the benthos, and throughout the water column in within each pond.

Differences Between Pond Classes: Macroinvertebrates

Stormwater ponds, stockponds, and natural ponds supported significantly different macroinvertebrate communities, differences associated with environmental variables, the majority of which were landscape level factors (Fig. 3.2). Specific conductance was highest in stormwater ponds, indirect evidence of poor water quality in these habitats due to higher concentrations of salts, nutrients, and other ionic compounds coming from return irrigation water and urban runoff; elevated conductivities have been linked to changes in invertebrate diversity and community structure through both direct and indirect effects (reviewed in Adamus et al., 2001; Makepeace et al., 1995). Stormwater ponds had the most invasive predators (fish or crayfish), contained the highest levels of productivity based on nutrient stoichiometry, and were perennial, additional factors that can potentially alter macroinvertebrate community structure (Della Bella et al., 2005; Knapp et al., 2001; Solimini et al., 2008; Trigal et al., 2009). In terms of macroinvertebrates, stormwater ponds had more worms, leeches, and water boatmen, taxa considered to be indicative of poor ecological condition (Adamus et al., 2001; U.S. EPA, 2002). According to the NMS ordination, there was almost no overlap between the cluster of stormwater sites and the natural ponds, indicating that the communities found at these sites was significantly different from stockponds and natural ponds, a result supported by MRPP analysis (Fig. 3.2). The four stormwater ponds with the biological communities most similar to natural ponds shared some similarities in that they were small (< 0.3 ha), have shallow littoral slopes, and support a higher degree of emergent vegetation emergent vegetation (e.g., *Typha* spp., *Scirpus* spp., *Eleocaris* spp.).

Stockponds also supported macroinvertebrate assemblages that differed from stormwater ponds but were more similar to natural ponds (Fig. 3.2). Stockponds tended to be small (< 0.2 ha) and deep (> 1 m) with moderate levels of invasive predators, and, surprisingly, the lowest productivity levels. However, in most respects, the environmental variables at stockponds and natural ponds were similar. Stockponds were the most likely ponds to support relatively large numbers mayfly and damselfly genera. These taxa are part of the Ephemeroptera-Odonata-Trichoptera (EOT) indicator, which is a common metric of pond biomonitoring programs that indicate a high level of ecological integrity (Helgen and Gernes, 2001, Dissertation Chapter 4). The moderate similarity between stockponds and natural ponds demonstrates that stockponds have higher conservation value than stormwater ponds. Of the five stockponds that supported a community most similar to natural ponds, four were seasonal and none were grazed by cattle.

Natural ponds tended to the smallest, shallowest habitats and typically would dry out seasonally. The five taxa most likely to be found at natural ponds did not share any pattern in functional feeding group or habitat association. Still, the general taxonomic associations across all three pond types can be used to develop metrics to determine how similar created ponds are to natural ones. The four vernal pools from the Central Valley and one from the North Coast showed the most dissimilarity from the other natural ponds, suggesting that duration of time the pond was dry will affect the macroinvertebrate assemblage. Unfortunately, the specific time of inundation could not be determined for every site in order to examine the hydroperiod relationship further. The two natural ponds with the most overlap with stormwater ponds and therefore assumed to have the worst condition were large perennial ponds, one of which was near an urban area and both contained large populations of invasive centrarchids and mosquitofish.

In terms of macroinvertebrate richness, the three variables with predictive power were all natural landscape or habitat variables. Therefore, attempts to maximize overall invertebrate diversity based on local habitat restoration or water quality improvements may not yield significant improvements in this metric. Macroinvertebrate richness showed a slight association with pond size as would be predicted by typical species-area relationships, and pond size was a significant predictor of taxa richness when incorporated in the general liner model with other parameters. Therefore, the weak species-area relationships identified in this study is similar to that reported by Oertli et al. (2002) which did not identify a size-area relationship for most taxa except odonates.

Differences Between Pond Classes: Amphibians

This study provides strong evidence that stockponds have a significant conservation value for amphibians in this region. Amphibian species richness was highest in the stockponds, whereas richness in both natural and stockponds was significantly greater than stormwater ponds (Table 3.5). Overall, Pacific chorus frogs and California newts were the most commonly encountered species and were found at most natural ponds and stockponds, which is expected because these species are both common and abundant throughout their ranges (Jennings and Hayes, 1994; Kuchta, 2005; Rorabaugh and Lannoo, 2005). These results reinforce anecdotal reports in California, which state that stockponds can support a diverse amphibian assemblage.

Amphibian richness across all sites increased in response the percent of natural habitat (non urban, non agricultural) in the 1 km surrounding landscape, and decreased in response to specific conductance and invasive predators. The invasive predator metric was composed of two classes of fish: sunfish (Centrarchidae), which have been shown to have negative effect on most amphibians (Adams, 2000; Boone et al., 2007; Kiesecker and Blaustein, 1998; Schilling et al., 2009; van Kleef et al., 2008; Werner and McPeek, 1994); and western mosquitofish (*Gambusia affinis*), which have been shown to negatively affect California red-legged frogs (Lawler et al., 1999). The predator metric also included crayfish, which have been shown to negatively affect amphibian populations (Kats and Ferrer, 2003; Riley et al., 2005; Rodriguez et al., 2005), and invasive American bullfrogs, which prey on native amphibians in the Western United States (Hayes and Jennings, 1986; Kiesecker and Blaustein, 1998; Lawler et al., 1999). Other studies have also observed reductions in amphibian populations with increasing specific conductance (Hamer and Parris, 2011; Karraker et al., 2008; Simon et al., 2009; Stumpel and van der Voet, 1998) . Specific conductance was highest in stormwater ponds, which might be a contributing factor why amphibians were rare in that pond type. Landscape factors such as percent natural within buffer zones around ponds has been identified as an important amphibian predictor in many regions (Loman and Lardner, 2006; Ostergaard et al., 2008; Simon et al., 2009). In addition, studies have shown that many stressors can act in a compounding manner on amphibian populations (e.g., Boone et al., 2007; Kiesecker and Blaustein, 1998; Reeves et al., 2010).

Rare amphibian species were encountered in this survey, and were present at created wetlands. Of the four sites with California red-legged frogs, three were artificial: two stockponds and one stormwater pond. California red-legged frogs are known to use stockponds (U.S. Fish and Wildlife Service, 2002) and have also been known to colonize water treatment ponds treatment (K Lunde, unpublished data). However, the presence of an endangered species at stormwater and treatment ponds can cause a conflict between pond management and safeguards against endangered species. Endangered California tiger salamanders were encountered at two sites in this survey, both of which were natural vernal pools. So this species appears to use created habitats less often than California red-legged frogs.

Effects of Pond Management: Cattle Grazing and Introduced Fish

Cattle grazing is a managed activity around wetlands that is generally perceived to negatively impact ecological condition, and there is evidence of this effect (e.g., Jansen and Healey, 2003; Knutson et al., 2004). In Belgium, farm ponds were found to have high conservation value when cattle access was limited (Declerck et al., 2006). However, other studies have shown mixed results from grazing depending on the amphibian focal species (Bull et al., 2001; Bull and Hayes, 2000; Burton et al., 2009; Schmutzer et al., 2008). In California, recent studies indicate that grazing of vernal pools increases the hydroperiod (time the pond is covered with surface water) long enough to significantly increase the acreage of suitable breeding habitat for the endangered California tiger salamander (Marty, 2005; Pyke and Marty, 2005).

In this study, cattle grazing showed significant associations with both macroinvertebrate and amphibian assemblages. In particular, ponds that were grazed had higher native amphibian species richness. In terms of macroinvertebrates, the effect of grazing was visible on the macroinvertebrate community, but the results were inconclusive whether the effect was positive or negative. *Lestes*, a genus of damselfly (Odonata) that are a component of the EOT metric used as a indicator of good wetland condition, was more common in non-grazed ponds. However, three of the other indicator taxa of non-grazed ponds were microcrustaceans, which are generally not sampled in wetland monitoring programs in the US, so there are no data to reinforce if the absence of these taxa should be considered a negative ecological effect. Microcrustaceans have been useful indicators of good wetland condition when used as a total abundance or richness metric (Boix et al., 2005), but others have found this assemblage to be unresponsive to cattle grazing (Bagella et al., 2010). Therefore, it is difficult to interpret the potential effect of grazing on microcrustaceans without more local data. Grazed ponds had slightly higher macroinvertebrate taxonomic richness, yet this difference was statistically inconclusive. Grazing was not associated with impacts to water quality, and thus does not appear to be causing eutrophication problems. Cattle presence did increase turbidity, a pattern observed in other studies (Schmutzer et al., 2008). It is important to note that grazing levels in this study were on the low end of the spectrum because ponds within open space districts and reserves had grazing management plans that prevent overgrazing.

The presence of introduced fish had mild impacts on both the macroinvertebrate and amphibian community among perennial ponds. Although the ordination figure and MRPP analysis showed what appears to be a biologically meaningful association with fish presence (Fig. 3.4), the difference was not statistically significant, which is likely a result of the small sample size (n=13). The three indicator species at fishless ponds use open water, and would be useful taxa to quantify as potential metric for an index of biotic integrity designed to quantify this stressor. Invasive bullfrogs were more common in ponds with introduced fish primarily as a result of these ponds being perennial, but this observation could also be related to their increased ability to colonize ponds where sunfish are present because sunfish eat dragonflies, which also are predators of larval bullfrogs (Werner and McPeek, 1994). Although the amphibian species richness metric did not significantly decrease in response to binary fish presence metric, the number of invasive species metric (which incorporates centrarchids, mosquitofish, crayfish, and bullfrogs) was significantly related to a decrease in amphibian richness when assessed in a general linear model. Therefore, the simple presence/absence metric for invasive fish was not highly sensitive, and future studies could collect fish abundance to better quantify the fish community.

Conservation Implications for Created Wetlands

A wide variety of created wetlands can provide habitat for aquatic species assemblages. For example, rice fields can provide habitat for waterfowl and wading birds (e.g., Elphick and Oring, 1998; Fasola and Ruiz, 1996), golf course ponds can provide valuable habitat to amphibians and invertebrates (Colding et al., 2009), and even roadside ponds can support abundant dragonfly, damselfly, and amphibian populations (Scher and Thiery, 2005). However, the conservation value of these created wetlands can depend on pond management as well as particular habitat, water chemistry, and landscape factors, some of which can be affected through restoration activities.

Recent studies have found that stormwater ponds have similar levels of amphibian diversity as natural ponds when a proportion of the surrounding landscape remains undeveloped (Ostergaard et al., 2008; Simon et al., 2009). For example, survey of created wetlands in England found that created farm ponds were colonized quickly by aquatic plants and invertebrates, that the amount of shading by riparian areas had a positive binomial effect on invertebrate diversity, and that fish stocking with low densities of trout had a mild effect on invertebrates (Gee et al., 1997). In regards to agricultural ponds, research in Minnesota showed that amphibian species richness at agricultural ponds was similar to natural ponds when the ponds were small and fish and cattle were absent (Knutson et al., 2004). A recent survey of livestock ponds in Europe concluded that created stockponds could be viable amphibian conservation habitats, even supporting rare species, but that cattle access to the pond did reduce water quality and habitat condition especially in late summer (Canals et al., 2011)

This study demonstrated that stockponds within Northern California are ecologically valuable aquatic resources for both amphibians and macroinvertebrates, and that light cattle grazing had a positive effect on amphibian diversity, while introduced invasive fish had a mild negative effect on the macroinvertebrate assemblage. Hydroperiod was an important variable that directly affected macroinvertebrate populations and amphibians in rural ponds, and can be manipulated in some wetlands. Perennial ponds generally supported bullfrogs and were often stocked with introduced fish, both of which have demonstrated negative impacts on native amphibians including the endangered California red-legged frog (Lawler et al., 1999). Therefore, allowing these created ponds to dry down once every few years would 1) prevent breeding populations of bullfrogs from becoming established, 2) remove any invasive fish if the pond were stocked, and 3) potentially provide the necessary environmental signals to allow egg hatching for populations of fairy shrimp or clam shrimp.

Stormwater ponds were found to have limited conservation value for amphibians and invertebrates in this study. This research provides some evidence that increased emergent and submergent vegetation in stormwater ponds will provide structure and habitat heterogeneity, which can foster macroinvertebrate communities more similar to natural ponds. However, the poor water quality (conductivity and nutrients), invasive species, rapidly changing hydrodynamics, limited aquatic connectivity may prevent these habitats from ever becoming ecological resources.

Mosquitoes were rare in both stormwater and stockponds, indicating that the risk of human and wildlife disease by vectors from these habitats is low. Vector control played an important role in reducing mosquito populations in stormwater ponds because these habitats were often monitored and treated with the bacterium *Bacillus thuringiensis israeliensis* or *Bacillus sphaericus* when mosquitoes are discovered (pers. com Alameda County Mosquito Abatement District, Contra Costa Mosquito & Vector Control District, Marin-Sonoma Mosquito & Vector Control District, Sacramento-Yolo Mosquito & Vector Control District).

Results and conclusions from this study are based on observations of correlation, and future experimental research is required to demonstrate causal relationships. However, small scale experiments in aquatic systems tend to lack the ecological realism to be useful in predicting whole ecosystem effects (Carpenter, 1996; Schindler, 1998). Although, it is possible that the absence of lentic taxa could be related to dispersal limitations and colonization processes, because ponds were generally surrounded by at least one stream and one or more ponds within a 1 km radius, dispersal opportunities do not appear to be limited. Macroinvertebrate communities in ponds are known to change throughout a season (e.g., Trigal et al., 2006), and this succession might have added noise to this dataset because the sample date was a significant variable in the ordination. However, despite these limitations, the results strongly indicate the value of stockponds as aquatic conservation resources within Northern California.

ACKNOWLEDGMENTS

I thank Jim Carter for assisting with subsampling methods; J Ball and S Feirer for assistance with GIS analyses; M Groff for assisting with the pilot study at Hog Lake, R Mazor for statistical advice; C Seibold for nutrient analyses; C Dunn, S Osman, K Yao, J Xin, M Aghaee, M Baragona, A Strother, for assistance with field and laboratory work; Hopland Research and Extension Center, East Bay Regional Parks, Alameda Flood Control and Water Conservation District, and Cities of Novato, Davis, Oakley for sites access. This work was funded with assistance from the Alameda Countywide Clean Water Program, National Science Foundation Graduate Research Fellowship Program and EPA STAR Fellowship Program.

LITERATURE CITED

ADAMS, M. J. 2000. Pond permanence and the effects of exotic vertebrates on anurans. Ecological Applications 10:559-568.

ADAMUS, P., T. J. DANIELSON, AND A. GONYAW. 2001. Indicators for monitoring biological integrity if inland, freshwater wetlands: A survey of the technical literature (1990-2000). Office of Water, US Environmental Protection Agency. Washington, DC. EPA-843-R-01. US Environmental Protection Agency Washington, DC, USA. http://www.epa.gov/owow/wetlands/bawwg/monindicators.pdf.

BAGELLA, S., S. GASCON, M. C. CARIA, J. SALA, M. A. MARIANI, AND D. BOIX. 2010. Identifying key environmental factors related to plant and crustacean assemblages in Mediterranean temporary ponds. Biodiversity and Conservation 19:1749-1768.

BARBOUR, M. T., J. GERRITSEN, B. D. SNYDER, AND J. B. STRIBLING. 1999. Rapid Bioassessment Protocols for Use in Streams and Wadeable Rivers: Periphyton, Benthic Macroinvertebrates and Fish, Second Edition. EPA 841-B-99-002. Office of Water, U.S. Environmental Protection Agency, Washington, DC, USA.

BARON, J. S., N. L. POFF, P. L. ANGERMEIER, C. N. DAHM, P. H. GLEICK, N. G. HAIRSTON, R. B. JACKSON, C. A. JOHNSTON, B. D. RICHTER, AND A. D. STEINMAN. 2002. Meeting ecological and societal needs for freshwater. Ecological Applications 12:1247-1260.

BOIX, D., S. GASCON, J. SALA, M. MARTINOY, J. GIFRE, AND X. D. QUINTANA. 2005. A new index of water quality assessment in Mediterranean wetlands based on crustacean and insect assemblages: the case of Catalunya (NE Iberian peninsula). Aquatic Conservation-Marine and Freshwater Ecosystems 15:635-651.

BOONE, M. D., R. D. SEMLITSCH, E. E. LITTLE, AND M. C. DOYLE. 2007. Multiple stressors in amphibian communities: Effects of chemical contamination, bullfrogs, and fish. Ecological Applications 17:291-301.

BRINSON, M. M., AND A. I. MALVAREZ. 2002. Temperate freshwater wetlands: Types, status, and threats. Environmental Conservation 29:115-133.

BULL, E. L., J. W. DEAL, AND J. E. HOHMANN. 2001. Avian and amphibian use of fenced and unfenced stock ponds in northeastern Oregon forests. Res. Pap. PNW-RP-539. US Department of Agriculture, Forest Service, Pacific Northwest Research Station, Portland, OR.

BULL, E. L., AND M. P. HAYES. 2000. Livestock effects on reproduction of the Columbia spotted frog. Journal of Range Management 53:291-294.

BURTON, E. C., M. J. GRAY, A. C. SCHMUTZER, AND D. L. MILLER. 2009. Differential responses of postmetamorphic amphibians to cattle grazing in wetlands. Journal of Wildlife Management 73:269-277.

CANALS, R. M., V. FERRER, A. IRIARTE, S. CARCAMO, L. SAN EMETERIO, AND E. VILLANUEVA. 2011. Emerging conflicts for the environmental use of water in high-valuable rangelands. Can livestock water ponds be managed as artificial wetlands for amphibians? Ecological Engineering 37:1443-1452.

CARPENTER, S. R. 1996. Microcosm experiments have limited relevance for community and ecosystem ecology. Ecology 77:677-680.

COLDING, J., J. LUNDBERG, S. LUNDBERG, AND E. ANDERSSON. 2009. Golf courses and wetland fauna. Ecological Applications 19:1481-1491.

CUKJATI, J., AND C. SEIBOLD. 2010. Kiowa Environmental Chemistry Laboratory Procedure Manual. Mountain Research Station & Institute of Arctic and Alpine Research, University of Colorado Boulder.
http://snobear.colorado.edu/Kiowa/Kiowaref/procedure.html.

DAHL, T. E. 1990. Wetland losses in the United States - 1780's to 1980's. U.S. Department of the Interior, Fish and Wildlife Service, Washington DC, Jamestown, ND: Northern Prairie Wildlife Research Center Online.
http://www.npwrc.usgs.gov/resource/wetlands/wetloss/index.htm.

DECLERCK, S., T. DE BIE, D. ERCKEN, H. HAMPEL, S. SCHRIJVERS, J. VAN WICHELEN, V. GILLARD, R. MANDIKI, B. LOSSON, D. BAUWENS, S. KEIJERS, W. VYVERMAN, B. GODDEERIS, L. DE MEESTER, L. BRENDONCK, AND K. MARTENS. 2006. Ecological characteristic's of small farmland ponds: Associations with land use practices at multiple spatial scales. Biological Conservation 131:523-532.

DELLA BELLA, V., M. BAZZANTI, AND F. CHIAROTTI. 2005. Macroinvertebrate diversity and conservation status of Mediterranean ponds in Italy: Water permanence and mesohabitat influence. Aquatic Conservation-Marine and Freshwater Ecosystems 15:583-600.

DIEHL, S. 1992. Fish predation and benthic community structure – The role of omnivory and habitat complexity. Ecology 73:1646-1661.

ELPHICK, C. S., AND L. W. ORING. 1998. Winter management of Californian rice fields for waterbirds. Journal of Applied Ecology 35:95-108.

ESRI. 2005. Environmental Systems Research Institute, ArcGIS 9.1. Redlands, CA.

FASOLA, M., AND X. RUIZ. 1996. The value of rice fields as substitutes for natural wetlands for waterbirds in the Mediterranean region. Colonial Waterbirds 19:122-128.

GARCIA-CRIADO, F., AND C. TRIGAL. 2005. Comparison of several techniques for sampling macroinvertebrates in different habitats of a North Iberian pond. Hydrobiologia 545:103-115.

GEE, J. H. R., B. D. SMITH, K. M. LEE, AND S. W. GRIFFITHS. 1997. The ecological basis of freshwater pond management for biodiversity. Aquatic Conservation-Marine and Freshwater Ecosystems 7:91-104.

GILLIAM, H. 2002. Weather of the San Francisco Bay Region. 2nd edition. University of California Press, Berkeley, CA.

GOOGLE INC. 2009. Google Earth (Version 5.1) Mountain View, CA.
http://www.google.com/earth/index.html.

GUILDFORD, S. J., AND R. E. HECKY. 2000. Total nitrogen, total phosphorus, and nutrient limitation in lakes and oceans: Is there a common relationship? Limnology and Oceanography 45:1213-1223.

HAMER, A. J., AND K. M. PARRIS. 2011. Local and landscape determinants of amphibian communities in urban ponds. Ecological Applications 21:378-390.

HAYES, M. P., AND M. R. JENNINGS. 1986. Decline of ranid frog species in Western North-America - Are bullfrogs (*Rana catesbeiana*) responsible. Journal of Herpetology 20:490-509.

HECNAR, S. J., AND R. T. MCLOSKEY. 1997. The effects of predatory fish on amphibian species richness and distribution. Biological Conservation 79:123-131.

HELFIELD, J. M., AND M. L. DIAMOND. 1997. Use of constructed wetlands for urban stream restoration: A critical analysis. Environmental Management 21:329-341.

HELGEN, J. C., AND M. C. GERNES. 2001. Monitoring the condition of wetlands: Indexes of biological integrity using invertebrates and vegetation. Pp. 167-185. *In* R. B. Rader, D. P. Batzer, and S. A. Wissinger (Eds.), Bioassessment and Management of North American Freshwater Wetlands. Wiley, New York, NY, USA.

HOBBS, R. J., S. ARICO, J. ARONSON, J. S. BARON, P. BRIDGEWATER, V. A. CRAMER, P. R. EPSTEIN, J. J. EWEL, C. A. KLINK, A. E. LUGO, D. NORTON, D. OJIMA, D. M. RICHARDSON, E. W. SANDERSON, F. VALLADARES, M. VILA, R. ZAMORA, AND M. ZOBEL. 2006. Novel ecosystems: theoretical and management aspects of the new ecological world order. Global Ecology and Biogeography 15:1-7.

HOMER, C., C. Q. HUANG, L. M. YANG, B. WYLIE, AND M. COAN. 2004. Development of a 2001 National Land-Cover Database for the United States. Photogrammetric Engineering and Remote Sensing. http://seamless.usgs.gov/.

JANSEN, A., AND M. HEALEY. 2003. Frog communities and wetland condition: Relationships with grazing by domestic livestock along an Australian floodplain river. Biological Conservation 109:207-219.

JENNINGS, M. R., AND M. P. HAYES. 1994. Amphibian and Reptile Species of Special Concern in California. California Department of Fish and Game, Rancho Cordova, CA.

JMP. 2010. JMP Version 9. SAS Institute Inc., Cary, NC, USA.

JOHNSON, P. T. J., J. M. CHASE, K. L. DOSCH, R. B. HARTSON, J. A. GROSS, D. J. LARSON, D. R. SUTHERLAND, AND S. R. CARPENTER. 2007. Aquatic eutrophication promotes pathogenic infection in amphibians. Proceedings of the National Academy of Sciences of the United States of America 104:15781-15786.

KARRAKER, N. E., J. P. GIBBS, AND J. R. VONESH. 2008. Impacts of road deicing salt on the demography of vernal pool-breeding amphibians. Ecological Applications 18:724-734.

KATS, L. B., AND R. P. FERRER. 2003. Alien predators and amphibian declines: Review of two decades of science and the transition to conservation. Diversity and Distributions 9:99-110.

KIESECKER, J. M., AND A. R. BLAUSTEIN. 1998. Effects of introduced bullfrogs and smallmouth bass on microhabitat use, growth, and survival of native red-legged frogs (*Rana aurora*). Conservation Biology 12:776-787.

KNAPP, R. A., C. P. HAWKINS, J. LADAU, AND J. G. MCCLORY. 2005. Fauna of Yosemite National Park lakes has low resistance but high resilience to fish introductions. Ecological Applications 15:835-847.

KNAPP, R. A., K. R. MATTHEWS, AND O. SARNELLE. 2001. Resistance and resilience of alpine lake fauna to fish introductions. Ecological Monographs 71:401-421.

KNIGHT, R. L., W. E. WALTON, G. F. O'MEARA, W. K. REISEN, AND R. WASS. 2003. Strategies for effective mosquito control in constructed treatment wetlands. Ecological Engineering 21:211-232.

KNUTSON, M. G., W. B. RICHARDSON, D. M. REINEKE, B. R. GRAY, J. R. PARMELEE, AND S. E. WEICK. 2004. Agricultural ponds support amphibian populations. Ecological Applications 14:669-684.

KUCHTA, S. R. 2005. *Taricha torosa*. Pp. 904-908. *In* M. J. Lannoo (Ed.), Amphibian Declines: The Conservation Status of United States Species. University of California Press, Berkeley, CA.

LAWLER, S. P., D. DRITZ, T. STRANGE, AND M. HOLYOAK. 1999. Effects of introduced mosquitofish and bullfrogs on the threatened California red-legged frog. Conservation Biology 13:613-622.

LEYSE, K. E., S. P. LAWLER, AND T. STRANGE. 2004. Effects of an alien fish, *Gambusia affinis*, on an endemic California fairy shrimp, *Linderiella occidentalis*: Implications for conservation of diversity in fishless waters. Biological Conservation 118:57-65.

LOMAN, J., AND B. LARDNER. 2006. Does pond quality limit frogs *Rana arvalis* and *Rana temporaria* in agricultural landscapes? A field experiment. Journal of Applied Ecology 43:690-700.

MAKEPEACE, D. K., D. W. SMITH, AND S. J. STANLEY. 1995. Urban stormwater quality - Summary of contaminant data. Critical Reviews in Environmental Science and Technology 25:93-139.

MARTY, J. T. 2005. Effects of cattle grazing on diversity in ephemeral wetlands. Conservation Biology 19:1626-1632.

MCCUNE, B., AND J. B. GRACE. 2002. Analysis of Ecological Communities. MjM Software Design, Gleneden Beach, OR, USA.

MCCUNE, B., AND M. J. MEFFORD. 2006. PC-ORD Multivariate Analysis of Ecological Data. Version 5.31. MjM Software Design, Gleneden Beach, OR, USA.

MITSCH, W. J., AND J. G. GOSSELINK. 2000. Wetlands. John Wiley & Sons, New York, NY, USA.

MORIN, P. J. 1984. The impact of fish exclusion on the abundance and species composition of larval Odonates results from short-term experiments in a North Carolina farm pond. Ecology 65:53-60.

NATIONAL RESOUCES AGENCY. 2010. State of the State's Wetlands. Natural Resources Agency, State of California, Sacramento, CA.
http://www.resources.ca.gov/docs/SOSW_report_with_cover_memo_10182010.pdf.

O'GEEN, A. T., R. BUDD, J. GAN, J. J. MAYNARD, S. J. PARIKH, AND R. A. DAHLGREN. 2010. Mitigating nonpoint source pollution in agriculture with constructed and restored wetlands. Pp. 1-76. *In* D. L. Sparks (Ed.), Advances in Agronomy, Vol 108. Elsevier Academic Press Inc, San Diego.

OERTLI, B., D. AUDERSET JOYE, E. CASTELLA, R. JUGE, D. CAMBIN, AND J. B. LACHAVANNE. 2002. Does size matter? The relationship between pond area and biodiversity. Biological Conservation 104:59-70.

OLSON, D. H., W. P. LEOARD, AND R. B. BURY (Eds.). 1997. Sampling Amphibians in Lentic Habitats: Methods and Approaches for the Pacific Northwest. Society for Northwestern Vertebrate Biology, Olympia, WA.

OSTERGAARD, E. C., K. O. RICHTER, AND S. D. WEST. 2008. Amphibian use of stormwater ponds in the Puget lowlands of Washington, USA. Pp. 259-270. *In* J. C. Mitchell, R. E. Jung Brown, and B. Bartholomew (Eds.), Urban Herpetology. Society for the study of Amphibians and Reptiles, Salt Lake City, Utah.

PASCOE, G. A., R. J. BLANCHET, AND G. LINDER. 1996. Food chain analysis of exposures and risks to wildlife at a metals-contaminated wetland. Archives of Environmental Contamination and Toxicology 30:306-318.

PYKE, C. R., AND J. MARTY. 2005. Cattle grazing mediates climate change impacts on ephemeral wetlands. Conservation Biology 19:1619-1625.

REEVES, M. K., P. JENSEN, C. L. DOLPH, M. HOLYOAK, AND K. A. TRUST. 2010. Multiple stressors and the cause of amphibian abnormalities. Ecological Monographs 80:423-440.

RICHARDS, A. B., AND D. C. ROGERS. 2006. List of freshwater macroinvertebrate taxa from California and adjacent states including standard taxonomic effort levels. Southwestern Association of Freshwater Invertebrate Taxonomists. http://www.safit.org/ste.html.

RILEY, S. P. D., G. T. BUSTEED, L. B. KATS, T. L. VANDERGON, L. F. S. LEE, R. G. DAGIT, J. L. KERBY, R. N. FISHER, AND R. M. SAUVAJOT. 2005. Effects of urbanization on the distribution and abundance of amphibians and invasive species in southern California streams. Conservation Biology 19:1894-1907.

RODRIGUEZ, C. F., E. BECARES, M. FERNANDEZ-ALAEZ, AND C. FERNANDEZ-ALAEZ. 2005. Loss of diversity and degradation of wetlands as a result of introducing exotic crayfish. Biological Invasions 7:75-85.

RORABAUGH, J. C., AND M. J. LANNOO. 2005. *Pseudacris regilla* (Baird and Girard, 1852[b]) Pacific treefrog. Pp. 478-484. *In* M. J. Lannoo (Ed.), Amphibian Declines: The Conservation Status of United States Species. University of California Press, Berkeley, CA.

SCHER, O., AND A. THIERY. 2005. Odonata, amphibia and environmental characteristics in motorway stormwater retention ponds (Southern France). Hydrobiologia 551:237-251.

SCHILLING, E. G., C. S. LOFTIN, AND A. D. HURYN. 2009. Effects of introduced fish on macroinvertebrate communities in historically fishless headwater and kettle lakes. Biological Conservation 142:3030-3038.

SCHINDLER, D. W. 1998. Replication versus realism: The need for ecosystem-scale experiments. Ecosystems 1:323-334.

SCHMUTZER, A. C., M. J. GRAY, E. C. BURTON, AND D. L. MILLER. 2008. Impacts of cattle on amphibian larvae and the aquatic environment. Freshwater Biology 53:2613-2625.

SGRILLO, R. 2009. GE-Path Version 1.4.4. http://www.sgrillo.net/googleearth/gepath.htm.

SIMON, J. A., J. W. SNODGRASS, R. E. CASEY, AND D. W. SPARLING. 2009. Spatial correlates of amphibian use of constructed wetlands in an urban landscape. Landscape Ecology 24:361-373.

SOLIMINI, A. G., M. BAZZANTI, A. RUGGIERO, AND G. CARCHINI. 2008. Developing a multimetric index of ecological integrity based on macroinvertebrates of mountain ponds in central Italy. Hydrobiologia 597:109-123.

STEBBINS, R. C. 2003. A Field Guide to Western Reptiles and Amphibians. 3rd edition. Houghton Mifflin Company, New York, NY, USA.

STUMPEL, A. H. P., AND H. VAN DER VOET. 1998. Characterizing the suitability of new ponds for amphibians. Amphibia-Reptilia 19:125-142.

TRIGAL, C., F. GARCIA-CRIADO, AND C. FERNANDEZ-ALAEZ. 2006. Among-habitat and temporal variability of selected macroinvertebrate based metrics in a Mediterranean shallow lake (NW Spain). Hydrobiologia 563:371-384.

TRIGAL, C., F. GARCÍA-CRIADO, AND C. FERNÁNDEZ-ALÁEZ. 2009. Towards a multimetric index for ecological assessment of Mediterranean flatland ponds: the use of macroinvertebrates as bioindicators. Hydrobiologia 618:109-123.

U.S. EPA. 2002. Methods for Evaluating Wetland Condition: Developing an Invertebrate Index of Biological Integrity for Wetlands. EPA-822-R-02-219. Office of Water, U.S. Environmental Protection Agency, Washington, DC.

U.S. FISH AND WILDLIFE SERVICE. 2002. Recovery Plan for the California Red-legged Frog (*Rana aurora draytonii*). U.S. Fish and Wildlife Service, Portland, OR.

U.S. GEOLOGICAL SURVEY AND U.S. ENVIRONMENTAL PROTECTION AGENCY. 1999. National Hydrography Dataset - Medium Resolution. Reston, Virginia. http://nhd.usgs.gov.

VAN KLEEF, H., G. VAN DER VELDE, R. LEUVEN, AND H. ESSELINK. 2008. Pumpkinseed sunfish (*Lepomis gibbosus*) invasions facilitated by introductions and nature management strongly reduce macroinvertebrate abundance in isolated water bodies. Biological Invasions 10:1481-1490.

VAN SICKLE, J., D. P. LARSEN, AND C. P. HAWKINS. 2007. Exclusion of rare taxa affects performance of the O/E index in bioassessments. Journal of the North American Benthological Society 26:319-331.

VENTURELLI, P. A., AND W. M. TONN. 2005. Invertivory by northern pike (*Esox lucius*) structures communities of littoral macroinvertebrates in small boreal lakes. Journal of the North American Benthological Society 24:904-918.

VREDENBURG, V. T. 2004. Reversing introduced species effects: experimental removal of introduced fish leads to rapid recovery of a declining frog. Proceedings of the National Academy of Sciences of the United States of America 101:7646-7650.

WERNER, E. E., AND M. A. MCPEEK. 1994. Direct and indirect effects of predators on 2 anuran species along an environmental gradient. Ecology 75:1368-1382.

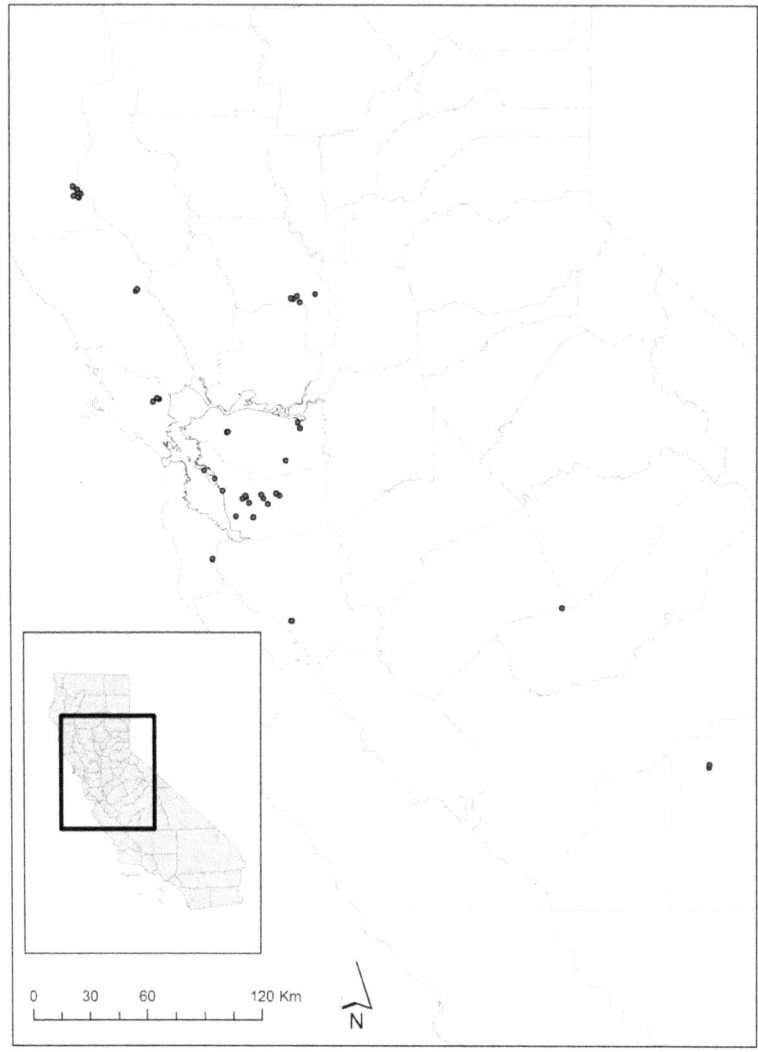

Figure 3.1. Map of 49 pond sampling locations across 9 counties in Northern California.

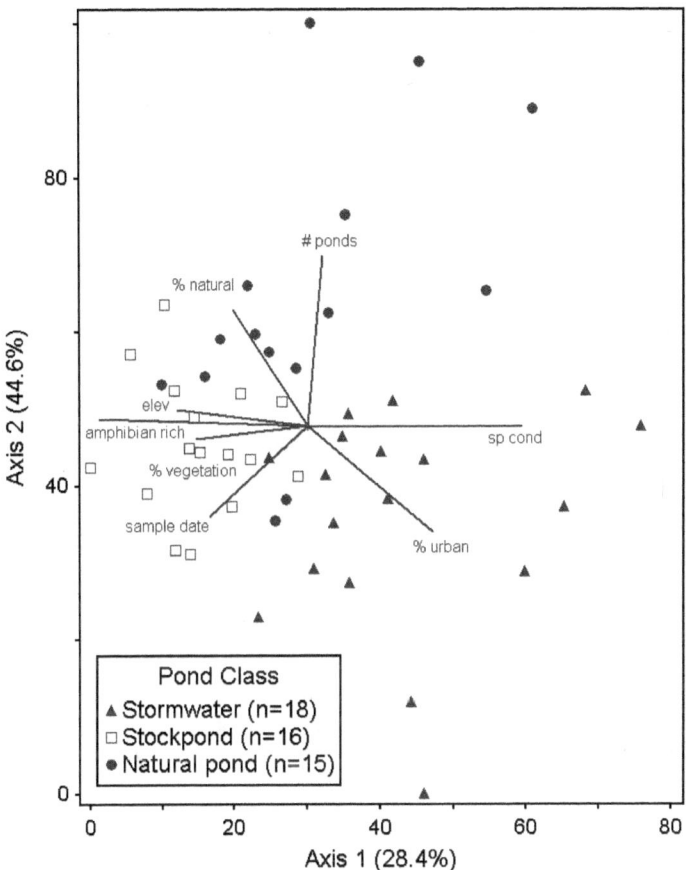

Figure 3.2. NMS ordination of all 49 sites by pond class (final stress = 23.5, instability < 0.0009). Axis 1 and 2 explain 28.4% and 44.6% of the variability in the data (total R^2 = 72.9). The length of vectors of stressors included on this diagram show the association with the biological community. All vectors with an $R^2 > 0.20$ with either axis are shown. MRPP showed a significant difference in the biological community between stormwater ponds, stockponds, and natural ponds ($A = 0.16, p < 0.00001$)

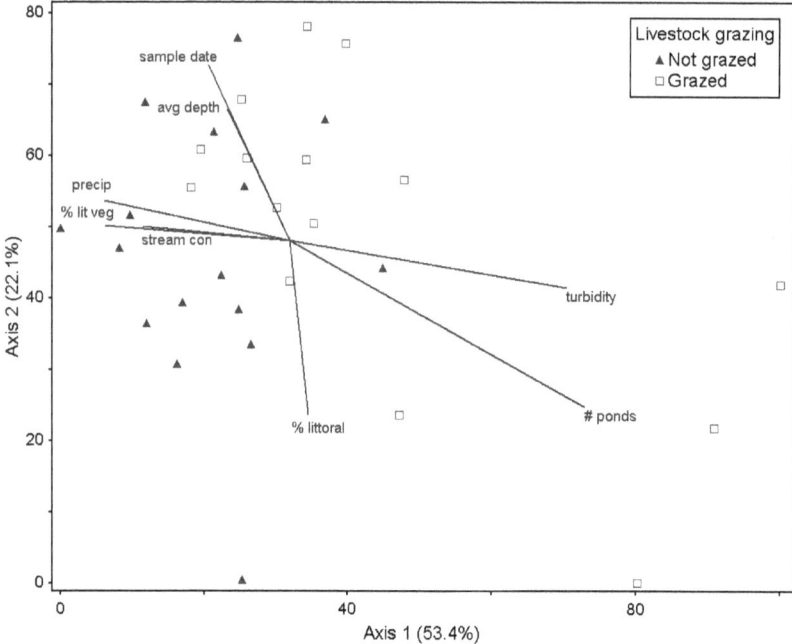

Figure 3.3. NMS ordination of 31 rural sites (excluding urban stormwater ponds) by pond class (final stress = 20.4, instability < 0.0004). Axis 1 and 2 explain 53.4% and 22.1% of the variability in the data (total R^2 = 75.5). The length of vectors of stressors included on this diagram show the association with the biological community. All vectors with an $R^2 > 0.25$ with either axis are shown. MRPP identified a significant difference in the variation of the macroinvertebrate community between ponds that were grazed and ungrazed ($A = 0.047$, $p < 0.025$).

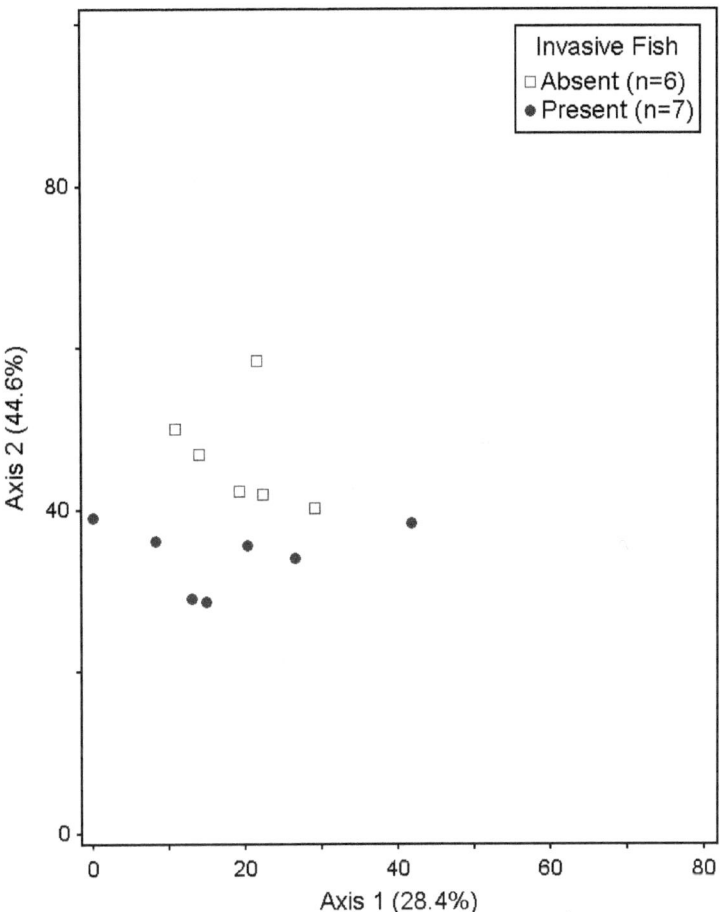

Figure 3.4. Stressor ranking and identification in NMS ordination space from ordination analysis of 49 sites (final stress = 23.1, instability < 0.0009). Axis 1 and 2 explain 28.4% and 44.6% of the variability in the data (total R^2 = 72.9). MRPP found a moderate difference in the biological community from 13 perennial ponds with invasive fish (n=6) compared to those without (n=7), yet this difference was marginally significant (A = 0.07, p < 0.08).

Table 3.1. Mean values and standard errors (in parentheses) of landscape, habitat and water chemistry variables according to pond type.

	Stormwater ponds (n=18)	Stockponds / Reservoirs (n=16)	Natural Ponds / Wetlands (n=15)
Landscape Variables			
Elevation (m)	47 (23)	311 (33)	330 (59)
Mean annual precipitation (cm)	53 (33)	74 (5)	76 (9)
Number of Ponds within 1 km	3.2 (0.6)	3.8 (0.7)	5.8 (1.4)
Meters of stream within 1 km	1513 (370)	3288 (586)	2856 (601)
Percent non-natural within 1 km	76 (6)	17 (8)	15 (7)
Percent urban within 1 km	54 (7)	5 (4)	7 (6)
Habitat Variables			
Percent perennial (within class)	100	62.5	30
Surface area (m^2)	5740 (5522)	218 (211)	135 (117)
Average depth (m)	0.9 (0.13)	1.0 (0.25)	0.6 (0.15)
Percent of littoral vegetation	63 (8)	80 (5)	74 (9)
Percent of total vegetation	45 (9)	52 (8)	60 (9)
Number of invasive predators	1.7 (0.3)	0.8 (0.3)	0.4 (0.3)
Water Chemistry			
Specific conductance (μS/cm^2)	2229 (651)	492 (113)	457 (110)
pH	8.8 (0.2)	8.6 (0.2)	8.1 (0.2)
Turbidity (NTU)	31 (14)	19 (10)	161 (83)
Total chromium (μg/L)	5 (2)	1 (0.5)	2 (0.5)
Total lead (μg/L)	5 (2)	2 (1)	5 (1)
Total dissolved nitrogen (TDN) (mg/L)	1.3 (0.2)	1.2 (0.2)	1.0 (0.1)
Total dissolved phosphorous (TDP) (mg/L)	0.17 (0.04)	0.07 (0.02)	0.11 (0.02)
Percent nitrogen limited	27	31	24
Percent phosphorous limited	10	2	6
Productivity scale	3.8 (0.6)	2.3 (0.5)	2.6 (0.4)

Table 3.2. Abundant taxa found in all 49 ponds. Average relative abundance was calculated as the overall sum of individuals found at each site divided by the number of organisms identified from each site.

Phylum/Subphylum	Class/subclass	Order/suborder	Family	Final taxa ID	Average Relative Abundance
Annelida	Oligochaeta	Haplotaxida	Naididae	*Dero* sp.	2.17%
Annelida	Oligochaeta	Haplotaxida	Tubificidae	*Limnodrilus* sp.	0.61%
Annelida	Oligochaeta	Lumbriculica	Lumbriculidae	*Lumbriculus* sp.	0.59%
Arthropoda	Insecta	Diptera	Chironomidae	Chironominae	3.67%
Arthropoda	Insecta	Diptera	Chironomidae	Orthocladiinae	2.93%
Arthropoda	Insecta	Diptera	Chironomidae	Tanypodinae	0.95%
Arthropoda	Insecta	Ephemeroptera	Baetidae	*Callibaetis* sp.	3.18%
Arthropoda	Insecta	Hemiptera	Corixidae	*Trichocorixa* sp.	2.86%
Arthropoda	Insecta	Hemiptera	Corixidae	*Corisella* sp.	0.92%
Arthropoda	Insecta	Hemiptera	Corixidae	*Cenocorixa* sp.	0.59%
Arthropoda	Insecta	Hemiptera	Notonectidae	*Notonecta* sp.	0.72%
Arthropoda	Insecta	Odonata/Zygoptera	Coenagrionidae	Coenagrionidae	6.73%
Arthropoda	Insecta	Odonata/Zygoptera	Lestidae	*Lestes* sp.	0.67%
Arthropoda/Crustacea	Maxillopoda/Copepoda	Calanoida	Diaptomidae	*Leptodiaptomus* sp.	1.92%
Arthropoda/Crustacea	Maxillopoda/Copepoda	Cyclopoida	Cyclopidae	*Macrocyclops* sp.	3.82%
Arthropoda/Crustacea	Maxillopoda/Copepoda	Cyclopoida	Cyclopidae	*Acanthocyclops* sp.	2.35%
Arthropoda/Crustacea	Branchiopoda	Cladocera	Daphniidae	*Moina* sp.	3.79%
Arthropoda/Crustacea	Branchiopoda	Cladocera	Daphniidae	*Ceriodaphnia* sp.	1.56%
Arthropoda/Crustacea	Branchiopoda	Cladocera	Daphniidae	*Simocephalus* sp.	25.67%
Arthropoda/Crustacea	Branchiopoda	Cladocera	Macrothricidae	Macrothricidae	0.83%
Arthropoda/Crustacea	Branchiopoda	Cladocera	Chydoridae	Chydoridae	0.69%
Arthropoda/Crustacea	Branchiopoda	Cladocera	Daphniidae	*Daphnia* sp.	2.20%
Arthropoda/Crustacea	Malacostraca	Amphipoda	Talitridae	*Hyalella* sp.	3.63%
Arthropoda/Crustacea	Malacostraca	Mysidacea	Mysidae	*Neomysis mercedis*	0.51%
Arthropoda/Crustacea	Ostracoda	Podocopida	Candoniidae	Candoniidae	0.63%
Arthropoda/Crustacea	Ostracoda	Podocopida	Cyprididae	Cyprididae	3.62%
Mollusca	Gastropoda	Basommatophora	Physidae	*Physa* sp.	4.33%
Mollusca	Gastropoda	Basommatophora	Planorbidae	*Planorbella* sp.	3.38%
Mollusca	Gastropoda	Basommatophora	Planorbidae	*Gyraulus* sp.	1.47%

Table 3.3. Benthic macroinvertebrate characteristics by pond class.

	Stormwater ponds (n=18)	Stockponds / Reservoirs (n=16)	Natural Ponds / Wetlands (n=15)
Unique benthic macroinvertebrate taxa	102	84	106
Benthic macroinvertebrate richness	18.5 (1.5)	20.3 (1.6)	20.1 (1.6)
Benthic macroinvertebrate density (# / m^2)	2926 (650)	2524 (690)	3385 (713)
Shannon-Weiner diversity index	3.54	3.10	3.28
Mosquito abundance (number / m^2)	10.5 (5.6)	0.3 (5.9)	7.5 (6.0)

Table 3.4. Most commonly encountered taxa found at each of the three pond classes.

Phylum/Subphylum	Class/subclass	Order/suborder	Family	Final Taxa ID	Prevalence
Stormwater ponds					
Arthropoda/Crustacea	Branchiopoda	Cladocera	Daphniidae	*Simocephalus* sp.	89%
Arthropoda	Insecta	Diptera	Chironomidae	Orthocladiinae	89%
Arthropoda	Insecta	Diptera	Chironomidae	Chironominae	78%
Arthropoda/Crustacea	Ostracoda	Podocopida	Cyprididae	Cyprididae	78%
Mollusca	Gastropoda	Basommatophora	Physidae	*Physa* sp.	78%
Annelida	Oligochaeta	Haplotaxida	Naididae	*Dero* sp.	67%
Arthropoda	Insecta	Odonata/Zygoptera	Coenagrionidae	Coenagrionidae	61%
Arthropoda/Crustacea	Malacostraca	Amphipoda	Talitridae	*Hyalella* sp.	56%
Annelida	Oligochaeta	Haplotaxida	Tubificidae	Tubificidae w/o cap setae	56%
Arthropoda	Maxillopoda/Copepoda	Cyclopoida	Cyclopidae	*Acanthocyclops* sp.	39%
Arthropoda	Insecta	Collembola	Isotomidae	Isotomidae	39%
Stockponds					
Arthropoda	Insecta	Odonata/Zygoptera	Coenagrionidae	Coenagrionidae	100%
Arthropoda/Crustacea	Branchiopoda	Cladocera	Daphniidae	*Simocephalus* sp.	94%
Arthropoda	Insecta	Diptera	Chironomidae	Tanypodinae	94%
Arthropoda	Insecta	Diptera	Chironomidae	Chironominae	81%
Mollusca	Gastropoda	Basommatophora	Planorbidae	*Planorbella* sp.	81%
Mollusca	Gastropoda	Basommatophora	Physidae	*Physa* sp.	75%
Arthropoda	Insecta	Ephemeroptera	Baetidae	*Callibaetis* sp.	75%
Arthropoda	Insecta	Diptera	Chironomidae	Orthocladiinae	63%
Arthropoda/Crustacea	Ostracoda	Podocopida	Cyprididae	Cyprididae	63%
Arthropoda	Insecta	Odonata/Anisoptera	Aeshnidae	Aeshnidae	63%
Arthropoda	Maxillopoda/Copepoda	Cyclopoida	Cyclopidae	*Macrocyclops* sp.	63%

Table 3.4 Cont.

Phylum/Subphylum	Class/subclass	Order/suborder	Family	Final Taxa ID	Prevalence
Natural ponds					
Arthropoda	Insecta	Diptera	Chironomidae	Chironominae	87%
Arthropoda	Insecta	Diptera	Chironomidae	Tanypodinae	87%
Arthropoda/Crustacea	Branchiopoda	Cladocera	Daphniidae	*Simocephalus* sp.	73%
Arthropoda	Insecta	Diptera	Chironomidae	Orthocladiinae	67%
Arthropoda/Crustacea	Ostracoda	Podocopida	Cyprididae	Cyprididae	67%
Arthropoda	Insecta	Odonata/Zygoptera	Coenagrionidae	Coenagrionidae	60%
Arthropoda	Insecta	Ephemeroptera	Baetidae	*Callibaetis* sp.	60%
Mollusca	Gastropoda	Basommatophora	Physidae	*Physa* sp.	47%
Arthropoda	Insecta	Odonata	Aeshnidae	Aeshnidae	47%
Arthropoda	Insecta	Hemiptera	Notonectidae	*Notonecta* sp.	47%
Arthropoda/Crustacea	Maxillopoda/Copepoda	Calanoida	Diaptomidae	*Leptodiaptomus* sp.	47%

Table 3.5. Amphibian species presence and total amphibian richness by pond class.

	Stormwater ponds (n=18)	Stockponds (n=16)	Natural ponds (n=15)	Total presence (n=49)
Pacific chorus frog (*Pseudacris regilla*)	8	14	11	33
Western toad (*Bufo boreas*)	1	5	2	8
California tiger salamander (*Ambystoma californiense*)	0	0	2	3
California red-legged frog (*Rana draytonii*)	1	2	1	4
California newt (*Taricha torosa*)	0	13	7	20
Western spadefoot (*Spea hammondii*)	0	0	1	1
American bullfrog (*Lithobates catesbeianus*)*	4	8	1	13
Native amphibian species richness (s.e. in parenthesis)	0.6 (0.2)	2.2 (0.2)	1.6 (0.2)	1.4 (0.15)

*Invasive species in California

CHAPTER 4

DEVELOPMENT AND VALIDATION OF A MACROINVERTEBRATE INDEX OF BIOTIC INTEGRITY (IBI) FOR ASSESSING ECOLOGICAL CONDITION OF NORTHERN CALIFORNIA FRESHWATER WETLANDS

Development and validation of a macroinvertebrate index of biotic integrity (IBI) for assessing ecological condition of Northern California freshwater wetlands

Abstract

Despite California policies requiring assessment of ambient wetland condition and compensatory wetland mitigations, no intensive monitoring tools have been developed to evaluate freshwater wetlands within the state. Therefore, we developed standardized, wadeable field methods to sample macroinvertebrate communities and evaluated 40 wetlands across Northern California to develop a macroinvertebrate index of biotic integrity (IBI). *A priori* reference sites were selected with minimal urban impacts, representing a best-attainable condition. We screened 56 macroinvertebrate metrics for inclusion in the IBI based on responsiveness to percent urbanization. Eight final metrics were selected for inclusion in the IBI: % 3 dominant species; scraper richness; % Ephemeroptera, Odonata, and Trichoptera (EOT); EOT richness; % Tanypodinae/Chironomidae; Oligochaeta richness; % Coleoptera; and predator richness. The IBI (potential range 0 to 100) demonstrated significant discriminatory power between the reference (mean=69) and impacted wetlands (mean=28). It also declined with increasing percent urbanization (R^2=0.53, p <0.005) among wetlands in an independent validation dataset (n=14). The IBI was robust in showing no significant bias with environmental gradients. This IBI is a functional tool to determine the ecological condition at urban (stormwater and flood control ponds), as well as rural freshwater wetlands (stockponds, seasonal wetlands, natural ponds). Biological differences between perennial and non-perennial wetlands suggest that developing separate indicators for these wetland types may improve applicability, although the existing data set was not sufficient for exploring this option.

Key words: IBI, lentic, pond, bioassessment, aquatic biomonitoring, multimetric index

INTRODUCTION

Biological monitoring has been successfully used to evaluate ecological integrity within a broad array of aquatic ecosystems and is an important component of programs that have previously focused on physical or chemical assessments (Resh, 2007; Yoder and Rankin, 1998). Biomonitoring is effective because aquatic organisms are cumulative indicators of overall environmental conditions, responding not only to pollutants but to changes of in-stream and watershed physical habitat conditions, which are difficult to assess with traditional chemical and toxicity monitoring tools (e.g., Rosenberg and Resh, 1993a). Programs to detect ecological impacts to streams and rivers that utilize biomonitoring methods have become well established world-wide (Barbour et al., 1999; Hering et al., 2004; Resh, 2007; Smith et al., 1999). A common approach has been to develop multimetric indicators commonly referred to as an index of biotic integrity (IBI) (Barbour et al., 1999; Carter et al., 2006; Karr and Chu, 1999).

Macroinvertebrates, including insects, snails, crustaceans, and worms, are the most commonly used indicator for aquatic biomonitoring in the United States, although some monitoring programs also use fish, diatoms, or a variety of other organisms (Resh, 2008). Macroinvertebrates are excellent indicators because the are ubiquitous, abundant, taxonomically diverse, and exhibit a wide range of tolerance to various stressors (Rosenberg and Resh, 1993b). Moreover, the macroinvertebrate community is responsive to multiple types of stressors including urbanization, agriculture, nutrients, sediment, and water diversions (e.g., Adamus et al., 2001; Berkman et al., 1986; Purcell et al., 2009; Rosenberg and Resh, 1993a; Roy et al., 2003; Smith et al., 2007). Besides being effective indicators, aquatic macroinvertebrates are an important food-base for vertebrates such as amphibians and waterbirds (Batzer and Wissinger, 1996; Murkin, 1989) and provide an essential energy subsidy for terrestrial ecosystems (Nakano and Murakami, 2001). Therefore, macroinvertebrates provide a direct measurement of many of the beneficial uses that must be supported under state and federal legislation (e.g., Clean Water Act, Porter-Cologne Act) and thus offer a useful and rational approach to aquatic ecosystem assessment.

Biomonitoring protocols based on lentic macroinvertebrates have been successfully applied in many localities to determine the ecological conditions of wetlands, ponds, and lakes. In Europe, for example, the Water Framework Directive has spurred efforts to develop indices that respond to various anthropogenic stressors (e.g., Boix et al., 2005; Solimini et al., 2008). Minnesota (Gernes and Helgen, 2002) along with some US states (U.S. EPA, 2003) have pilot tested and developed biomonitoring protocols for wetland habitats. The U.S. EPA (1998,2002a) has also established guidelines to assist states with developing locally relevant lentic monitoring programs. Such field protocols and corresponding biological indicators are designed to assist with Clean Water Act (CWA) 303(d) listings of impairment, CWA 305(b) National Water Quality Inventory Report to Congress, as well as CWA 401 certifications (Brown et al., 2005).

California lacks an intensive wetland bioassessment tool to support environmental monitoring and regulatory programs. Although macroinvertebrate indicators for stream habitats have been developed for many regions (Herbst and Silldorff, 2009; Ode et al., 2005; Rehn et al., 2005,2008), ponds, marshes, and wetland habitats are not intensively monitored despite the 708,000 hectares of freshwater wetlands throughout the state (National Resouces Agency, 2010). Existing wetland assessment tools such as the California Rapid Assessment Method (CRAM) (Collins et al., 2008; Stein et al., 2009; Sutula et al., 2006) provide an assessment of general condition, but may not be sensitive to water quality or water chemistry perturbations. Thus, a macroinvertebrate-based bioassessment indicator for wetland habitats would provide a much needed tool and be used to validate existing rapid assessment protocols.

This study was designed to determine if macroinvertebrates could be used as an integrative indicator of the ecological condition of Northern California wetlands. We sought to develop an IBI that was suitable across a range of lentic habitats and could apply to both artificial (i.e., stormwater, irrigation reservoirs, stockponds) and natural (i.e., ephemeral wetlands, and ponds) ecosystems. The three main goals of this study were to: (1) develop standardized macroinvertebrate collection and physical habitat assessment methods that were rapid (< 4hs) and applicable across diverse habitat types; (2) develop a macroinvertebrate-based indicator of biotic integrity (IBI) to determine aquatic condition of lentic ecosystems in California; (3) evaluate the accuracy, bias, and precision of the IBI; and (4) determine how well a macroinvertebrate-based IBI could serve as an indicator for other pond assemblages (i.e., amphibians) in these habitats.

METHODS

Site Selection

The sampling region of this study encompassed eight counties within the Central and Northern Coast of California (Fig. 4.1). A total of 40 sites were selected by targeted sampling to encompass a wide range of natural variability and anthropogenic stressors, with a focus on capturing an urbanization gradient. Habitats included seasonal wetlands, natural ponds, stock ponds, stormwater retention ponds, and flood control basins. These habitats were hydrologically isolated (i.e., not riparian or connected via a floodplain) freshwater systems with salinities less than 6 ppt. Site selection focused on small wetlands, generally 0.1 - 2 hectares in size. Samples were collected in 2007 (n = 4), 2008 (n = 3), and 2009 (n = 33).

In order to limit the effects of seasonality (i.e., intra-annual variability), we restricted sampling to a specific index period, as is recommended for aquatic macroinvertebrate biomonitoring protocols in streams and wetlands (Barbour et al., 1999; Trigal et al., 2006). Sample dates of the main study were restricted to late spring and summer (May 10 – July 13), at which time most macroinvertebrates captured would be large enough to identify but most taxa would not have already emerged.

Development of Field Sampling Protocols

To determine the number of macroinvertebrate collection sweeps and area to sample at each site, a pilot study was undertaken at Hog Lake, a seasonal wetland in Mendocino County in 2007. Samples were collected with a 500-μm D-frame dipnet on 22 May, 2007 and 3 June, 2007. On each date, 10 individual sweeps (each 1 m long) were taken. All collected macroinvertebrates were stored in alcohol in the field and every individual was identified to family (order for micro-crustaceans), and the data were kept separate by sweep.

Similarity among the macroinvertebrate community found in each sweep was compared using three methods. The first was a (1) A Percent Similarity Index (PSI) calculated by the equation $PSI = \sum_{j=1}^{10} \min(p_{ij}, p_{ik}) \times 100$ where p_{ij}, is the proportion of individuals for species i at sweep combination j, p_{ik} is the proportion of species i when grouping all 10 sweeps (Wolda,

1981). The second and third similarity comparisons involved calculating the dissimilarity index based on Bray Curtis/Sørensen distance and a liner correlation matrix calculated with PC-ORD (McCune and Mefford, 2006).

Macroinvertebrate Sampling and Laboratory Methods

Freshwater wetlands were sampled to determine the composition of the overall aquatic macroinvertebrate community, which including all crustaceans greater than 500 µm, mollusks, and insects. Macroinvertebrates were sampled using 20 active netsweeps with a 500-µm D-frame dipnet by the same person (KBL). Each sweep involved a 1 m long pull that sampled organisms through the water surface, limnetic zone, and benthic zone, thereby sampling neuston, nekton/zooplankton, and benthos respectively. In total, the sampling encompassed 6 m^2 of pond area, collected at various depths throughout the littoral zone.

Macroinvertebrates were collected using a novel, standardized multi-habitat sampling approach. We sampled different microhabitats present in lentic habitats in proportion to their relative abundance because taxonomic groups show strong affinities to vegetation and sediment structure (e.g., Garcia-Criado and Trigal, 2005; Trigal et al., 2006). Sampling was focused throughout the wadeable littoral zone because that area was accessible by wading and contains the majority of species found in lentic habitats (Garcia-Criado and Trigal, 2005; Trigal et al., 2006). The sampling area was classified into four habitat types prior to sampling: emergent vegetation (e.g., *Typha* spp., *Scirpus* spp., *Eleocaris* spp.), submerged vegetation (e.g., *Ceratophyllum* spp., *Myriophyllum* spp., *Potamogeton* spp.), floating vegetation (e.g., *Lemna* spp., *Azola* spp., algae), and open areas (absence of vegetation). The 20 total samples were stratified according to percent occupied by the four sample types. For example, if 30% of the littoral zone was occupied with emergent vegetation, then 6 of the 20 sweeps (30%) were taken from that habitat class. For wetlands that were very small (0.01 - 0.03 ha), we took a composite sample based on only 10 total sweeps. In the field, composite macroinvertebrate samples were double-elutriated to reduce the amount of aquatic vegetation and organic debris in the sample. Macroinvertebrates were preserved with 95% ethanol in the field for a final concentration of 70%.

In the laboratory, macroinvertebrate samples were randomly subsampled to a fixed count of 500 organisms and identified to genera. Subsampling was accomplished using a custom-made 30.5 x 35.5 cm Caton-type tray. At least 3 out of 42 total 5 x 5-cm sections were sampled and then each of those was randomly subsampled using a 5-cm square Petri dish divided into 16 subsections. Picked individuals were identified to SAFIT Standard taxonomic effort (STE) Level I (Richards and Rogers, 2006) with additional resolution for Chironomidae (subfamily), Oligochaeta (order), Hirudenia (genus), Copepoda (genus), Cladocera (genus), and Ostracoda (order/family) by EcoAnalysts Inc. Obligate terrestrial Coleoptera as well as all pupal and adult Diptera were excluded from the study. To test for quality assurance three samples were selected for a replicate susbsample and identification.

Environmental and Stressor Variables

To determine how water quality, local physical habitat, landscape, human altered biotic variables affect the macroinvertebrate community, we recorded a number of variables in the field or used geographic information systems (GIS). In the field we measured temperature (°C) and specific conductance (conductivity calibrated to 25°C) using a YSI MP 556 meter, and pH using Oakton pHTstr 3. Turbidity (NTU) was measured with a HACH 2100P turbidity meter.

Water samples were collected from the littoral area within each pond. Water samples for total Chromium and total Lead were stored at 5°C until testing by the Davis DANR Laboratory. Water samples for total dissolved nitrogen (TDN), and total dissolved phosphorous (TDP) were frozen within 8 hrs of collection, then thawed and filtered using glass fiber filter (Whatman GF/D 2.7 μm) prior to analysis (Cukjati and Seibold, 2010). The N:P ratio was calculated as a stoichiometric atomic ratio to evaluate N or P limitation in the systems (Guildford and Hecky, 2000).

The number of invasive predators metric (N predator) was calculated using field observed and reports from landowners or managers regarding the presence of (1) any Centrarchidae (e.g., *Micropterus* spp., *Lepomis* spp.), (2) Western mosquitofish (*Gambusia affinis*), (3) predatory larval amphibians (i.e., *Rana catesbeiana*), or (4) invasive crayfish (e.g., *Pacifastacus leniusculus, Procambarus clarkii*). Each invasive predator received a score of 1 for present or 0 for absent. Therefore, the total score could range from 0 to 4.

Landscape variables were calculated with ESRI ArcInfo v9.2 or Google Earth. The effect of landscape variables were assessed at two spatial scales using concentric buffer zones from the wetland center point at a "local" (500-m radius), and "watershed " (1-km radius) scale because biological metrics may respond to anthropogenic stressors at various spatial scales (Brazner et al., 2007). The proportion of urbanization within these zones (percent urban) was calculated from the National Land Cover Dataset 2001 dataset (Homer et al., 2004). The NLCD categories of low, medium and high intensity developed were collapsed into a single urban category. Pond size (surface area) was determined using Google Earth Professional and the most currently available imagery during the wet season (December-May).

To assess the importance of connectivity to other aquatic habitats two variables were calculated: (1) the influence of proximate stream habitats measured as the amount of stream habitat from the National Hydrography Dataset (US Geolgical Survey and US Environmental Protection Agency, 1999) within each buffer zone; and (2) the importance of lentic habitats measured as the number of natural or artificial wetlands, ponds, and reservoirs within the 1-km buffer that were visible in Google Earth imagery from the wet season. Buffers of 1 km were calculated around the midpoint of the wetland using the GE-Path 1.4.4 extension in Google Earth (Sgrillo, 2009).

Index of Biotic Integrity (IBI) Development

Successful biomonitoring programs require standardized field methods and indicators that are both precise and accurate. An ideal sampling method provides a quantitative or semi-quantitative density estimate and also accurately captures the relative community composition. Macroinvertebrate indicators, whether an index of biotic integrity or multivariate O/E model, should be precise (low variability), unbiased towards natural gradients, and respond to anthropogenic stress gradients (Klemm et al., 2003; U.S. EPA, 2002a). Some univariate metrics that are typically useful in stream IBIs (e.g., tolerance values, Richness of Ephemeroptera, Trichoptera, and Plecoptera) are generally not applicable for lentic ecosystems (Helgen and Gernes, 2001) due to different biota and physiological limitations. Therefore, when developing a lentic multimetric index or IBI, a wide range of lentic-based metrics are typically explored, which calculate richness and percent composition of particular taxonomic groups and functional feeding groups for common taxa (Karr and Chu, 1999).

Influence of Environmental Variability

Reference sites were identified based on *a priori* targeted sampling of urban ponds (n=18) and rural ponds (n=22), with the intention of capturing the full range of an urban gradient. Reference sites are used as the unperturbed, expected biological community for all future steps in the IBI development. They represent a "best attainable condition" because reference sites included both natural and created wetlands (Bailey et al., 2004; Stoddard et al., 2006). Variables were examined for differences between the reference and test groups using *t*-tests for continuous variables or Chi-squared tests for categorical variables.

We assessed if distinct biological groups existed within the reference pool, which determined if a single IBI was be suitable for the range of sampled lentic habitats (Bailey et al., 2004). This was done by exploring environmental variability and looking for clustering based on the macroinvertebrate communities using NMS ordination for all 22 reference sites based on Sørenson/ Bray Curtis distance measures in PC-ORD (McCune and Mefford, 2006). Categorical variables such as hydroperiod (seasonal vs. perennial), and ecoregion (USDA Forest Service 2006) were compared using multi-response permutation procedures (MRPP) in PC-ORD (McCune and Grace, 2002). Continuous variables such as average annual rainfall (PRISM Climate Group, 2010), elevation, wetland average depth, wetland surface area, cumulative stream length and number of ponds in a 1-km buffer, and sample date (Julian date - mean Julian date) were ranked using weighted R^2 values for each ordination axis. Thresholds of importance for continuous variables were R^2 value ≥ 0.20, whereas the categorical variable criterion for MRPP tests was a p value ≤ 0.05.

Metric Selection and Scoring

To test the predictive ability of the IBI, all sites were randomly assigned to either a development or validation group within this dataset. The development set was used to create the IBI, which involved identifying metrics responsive to stress, scoring the metrics and calculating the IBI (Klemm et al., 2003). Therefore, the reference and impacted set (as determined by % urbanization described above) were divided into a development (14 reference / 12 impacted) and validation set (8 reference / 6 impacted), which corresponds a 65% development and 35% test set allocation.

We compiled a list of macroinvertebrate metrics and examined them for appropriateness to be included in the IBI (Appendix I). Functional feeding group and tolerance value designations are noted for taxa in Appendix II. Metrics responsive to various anthropogenic stressors of lentic habitats (lakes and reservoirs, prairie potholes, wetlands) were selected from the literature as well as from those created by state and federal resource (e.g., Adamus et al., 2001; Gernes and Helgen, 2002; Tangen et al., 2003; U.S. EPA, 1998,2002b). Metrics were then calculated and examined using the development dataset (n = 26).

To be included in the IBI, a given metric needed to meet three criteria with the developmental dataset: 1) correlation with percent urbanization; 2) have adequate range; and 3) lack redundancy with other significant metrics. The metric needed to show a relationship with percent urbanization within a 1-km buffer around the pond, which was evaluated using ordinary least squares (OLS) regression. Selection criteria included identifying a "wedge" or linear relationship, as well as an $R^2 \geq 0.10$. A wedge-type response is common because a single stressor may be a generalized limiting factor for a given metric, but the metric is also sensitive to additional stressors not evaluated in an OLS regression (Carter and Fend, 2005; Purcell et al., 2009; Thomson et al., 1996). The minimum range criteria was that each metric must support at least three categories of scoring as has been used in other wetland metrics (Gernes and Helgen, 2002). If two metrics were highly correlated ($r > 0.7$), then one with a lower R^2 was removed.

Metrics that passed all three screens were selected for inclusion in the IBI and scored on a 0 to 10 scale. For metrics with a negative response to stress (i.e., values decrease with increasing urbanization) values $\geq 80^{th}$ percentile of the reference group were assigned the maximum score of 10. A score of zero was assigned to values $\leq 10^{th}$ percentile of the impacted group. Values in between these upper and lower limits were scored by evenly dividing the value range into 9 equal portions and scoring them from 1 – 9 (Table 4.1). For metrics that increase with increasing urbanization, the score of ten was assigned to the $\leq 20^{th}$ percentile of the reference group, and zero to the $\geq 90^{th}$ percentile of the impacted group with the remainder scored into 9 equal portions.

IBI scores were calculated for all 40 sites according to the scoring thresholds for each of the 8 metrics that passed all three screens (Table 4.1). The average of all 8 metric scores was multiplied by 10 so that the metrics were evenly weighted and the final IBI would be scaled from 0 – 100. Higher IBI scores signal a less disturbed community, and lower IBI scores indicate a community response to urban stress.

IBI Validation

The IBI created using the developmental dataset was validated with the independent dataset (n=14), a process which indicates how well the IBI would be expected to work with novel sample sites. The validation set was tested with *a priori* performance thresholds: 1) a significant *t*-test ($p < 0.05$) comparing the scores from reference and impacted sites; and 2) a significant negative linear relationship between overall IBI scores and % urbanization (e.g., Ode et al., 2005). To investigate the possibility that an individual metric might have been selected by chance, we conducted two way *t*-tests of discriminatory power between the eight IBI subcomponent metrics at urban and reference sites, and OLS regressions to test responsiveness of the metrics against % urbanization.

Precision of the IBI score was evaluated with duplicate laboratory samples from three sites and replicate field samples taken from Hog Lake, a seasonal wetland, on four separate occasions by the same field crews. We calculated standard deviation of the two scores, and then took the average deviation to document how spatial variability within a pond and the random selection of macroinvertebrates and identification error affects IBI score precision. Following protocols outlined in Rehn (2005), we used an ANOVA with site as the independent variable to calculate the mean squared error (MSE) as a measure of within-site variability of the IBI score. The MSE was incorporated as s^2 used in a power analysis to calculate the minimum detectable difference (MDD) for a two sample *t*-test following Formula 8.23 in Zar (1999). A sample size of $n = 3$ for each sample, $df = 4$ (total $n - 2$), $\alpha = 0.1$, and $\beta = 0.1$ was used to be comparable to California stream assessments (Mazor et al., 2010; Ode et al., 2005; Rehn et al., 2005).

We measured robustness of the IBI by examining (1) potential bias along natural gradients among all reference sites, and (2) intra-annual variability of the IBI. To determine if the IBI was robust to natural gradients, reference site scores (n=22) were examined for association using *t*-tests or OLS regressions with the same variables examined in the reference NMS ordination. Intra-annual variability of the IBI was examined at Hog Lake, a seasonal wetland that typically dries out in July. Three samples with replicates were taken as the pond experienced seasonal drying succession in 2008 on 20 April, 19 May, and 02 June, ranging from 78%, 54%, and 41% of maximum depth, respectively.

An implicit assumption to biomonitoring is that he group being sampled is an overall indicator of all taxonomic groups in the ecosystem of interest. To test this assumption, if the macroinvertebrate community was a valid indictor for another aquatic group, we compared the macroinvertebrate IBI results with pond-breeding amphibian species richness, including frogs, toads, and salamanders. Amphibian presence or absence was evaluated by sampling for larval amphibians using the same 20 netsweeps used for macroinvertebrates. Metamorphic (emerged that summer) and adult life stage were sampled visually by inspecting a survey zone 2 meters in either direction of the water line (Olson et al., 1997). Additionally, bullfrogs (*Lithobates catesbeiana*) or Pacific chorus frogs (*Pseudacris regilla*). If any life stage of any species was observed, that species was recorded as present. Native amphibian species richness metric was calculated from these data.

Stressor Analysis

A stressor analysis was conducted to determine the sensitivity of the macroinvertebrate community to anthropogenic stress. Ten stressors within these habitats that were anthropogenic in nature or could be affected by anthropogenic activities (e.g., % urbanization, heavy metal and nutrient concentrations, conductivity, pH, and turbidity) were examined using a NMS ordination for all 40 sites using Sørensen / Bray Curtis distance measures in PC-ORD (McCune and Mefford, 2006). We ranked the stressors in order of importance using the cumulative weighted R^2 values for each ordination axis.

RESULTS

Development of Field Sampling Protocols

Data collected in the field study at Hog Lake indicated that a composite sample of more than 6 sweeps adequately represents the community composition (Fig. 4.2). All three similarity metrics showed over 95% agreement with composite sweeps composed of 6 or more out of the 10 total sweeps. However, to be certain to capture 500 individuals at sites with lower abundance, we decided that 20 habitat stratified netsweeps (6 m^2 sampled area) would be used to sample the macroinvertebrate community composition, followed by subsampling to the 500 individual threshold.

Data Collection

For the main study, a total of 40 freshwater wetlands were assessed in terms of macroinvertebrates, water chemistry, and physical habitat in the field, along with landscape level attributes calculated using laboratory-based procedures (Fig. 4.1). The subsampling procedure used to estimate the total number of individuals in the composite sample indicated that the approach showed similar or lower variability than commonly found in estimates of lotic abundance. In this study, coefficients of variation for abundance counts were approximately 20.5% and ranged from 5.8 to 58.3%. Wetlands examined supported an average abundance of 3455 organisms/m^2 (95% CI 2726 – 4404), which ranged from 275 to 22,978 organisms/m^2. A total of 116 unique taxa were observed at the 40 sites. Taxonomic richness of the individuals identified ranged from 9 to 36, with a median value of 19. The most common taxa included a wide array of organisms including small Crustaceans (Cladocera, Copepoda), Insects (Chironomidae, Ephemeroptera), Gastropods (*Physa*), and Annelids (Tubificidae) (Appendix II).

IBI Development
Evaluation of environmental variability

Sites were classified as reference condition (best attainable condition) based on *a priori* targeted sampling of rural, open space wetlands in contrast to wetlands in highly urbanized areas. The cutoff between reference and urban sites corresponded to an 11% threshold based on the persistent but low levels of urbanization found at *a priori* reference sites (near borders of open space districts or within private, rural properties) and it also provided an adequate number of reference and impacted sites for the analysis. Thus, sites with less than 11% of the 1-km buffer was urbanized were considered reference (n = 22) and sites with ≥ 11% urbanization were considered impacted (n = 18). Many significant differences existed between the reference and impacted sites (Table 4.2). Overall, urban wetlands tended to be man-made, larger, perennial, and have higher conductivities.

We analyzed the reference dataset to look for distinct clusters of sites based on biological data. Most environmental gradient variables were not significantly associated with changes in the biological community, suggesting that one IBI could suffice for the broad array of habitats and regions sampled. Precipitation, elevation, pond depth, pond surface area, sample date, and connectivity (stream length and number of ponds in 1 km buffer) all had an average R^2 below the 0.2 the threshold of importance established previously (Table 4.3). Of the three categorical variables tested, only hydroperiod showed a significant MRPP result (T = -5.6, $p < 0.002$). This difference could justify splitting the dataset into seasonal and perennial groups. However, creating an IBI for both perennial and seasonal wetlands was not possible because there were no urban-impacted seasonal wetlands. Therefore, the entire reference pool was treated as a single cluster for further analyses.

Metric selection and Scoring

Out of 56 macroinvertebrate metrics screened for inclusion in the IBI, 13 showed significant associations with urbanization. After removal of metrics that were correlated with each other (r ≥ 0.7) or lacked adequate range, 8 metrics remained as final candidates for inclusion in the IBI: % 3 dominant species; scraper richness; % Ephemeroptera, Odonata, and Trichoptera (EOT); EOT richness; % Tanypodinae/Chironomidae; Oligochaeta richness; % Coleoptera; and predator richness (Fig. 4.3).

IBI Performance and Validation

IBI performance was successfully validated using *a priori* threshold from independent dataset. The MRPP test showed no significant difference in the biological community between the development set and validation set, indicating a successful random selection process ($T = -0.91$, p = 0.17). Within the validation dataset, IBI scores for reference sites (mean = 69.3) were significantly higher than for impacted sites (mean = 27.9) within the validation set, demonstrating adequate discriminatory ability ($t = -7.36$, p < 0.001; Fig. 4.4). Similarly, the IBI showed a strong negative relationship with percent urbanization demonstrating strong responsiveness to this dominant stressor ($R^2=0.53$, $F = 13.4$, p < 0.005; Fig. 4.5).

An analysis of the subcomponent metrics determined that some metrics may have met the inclusion criteria by chance. Five of the 8 metrics that composed the IBI could independently differentiate between reference and urban wetlands in the validation set (Table 4.4). However, % 3 dominant taxa, scraper richness, and % Tanypodinae/Chironomidae did not show a significant discrimination or responsiveness (Table 4.4), and thus are less likely to be useful components of an ultimate wetland IBI for this region.

Precision of the IBI based on replicate samples from a single site was within an acceptable range. For example, the mean square error (MSE) of replicate field samples at Hog Lake was 59.75, which corresponded to a minimum detectable difference (MDD) of 27.2 IBI points, or 57.7% of the mean. Such an MDD can justify dividing the IBI into three or four distinct subcategories of condition such as poor, fair, and good (Fore et al., 2001).

Precision error appears to stem equally from both field and subsampling variability. For example, three laboratory duplicate subsamples of 500 organisms, each taken from the same composite macroinvertebrate sample as the original, had a mean standard deviation of 3.2 IBI points (CV = 6.9) compared to the original. This variability results from error in sampling the same 500 organisms and identification error. At Hog Lake, replicate field samples collected four times over two years had a mean standard deviation of 6.2 IBI points (CV = 11.9), which incorporated both intra-wetland spatial variability as well as the subsampling variability.

The IBI was robust against environmental variability and natural bias. For example, we found no significant effect between IBI score and all environmental variables: sample date ($R^2 = 0.002$, $p = 0.83$); Ecoregion ($R^2 = 0.089$, $p = 0.41$); pond size ($R^2 = 0.001$, $p = 0.89$); precipitation ($R^2 = 0.013$, $p = 0.61$); elevation ($R^2 = 0.084$, $p = 0.19$); connectivity to other ponds ($R^2 = 0.007$, $p = 0.71$); or hydroperiod (seasonal vs. ephemeral) ($R^2 = 0.005$, $p = 0.75$). However, IBI scores from samples collected at Hog Lake in April, May, and June changed consistently and significantly over time (Fig. 4.6), indicating that season can affect IBI scores.

The macroinvertebrate-based IBI was predictive of ecosystems condition as measured by the amphibian community. The ponds with higher IBI scores supported significantly more native amphibian species (Fig. 4.7). A minimum of 0 and maximum of 4 native amphibian species were recorded at the 40 wetlands. The Pacific chorus frog (*Pseudacris regilla*) was most common and found at 28 sites, followed by the coast range news (*Taricha torosa*) (n=18), invasive American Bullfrog (*Rana catesbeiana*) (n=12), California red-legged frog (*Rana draytonii*) (n=4), and California tiger salamander (*Ambystoma californiense*) (n=1).

Stressor Analysis

Across all sites, urbanization was the most important stressor associated with differences in the biological community (Fig. 4.8). The proportion of urbanization within a 1-km buffer and specific conductance both had an average $R^2 > 0.2$, which was the threshold of importance used throughout this study (Table 4.5). The number of invasive predators metric, chromium concentration, lead concentration, turbidity, pH, nutrients (TDP, TDN, N:P ratio) all had R^2 values below this threshold. Percent urban showed a moderate correlation ($r = 0.54$) with specific conductance, and thus might be a mechanism affecting the biological community. In terms of spatial scales, the 1 km watershed scale sphere of influence was slightly more important than the local 50 m buffer. For example, percent urbanization within 50 m had a slightly lower R^2 (0.244) compared to the 1 km buffer (0.262).

DISCUSSION

This study indicates that macroinvertebrates were successful bioindicators of urban stress in wetland ecosystems within Northern California. The field and laboratory methods worked well within the range of habitats, capturing 500 organisms or more and with adequate precision. The IBI was successfully validated with an independent dataset and robust against environmental variability within the region. The developed IBI is a proof of concept for applying biomonitoring protocols to wetland habitats in California.

Evaluation of Field and Laboratory Methods

On average, the field methods required 3.5 hours of field work (with two people), 4 hours to subsample 500 organisms, and 3 hours for taxonomic experts to identify 500 individuals, which is nearly in line with rapid assessment protocols even though this is an intensive (Level III) procedure (Fennessy et al., 2004). Sites with >50% surface or submergent vegetation took 4-5 hours in the field owing to the large amount of time required to elutriate the sample and separate the invertebrates from debris and vegetation. Considering results from the pilot study and high densities of organisms observed in general, it is possible that a total of 10 sweeps (3 m^2 area) could be used to survey for macroinvertebrates, especially for smaller wetlands (generally < 0.5 ha).

The timing (May - July) and length (two months) of the index period used appears appropriate for these habitat types in a mediterranean climate. For example, Julian date was not a significant factor affecting the biological community in the NMS ordination of reference sites, nor was it significantly associated with final IBI scores among the reference pool. However, IBI scores increased by nearly 30 points at a single wetland sampled between April 20 (which was outside of the index period) and June 2 (inside the index period), indicating site-specific effects of season and justifies a narrow index period. Differences in IBI scores were probably influenced by annual colonization patterns, selective predation, and emergence. Phenological shifts are likely to be most pronounced in seasonal wetland and vernal pools as compared to perennial ponds or lakes (Rogers, 1998; Williams, 2006)

Evaluation of the IBI

Based on the strong discriminatory power of the IBI and its robustness across environmental gradients, we conclude that macroinvertebrates are effective indicators of the ecological condition of wetlands, ponds, and reservoirs in Northern California. In particular, the multimetric IBI developed in this study successfully differentiated between reference quality and urban-impacted sites in the development and validation datasets and showed an overall significant decrease with increasing urbanization (Figs. 5.4, 5.5). It is important to note that metrics based on stream tolerance values (e.g., % sensitive, Hilsenhoff Biotic Index) were difficult to apply because many taxa were not listed in the SAFIT database describing tolerance values and functional feeding groups for local taxa (Richards and Rogers, 2006). Interestingly, none of the component metrics included data on the abundant zooplankton community (e.g., copepods, cladocerans). Removing this group from the subsampling and identification process could reduce costs perhaps increase accuracy, as has been done by other wetland biomonitoring programs (e.g., U.S. EPA, 2002a)

The IBI developed in this study can be further refined. First, this IBI is based only on urbanization yet other stressors are important in lentic habitats (see below). Second, some metrics were only marginally useful in terms of discriminatory power. In particular, scraper richness, % 3 dominant taxa, and % Tanypodinae/Chironomidae did not show satisfactory discriminatory power comparing reference and impacted sites in the validation dataset, The lack of statistical significance may indicating their inclusion could have been resulted from spurious associations in the developmental set, inaccurate scoring of maximum and minimum thresholds based on the development set, or the small sample size of the validation set (n=14).

Although this IBI was robust in both seasonal and perennial wetlands and found no distinction between the two, future efforts towards developing a lentic IBI should consider formulating one for each type of wetland, especially considering insect, crustacean, and gastropod taxa in ephemeral habitats can be unique (Della Bella et al., 2005; Williams, 1997). In addition, the two lowest scoring reference sites were seasonal ponds, providing additional evidence that IBI sensitivity could be improved by developing an IBI specifically for seasonal water bodies. Novel metrics might include the presence of branchiopods (e.g., fairy shrimp) or other obligate species of seasonal habitats.

The precision of the IBI developed in this study, as determined from a single site, is within a range observed for multimetric indices. The minimum detectable difference (MDD) of 27 IBI points was greater than MDD's observed in stream studies in California, which ranged from 13-22 (Mazor et al., 2010; Ode et al., 2005; Rehn et al., 2005), but similar to the 18-30 range observed with the Virginia Stream Condition Index (Mazor et al., 2010). Excluding large zooplankton from the identification process may improve precision because no zooplankton-based metrics were used in the IBI. Replicate samples from multiple wetlands in future studies will be necessary to confirm the MDD estimates for the field protocol and IBI.

This IBI based on macroinvertebrate community structure was useful in predicting native amphibian richness, justifying the use of macroinvertebrates as overall aquatic indicators. However, there remains unexplained variation in this relationship, indicating that a multi-group indicator could be a more robust and useful assessment tool. For example, Hughes et al. (2004) developed a more robust and inclusive indicator by incorporated amphibians with fish to develop a stream multimetric index. Although amphibians are considered an important indicator group sensitive to various terrestrial and aquatic stressors, few aquatic IBIs incorporate using amphibians (Adamus et al., 2001). Therefore, it may be prudent to consider incorporating amphibians and macroinvertebrates into a multi-guild index, especially considering that two endangered species in this region of California are common to pond habitats (Jennings and Hayes, 1994). Also, these taxa are observed during the physical habitat assessments and during the field elutriation process, thus do not require additional time to survey.

Stressor Analysis

Urbanization was the stressor most significantly associated with changes in community structure within this study. Conductivity was also associated with changes in community structure and correlated with urbanization, offering a potential mechanism for the water chemistry variable most affected by urbanization. Other water chemistry stressors showed minor association with the macroinvertebrate community despite existing evidence of their influence. In terms of biotic factors, the presence of invasive species was not an important stressor in this dataset, but fish can alter both amphibian and insect communities in high elevation California lakes (Knapp et al., 2001). A predator metric that incorporates abundance and not solely presence of predators might be a more responsive indicator. Considering bottom-up dynamics, nutrients alone or in combination did not appear to affect macroinvertebrate community structure or abundance in this study, even tough they can significantly increase wetland productivity or biomass (Adamus et al., 2001).

Applicability of a Lentic IBIs in California
California's lentic habitats are important to evaluate and monitor not only because they are protected under state and federal policies, but also because they are integral components of our natural environment. Intensive bioassessment protocols can be used to determine the ambient condition of California's freshwater wetlands, and to assist regulators evaluate current wetland mitigation and restoration projects. In addition, wetland monitoring tools could determine habitat quality of mitigation banks, ensuring that either man-made or natural wetlands were of sufficient condition to replace a functioning ecosystem. Finally, a large number of seasonal and perennial wetlands have been created in California (e.g., cattle ponds, flood control ponds, stormwater ponds, and irrigation reservoirs). Assessment of these created wetlands could confirm if these habitats are also providing valuable ecological services, which is a high priority for multiple-objective stormwater detention ponds.

ACKNOWLEDGMENTS

I thank R Mazor and E Stein for constructive comments on the manuscript; Jim Carter for assisting with subsampling methods; J Ball and S Feirer for assistance with GIS analyses; M Groff for assisting with the pilot study at Hog Lake, R Mazor and A Rehn for statistical advice; C Seibold for nutrient analyses; C Dunn, S Osman, K Yao, J Xin, M Aghaee M Baragona, A Strother, for assistance with field and laboratory work; Hopland Research and Extension Center, East Bay Regional Parks, Alameda Flood Control and Water Conservation District, and Cities of Novato, Davis, Oakley for sites access. This work was funded with assistance from the Alameda Countywide Cleanwater Program, National Science Foundation Graduate Research Fellowship Program and EPA STAR Fellowship Program.

LITERATURE CITED

ADAMUS, P., T. J. DANIELSON, AND A. GONYAW. 2001. Indicators for monitoring biological integrity if inland, freshwater wetlands: A survey of the technical literature (1990-2000). Office of Water, US Environmental Protection Agency. Washington, DC. EPA-843-R-01. US Environmental Protection Agency Washington, DC, USA.
http://www.epa.gov/owow/wetlands/bawwg/monindicators.pdf.

BAILEY, R. C., R. H. NORRIS, AND T. B. REYNOLDSON. 2004. Bioassessment of freshwater ecosystems: Using the reference condition approach. Kluwer Academic, Boston, MA, USA.

BARBOUR, M. T., J. GERRITSEN, B. D. SNYDER, AND J. B. STRIBLING. 1999. Rapid Bioassessment Protocols for Use in Streams and Wadeable Rivers: Periphyton, Benthic Macroinvertebrates and Fish, Second Edition. EPA 841-B-99-002. Office of Water, U.S. Environmental Protection Agency, Washington, DC, USA.

BATZER, D. P., AND S. A. WISSINGER. 1996. Ecology of insect communities in nontidal wetlands. Annual Review of Entomology 41:75-100.

BERKMAN, H. E., C. F. RABENI, AND T. P. BOYLE. 1986. Biomonitors of stream quality in agricultural areas: Fish versus invertebrates. Environmental Management 10:413-419.

BOIX, D., S. GASCON, J. SALA, M. MARTINOY, J. GIFRE, AND X. D. QUINTANA. 2005. A new index of water quality assessment in Mediterranean wetlands based on crustacean and insect assemblages: the case of Catalunya (NE Iberian peninsula). Aquatic Conservation-Marine and Freshwater Ecosystems 15:635-651.

BRAZNER, J. C., N. P. DANZ, A. S. TREBITZ, G. J. NIEMI, R. R. REGAL, T. HOLLENHORST, G. E. HOST, E. D. REAVIE, T. N. BROWN, J. M. HANOWSKI, C. A. JOHNSTON, L. B. JOHNSON, R. W. HOWE, AND J. J. H. CIBOROWSKI. 2007. Responsiveness of Great Lakes wetland indicators to human disturbances at multiple spatial scales: A multi-assemblage assessment. Journal of Great Lakes Research 33:42-66.

BROWN, B. S., N. E. DETENBECK, AND R. ESKIN. 2005. How probability survey data can help integrate 305(b) and 303(d) monitoring and assessment of state waters. Environmental Monitoring and Assessment 103:41-57.

CARTER, J. L., AND S. V. FEND. 2005. Setting limits: The development and use of factor-ceiling distributions for an urban assessment using macroinvertebrates. Effects of Urbanization on Stream Ecosystems 47:179-191.

CARTER, J. L., V. H. RESH, M. J. HANNAFORD, M. J. MYERS, F. R. HAUER, AND G. A. LAMBERTI. 2006. Macroinvertebrates as biotic indicators of environmental quality. Pp. 805-833. In F. R. Hauer, and G. A. Lamberti (Eds.), Methods in Stream Ecology. Second Edition. Academic Press/Elsevier, San Diego, CA, USA.

COLLINS, J. N., E. D. STEIN, M. SUTULA, R. CLARK, A. E. FETSCHER, L. GRENIER, C. GROSSO, AND A. WISKIND. 2008. California Rapid Assessment Method (CRAM) for Wetlands and Riparian Areas. www.cramwetlands.org. .

CUKJATI, J., AND C. SEIBOLD. 2010. Kiowa Environmental Chemistry Laboratory Procedure Manual. Mountain Research Station & Institute of Arctic and Alpine Research, University of Colorado Boulder.
http://snobear.colorado.edu/Kiowa/Kiowaref/procedure.html.

DELLA BELLA, V., M. BAZZANTI, AND F. CHIAROTTI. 2005. Macroinvertebrate diversity and conservation status of Mediterranean ponds in Italy: water permanence and mesohabitat influence. Aquatic Conservation-Marine and Freshwater Ecosystems 15:583-600.

FENNESSY, M. S., A. D. JACOBS, AND M. E. KENTULA. 2004. Review of Rapid Methods for Assessing Wetland Condition. EPA/620/R-04/009. U.S. Environmental Protection Agency, Washington, D.C. USA.

FORE, L. S., K. PAULSEN, AND K. O'LAUGHLIN. 2001. Assessing the performance of volunteers in monitoring streams. Freshwater Biology 46:109-123.

GARCIA-CRIADO, F., AND C. TRIGAL. 2005. Comparison of several techniques for sampling macroinvertebrates in different habitats of a North Iberian pond. Hydrobiologia 545:103-115.

GERNES, M. C., AND J. C. HELGEN. 2002. Indexes of biological integrity (IBI) for large depressional wetlands in Minnesota. Final Report to U.S. Environmental Protection Agency. Minnesota Pollution Control Agency. St Paul, Minnesota.
http://www.pca.state.mn.us/index.php/water/water-monitoring-and-reporting/biological-monitoring/wetland-monitoring/wetland-monitoring-aquatic-invertebrates.html.

GUILDFORD, S. J., AND R. E. HECKY. 2000. Total nitrogen, total phosphorus, and nutrient limitation in lakes and oceans: Is there a common relationship? Limnology and Oceanography 45:1213-1223.

HELGEN, J. C., AND M. C. GERNES. 2001. Monitoring the condition of wetlands: Indexes of biological integrity using invertebrates and vegetation. Pp. 167-185. *In* R. B. Rader, D. P. Batzer, and S. A. Wissinger (Eds.), Bioassessment and Management of North American Freshwater Wetlands. Wiley, New York, NY, USA.

HERBST, D. B., AND E. L. SILLDORFF. 2009. Development of a Benthic Macroinvertebrate Index of Biological Integrity (IBI) for Stream Assessments in the Eastern Sierra Nevada of California Unpublished technical report for the California State Water Quality Control Board, Sacramento, CA.
http://www.waterboards.ca.gov/water_issues/programs/swamp/tools.shtml#indicator.

HERING, D., O. MOOG, L. SANDIN, AND P. F. M. VERDONSCHOT. 2004. Overview and application of the AQEM assessment system. Hydrobiologia 516:1-20.

HOMER, C., C. Q. HUANG, L. M. YANG, B. WYLIE, AND M. COAN. 2004. Development of a 2001 National Land-Cover Database for the United States. Photogrammetric Engineering and Remote Sensing. http://seamless.usgs.gov/.

HUGHES, R. M., S. HOWLIN, AND P. R. KAUFMANN. 2004. A biointegrity index (IBI) for coldwater streams of Western Oregon and Washington. Transactions of the American Fisheries Society 133:1497-1515.

JENNINGS, M. R., AND M. P. HAYES. 1994. Amphibian and Reptile Species of Special Concern in California. California Department of Fish and Game, Rancho Cordova, CA.

KARR, J. R., AND E. W. CHU. 1999. Restoring Life in Running Waters. Island Press, Washington, DC.

KLEMM, D. J., K. A. BLOCKSOM, F. A. FULK, A. T. HERLIHY, R. M. HUGHES, P. R. KAUFMANN, D. V. PECK, J. L. STODDARD, W. T. THOENY, M. B. GRIFFITH, AND W. S. DAVIS. 2003. Development and evaluation of a Macroinvertebrate Biotic Integrity Index (MBII) for regionally assessing Mid-Atlantic Highlands streams. Environmental Management 31:656-669.

KNAPP, R. A., K. R. MATTHEWS, AND O. SARNELLE. 2001. Resistance and resilience of alpine lake fauna to fish introductions. Ecological Monographs 71:401-421.

MAZOR, R. D., K. SCHIFF, K. RITTER, A. REHN, AND P. ODE. 2010. Bioassessment tools in novel habitats: An evaluation of indices and sampling methods in low-gradient streams in California. Environmental Monitoring and Assessment 167:91-104.

MCCUNE, B., AND J. B. GRACE. 2002. Analysis of Ecological Communities. MjM Software Design, Gleneden Beach, OR, USA.

MCCUNE, B., AND M. J. MEFFORD. 2006. PC-ORD Multivariate Analysis of Ecological Data. Version 5.31. MjM Software Design, Gleneden Beach, OR, USA.

MURKIN, H. R. 1989. The basis for food chains in prairie wetlands. Pp. 316-339. *In* A. Van Der Valk (Ed.), Northern Prairie Wetlands. Iowa State University, Ames, IA, USA.

NAKANO, S., AND M. MURAKAMI. 2001. Reciprocal subsidies: Dynamic interdependence between terrestrial and aquatic food webs. Proceedings of the National Academy of Sciences of the United States of America 98:166-170.

NATIONAL RESOUCES AGENCY. 2010. State of the State's Wetlands. Natural Resources Agency, State of California, Sacramento, CA.
http://www.resources.ca.gov/docs/SOSW_report_with_cover_memo_10182010.pdf.

ODE, P. R., A. C. REHN, AND J. T. MAY. 2005. A quantitative tool for assessing the integrity of southern coastal California streams. Environmental Management 35:493-504.

OLSON, D. H., W. P. LEOARD, AND R. B. BURY (Eds.). 1997. Sampling Amphibians in Lentic Habitats: Methods and Approaches for the Pacific Northwest. Society for Northwestern Vertebrate Biology, Olympia, WA.

PRISM CLIMATE GROUP. 2010. Precipitation 800m annual normals (1971-2000). Oregon State University. http://www.prism.oregonstate.edu/.

PURCELL, A. H., D. W. BRESSLER, M. J. PAUL, M. T. BARBOUR, E. T. RANKIN, J. L. CARTER, AND V. H. RESH. 2009. Assessment tools for urban catchments: developing biological indicators based on benthic macroinvertebrates. Journal of the American Water Resources Association 45:306-319.

REHN, A. C., P. R. ODE, AND J. T. MAY. 2005. Development of a benthic index of biotic integrity (B-IBI) for wadeable streams in northern coastal California and its application to regions 305(b) assessment. Technical report for the California State Water Quality Control Board. California Department of Fish and Game Aquatic Bioassessment Laboratory, Rancho Cordova, CA.
http://www.swrcb.ca.gov/water_issues/programs/swamp/docs/reports/final_north_calif_ibi.pdf.

REHN, A. C., P. R. ODE, AND J. T. MAY. 2008. An index of biotic integrity (IBI) for perennial streams in California's Central Valley. Unpublished technical report for the California State Water Quality Control Board Sacramento, California.
http://www.swrcb.ca.gov/water_issues/programs/swamp/docs/reports/ibi_perstrms_cen_val.pdf.

RESH, V. H. 2007. Multinational, freshwater biomonitoring programs in the developing world: Lessons learned from African and Southeast Asian river surveys. Environmental Management 39:737-748.

RESH, V. H. 2008. Which group is best? Attributes of different biological assemblages used in freshwater biomonitoring programs. Environmental Monitoring and Assessment 138:131-138.

RICHARDS, A. B., AND D. C. ROGERS. 2006. List of freshwater macroinvertebrate taxa from California and adjacent states including standard taxonomic effort levels. Southwestern Association of Freshwater Invertebrate Taxonomists. http://www.safit.org/ste.html.

ROGERS, D. C. 1998. Aquatic macroinvertebrate occurrences and population trends in constructed and natural vernal pools in Folsom, California. *In* Proceedings: Ecology, conservation and management of vernal pool ecosystems. Proceedings from a 1996 conference., C. W. Witham, E. T. Bauder, D. Belk, W. R. Ferren, Jr., and R. Ornduff (Eds.). California Native Plant Society. pp. 224-235.

ROSENBERG, D. M., AND V. H. RESH. 1993a. Freshwater Biomonitoring and Benthic Macroinvertebrates. Chapman & Hall, New York, NY, USA.

ROSENBERG, D. M., AND V. H. RESH. 1993b. Introduction to freshwater biomonitoring and benthic macroinvertebrates. Pp. 1 - 9. *In* D. M. Rosenberg, and V. H. Resh (Eds.), Freshwater Biomonitoring and Benthic Macroinvertebrates. Chapman & Hall, New York.

ROY, A. H., A. D. ROSEMOND, M. J. PAUL, D. S. LEIGH, AND J. B. WALLACE. 2003. Stream macroinvertebrate response to catchment urbanisation (Georgia, USA). Freshwater Biology 48:329-346.

SGRILLO, R. 2009. GE-Path Version 1.4.4. http://www.sgrillo.net/googleearth/gepath.htm.

SMITH, A. J., R. W. BODE, AND G. S. KLEPPEL. 2007. A nutrient biotic index (NBI) for use with benthic macroinvertebrate communities. Ecological Indicators 7:371-386.

SMITH, M. J., W. R. KAY, D. H. D. EDWARD, P. J. PAPAS, K. S. RICHARDSON, J. C. SIMPSON, A. M. PINDER, D. J. CALE, P. H. J. HORWITZ, J. A. DAVIS, F. H. YUNG, R. H. NORRIS, AND S. A. HALSE. 1999. AusRivAS: using macroinvertebrates to assess ecological condition of rivers in Western Australia. Freshwater Biology 41:269-282.

SOLIMINI, A. G., M. BAZZANTI, A. RUGGIERO, AND G. CARCHINI. 2008. Developing a multimetric index of ecological integrity based on macroinvertebrates of mountain ponds in central Italy. Hydrobiologia 597:109-123.

STEIN, E. D., A. E. FETSCHER, R. P. CLARK, A. WISKIND, J. L. GRENIER, M. SUTULA, J. N. COLLINS, AND C. GROSSO. 2009. Validation of a wetland rapid assessment method: Use of EPA's Level 1-2-3 framework for method and testing and refinement. Wetlands 29:648-665.

STODDARD, J. L., D. P. LARSEN, C. P. HAWKINS, R. K. JOHNSON, AND R. H. NORRIS. 2006. Setting expectations for the ecological condition of streams: The concept of reference condition. Ecological Applications 16:1267-1276.

SUTULA, M. A., E. D. STEIN, J. N. COLLINS, A. E. FETSCHER, AND R. CLARK. 2006. A practical guide for the development of a wetland assessment method: The California experience. Journal of the American Water Resources Association 42:157-175.

TANGEN, B. A., M. G. BUTLER, AND J. E. MICHAEL. 2003. Weak correspondence between macroinvertebrate assemblages and land use in Prairie Pothole Region wetlands, USA. Wetlands 23:104-115.

THOMSON, J. D., G. WEIBLEN, B. A. THOMSON, S. ALFARO, AND P. LEGENDRE. 1996. Untangling multiple factors in spatial distributions: Lilies, gophers, and rocks. Ecology 77:1698-1715.

TRIGAL, C., F. GARCIA-CRIADO, AND C. FERNANDEZ-ALAEZ. 2006. Among-habitat and temporal variability of selected macroinvertebrate based metrics in a Mediterranean shallow lake (NW Spain). Hydrobiologia 563:371-384.

U.S. EPA. 1998. Lake and Reservoir Bioassessment and Biocriteria. EPA-841-B-98-007. Office of Water, U.S. Environmental Protection Agency, Washington, DC, USA.

U.S. EPA. 2002a. Methods for Evaluating Wetland Condition: Developing an Invertebrate Index of Biological Integrity for Wetlands. EPA-822-R-02-219. Office of Water, U.S. Environmental Protection Agency, Washington, DC

U.S. EPA. 2002b. Methods for Evaluating Wetland Condition: Using Amphibians in Bioassessments of Wetlands. EPA-822-R-02-022. Office of Water, U.S. Environmental Protection Agency, Washington, DC

U.S. EPA. 2003. Wetland Bioassessment Case Studies. http://water.epa.gov/type/wetlands/assessment/case.cfm.

US GEOLGICAL SURVEY AND US ENVIRONMENTAL PROTECTION AGENCY. 1999. National Hydrography Dataset - Medium Resolution. Reston, Virginia. http://nhd.usgs.gov.

USDA FOREST SERVICE - PACIFIC SOUTHWEST REGION - REMOTE SENSING LAB. 2006. CalvegTiles Ecoregions. McClellan, CA. http://www.fs.fed.us/r5/rsl/clearinghouse/gis-download.shtml.

WILLIAMS, D. D. 1997. Temporary ponds and their invertebrate communities. Aquatic Conservation-Marine and Freshwater Ecosystems 7:105-117.

WILLIAMS, D. D. 2006. The Biology of Temporary Waters. Oxford University Press, Oxford, UK.

WOLDA, H. 1981. Similarity indexes, sample-size and diversity. Oecologia 50:296-302.

YODER, C. O., AND E. T. RANKIN. 1998. The role of biological indicators in a state water quality management process. Environmental Monitoring and Assessment 51:61-88.

ZAR, J. H. 1999. Biostatistical Analysis. 4th edition. Prentice Hall, Upper Saddle River, New Jersey, USA.

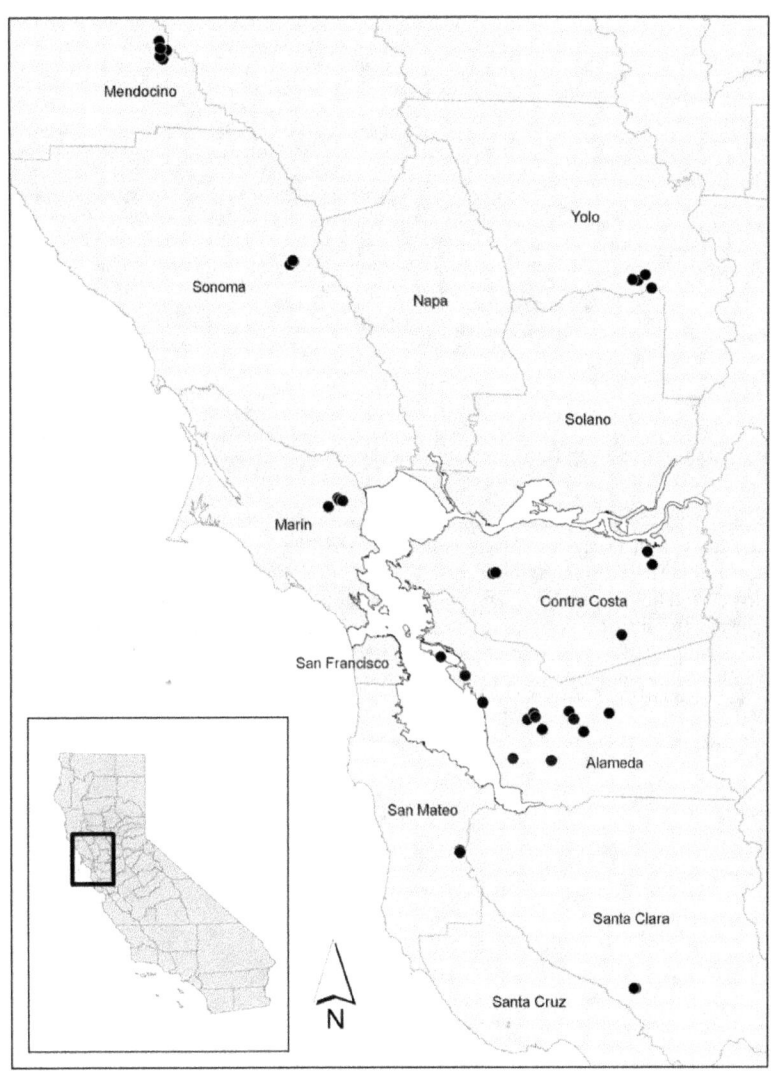

Figure 4.1. Map of 40 wetland biomonitoring sites across 8 counties in Northern California.

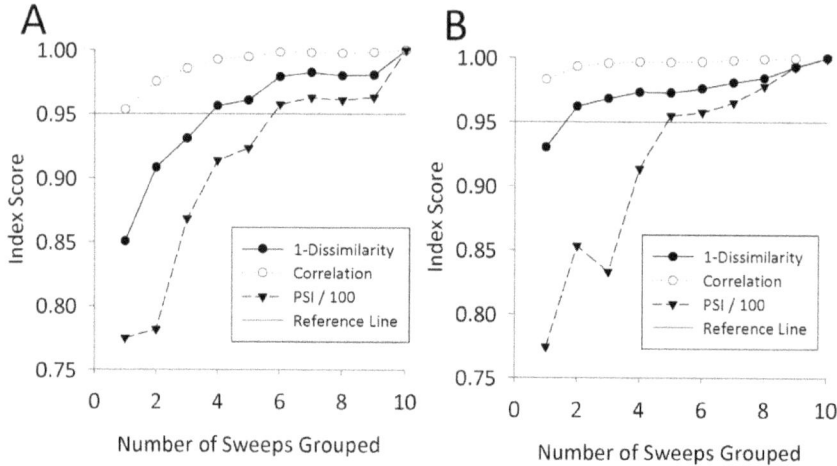

Figure 4.2. Similarity comparisons of taxonomic composition of replicate samples collected as part of a pilot study. Ten sweeps each were collected on 05/22/07 (A) and 06/03/07 (B), and identified to family. Three similarity metrics were scaled to fit on the same graph: 1 – Sørensen Dissimilarity, correlation (no scaling), and percent similarity index (PSI)/100. Each metric was calculated for the group with a composite sample size (n), against the total sample composite of 10. Composite samples of 6 sweeps or greater consistently scored above 95% (Reference Line) agreement with all three similarity metrics in both samples.

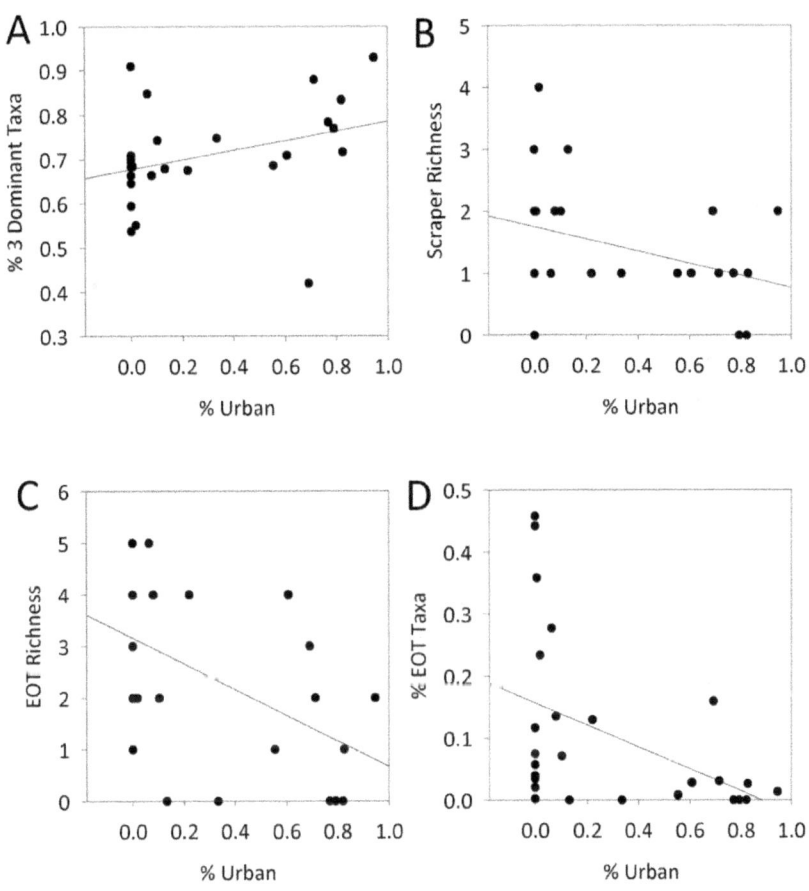

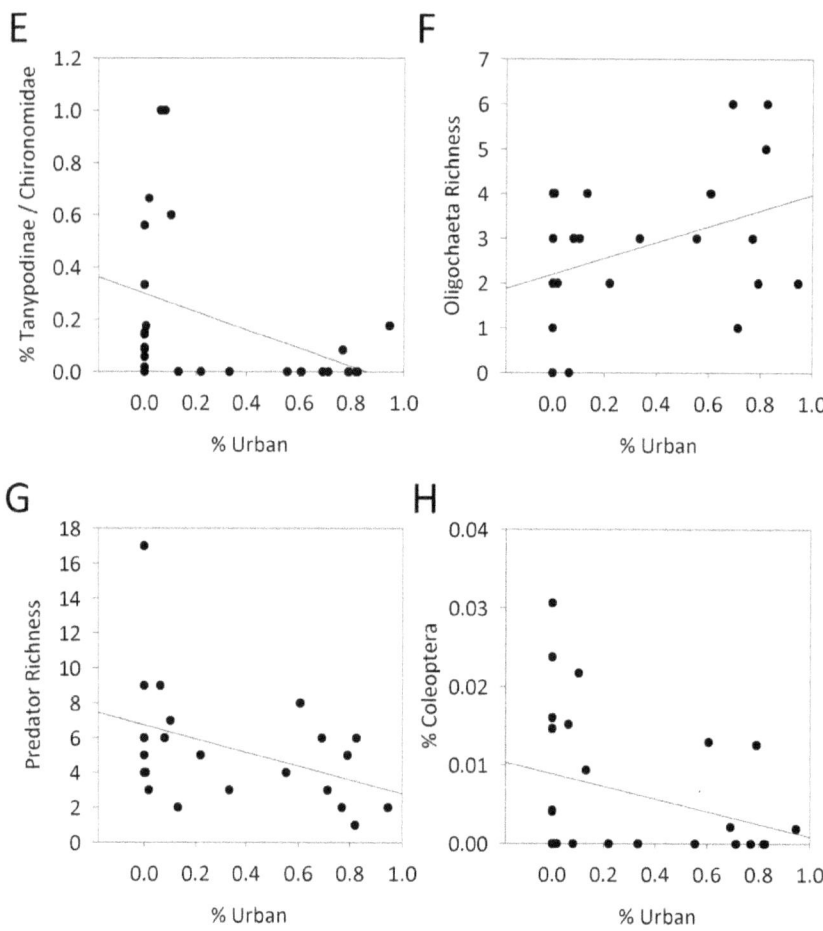

Figure 4.3. Associations of 8 final metrics with % urbanization within a 1km buffer around the site. All sites had an OLS regression R^2 value of ≥ 0.1, lacked redundancy with the other seven metrics, and had adequate range for proper scoring.

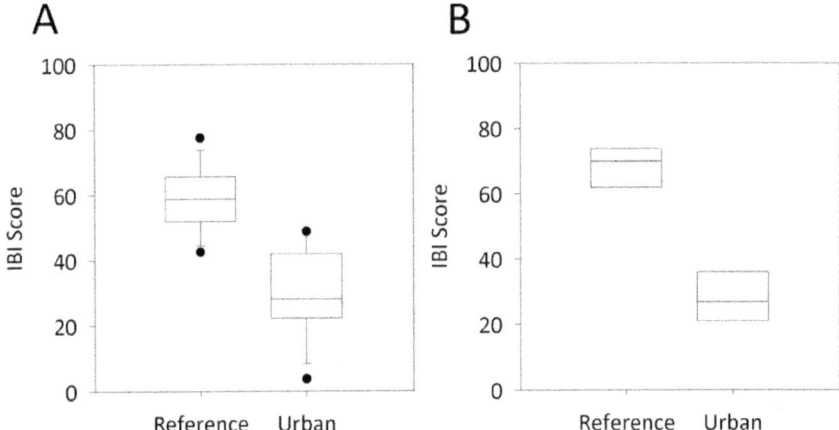

Figure 4.4. (A) Comparison of IBI scores for the development data set (n = 26, t = -6.5, $p <$ 0.001). (B) Comparison of IBI scores for the validation data set (n = 14, t = -6.9, p <0.001). The significant difference between Reference (mean = 67.8) and Urban (mean = 28.1) IBI scores validates the discriminatory power of the IBI on a novel set of wetlands.

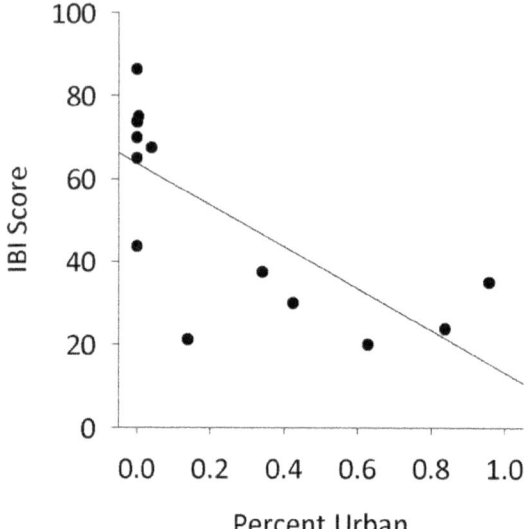

Figure 4.5. Ordinary least squares (OLS) regression of IBI scores against percent urbanization within the 1km buffer of each wetland based on the validation dataset (n = 14, R^2 = 0.53, p = 0.003). The significant negative relationship represents responsiveness of the IBI to urbanization using a novel set.

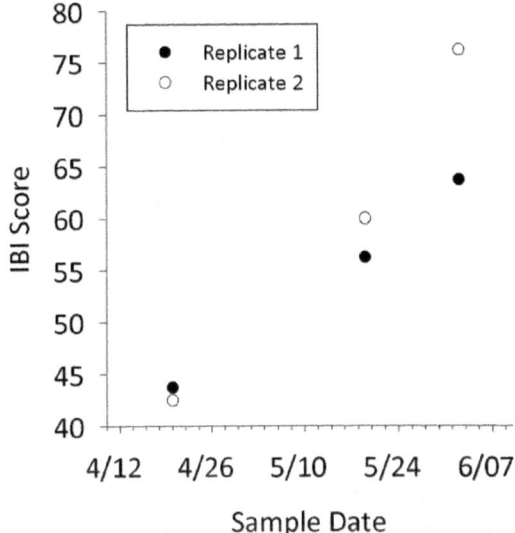

Figure 4.6. Changes in IBI score based on sampling date at a seasonal wetland. Duplicate samples were taken on each sample period April 20, May 19 and June 2. Score significantly increased over this time (logistic regression, $n = 6$, $p < 0.05$).

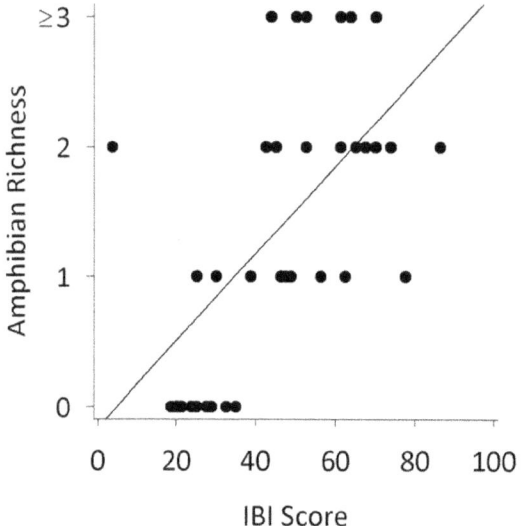

Figure 4.7. Correlation between the macroinvertebrate IBI and a metric based on a different aquatic assemblage, native amphibian species richness ($r = 0.63$, $p < 0.001$). Because only one wetland had 4 native amphibian species, this category was merged with 3 to become greater than or equal to three species.

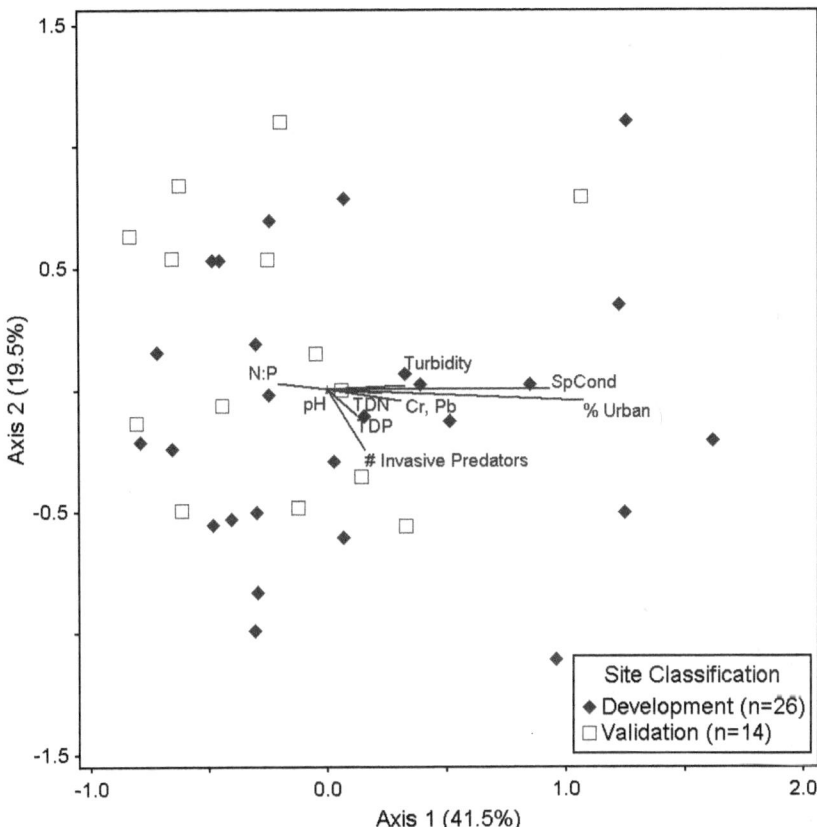

Figure 4.8. Stressor ranking and identification in NMS ordination of 40 sites (Final stress = 15.8, Instability < 0.00001). Axis 1, 2, and 3, explain 41.5%, 19.5%, and 18.5% of the variability in the data (Axis 3 not shown). The length of vectors of stressors included on this diagram show the association with the biological community. The similar vector direction of % urban and specific conductance (SpCond) implies a strong correlation between the two. MRPP showed a significant difference in the biological community between the perennial and non-perennial ponds ($A = 0.05$, $p < 0.002$)

Table 4.1. Scoring criteria for the IBI

Score	% 3 Dominant taxa	% Tanypodinae /Chironomidae	% Coleoptera	% EOT	Scraper richness	EOT richness	Oligochaeta richness	Predator richness
10	≤ 65.3	≥ 62.6	≥ 1.8	≥ 31.0	≥ 2	≥ 5	0	≥ 9
9	65.4 - 67.5	56.3 – 62.5	1.6 – 1.7	27.9 – 30.9			1	8
8	67.6 - 69.8	50.1 – 56.2	1.5	24.8 – 27.8		4		
7	69.9 - 72.0	43.8 – 50.0	1.3 – 1.4	21.9 – 24.7			2	7
6	72.1 - 74.2	37.5 – 43.7	1.1 – 1.2	18.6 – 21.6		3		6
5	74.3 - 76.4	31.3 – 37.4	0.9 – 1.0	15.5 – 18.5	1		3	
4	76.5 - 78.6	25.0 – 31.2	0.7 – 0.8	12.4 – 15.4		2		5
3	78.7 - 80.9	18.8 – 24.9	0.5 – 0.6	9.3 – 12.3			4	4
2	81.0 - 83.1	12.5 – 18.7	0.4	6.2 – 9.2		1	5	
1	83.2 - 87.5	6.3 – 12.4	0.2 – 0.3	3.1 – 6.1				3
0	≥ 87.6	0.0 – 6.2	0.0 – 0.1	0.0 – 3.0	0	0	≥ 6	≤ 2

Table 4.2. Mean values and standard deviations (in parentheses) for ponds in the Reference (best-attainable condition) and Urban-impacted classifications with associated *t*-test results comparing the two groups. Wetlands were *a priori* classified as Urban or Reference, which subsequently corresponded to the proportion of urbanization within a 1 km buffer of 11% or greater for the urban group. The groupings of natural variables refers to variables that are not considered anthropogenic stressors but may influence macroinvertebrate community composition while the stressor variables are mostly affected by anthropogenic activities.

	Reference (n=22)	Urban (n=18)	*p*
Natural Variables			
% Perennial	41	100	<0.001
Surface area (hectares)	0.2 (0.3)	1.9 (2.8)	0.011
Average depth (m)	1.0 (0.73)	0.97 (0.53)	n.s.
Elevation (m)	364 (160)	48 (99)	<0.001
Mean annual precipitation (cm)	76.6 (22.6)	56.1 (8.2)	<0.002
Stressor Variables			
% Urban within 1 km buffer	1.4 (3.0)	59.6 (26.9)	<0.001
# Invasive predators	0.6 (1.1)	1.7 (1.1)	0.002
% Created	64	94	0.014
Specific conductance (µS/cm^2)	390 (359)	2140 (2800)	0.006
pH	8.44 (0.98)	8.71 (0.97)	n.s.
Turbidity (NTU)	14.6 (33.6)	29.3 (59.8)	n.s.
Total Chromium (µg/L)	1.2 (1.8)	4.6 (6.9)	0.033
Total Lead (µg/L)	3.0 (4.6)	5.4 (7.6)	n.s.
Total dissolved Nitrogen (TDN) (mg/L)	1.21 (0.60)	1.26 (0.94)	n.s.
Total dissolved Phosphorous (TDP) (mg/L)	0.09 (0.07)	0.14 (0.13)	n.s.
TDN:TDP molar ratio	45.9 (25.6)	24.5 (15.1)	0.003

Table 4.3. Association between natural variables independent of anthropogenic disturbance and macroinvertebrate community structure at all 22 reference sites. Values represent squared correlation coefficients (R^2) based on the association between nonmetric multidimensional scaling (NMS) scores and each environmental variable. Rank of importance was based on the weighted average of the squared correlation coefficient (R^2) and the NMS model coefficients of determination for that axis: Axis 1, 2, and 3, explained 10.2%, 26.5%, and 46.6% of the variance, respectively.

	Axis 1 R^2	Axis 2 R^2	Axis 3 R^2	Weighted R^2	Rank
Average pond depth	0.00	0.51	0.01	0.17	1
Ln (Size (surface area))	0.01	0.39	0.04	0.15	2
Elevation	0.00	0.33	0.01	0.11	3
Number of ponds within 1 km	0.18	0.05	0.13	0.11	4
Sample (Julian) date	0.00	0.20	0.06	0.10	5
Stream length within 1 km	0.00	0.00	0.11	0.06	6
Average annual precipitation	0.01	0.00	0.05	0.03	7

Table 4.4. Performance of individual metrics composing the IBI among the development and validation sets. Results displayed are R^2 values from ANOVA or OLS regression of non-transformed raw data. The metrics with significant differences in all four tests were considered to have strong discriminatory power.

8 metric components of the IBI	R^2 from IBI against % urban (OLS regression)		R^2 of Urban vs. Reference (ANOVA)		Discriminatory power of indicator
	Development (n=26)	Validation (n=14)	Development (n=26)	Validation (n=14)	
% 3 Dominant taxa	0.11	0.13	0.05	0.26	weak
Scraper richness	0.12	0.09	0.08	0.12	weak
%EOT	0.20*	0.29*	0.24*	0.40*	strong
EOT richness	0.25*	0.37*	0.30*	0.71*	strong
% Tanypodinae/Chironomidae	0.16*	0.04	0.29*	0.12	inconsistent
Oligochaeta richness	0.14	0.37*	0.15*	0.33*	inconsistent
% Coleoptera	0.10	0.18	0.12	0.25	weak
Predator richness	0.17*	0.56*	0.22*	0.69*	strong

* denotes significance at $p < 0.05$.

Table 4.5. Stressor analysis rankings. Results of nonmetric multidimensional scaling (NMS) ordination of all 40 sites examining the correlation between explanatory variables and changes in macroinvertebrate community structure. Values represent squared correlation coefficients (R^2) based on the association between nonmetric multidimensional scaling (NMS) scores and each environmental variable. Rank of importance was based on the weighted average of the squared correlation coefficient (R^2) and the NMS model coefficients of determination for that axis: Axis 1, 2, and 3, explained 41.5, 19.5, and 18.8% of the variance, respectively.

Anthropogenic Stressor	Axis 1 R^2	Axis 2 R^2	Axis 3 R^2	Weighted R^2	Rank
*(% Urban within 1 km)	0.49	0.00	0.00	0.26	1
Ln (Specific conductance)	0.40	0.02	0.02	0.22	2
Total Lead	0.15	0.00	0.01	0.08	3
# Invasive predators	0.10	0.07	0.03	0.08	4
Ln (Turbidity)	0.13	0.03	0.00	0.08	5
Total Chromium	0.11	0.00	0.07	0.07	6
N:P ratio	0.10	0.00	0.06	0.07	7
Total dissolved Phosphorous	0.07	0.02	0.02	0.05	8
Total dissolved Nitrogen	0.07	0.00	0.06	0.05	9
pH	0.00	0.01	0.03	0.01	10

*ArcSine square root transformed

Appendix 4.I. All 56 macroinvertebrate based metrics analyzed for inclusion in the Index of Biotic Integrity.

Abundance Metrics
Individuals / m^2

Total Diversity/ Richness Metrics
Taxonomic Richness
Shannon-Weaver H'
Margalef's Richness
Pielou's J'
Simpson's Heterogeneity

Sensitivity Metrics
Hilsenhoff Biotic Index (HBI)
% Dominant Taxon
% 2 Dominant Taxa
% 3 Dominant Taxa

Functional Feeding Group Metrics
% Filterers
Filterer Richness
% Gatherers
Gatherer Richness
% Predators
Predator Richness
% Scrapers
Scraper Richness
% Shredders
Shredder Richness
% Macrophyte-Herbivores
Macrophyte-Herbivores Richness

Taxonomic Composition Metrics
% Insecta
% Ephemeroptera
% Baetidae
% Coleoptera
% Hemiptera
% Corixidae
Corixidae Richness
% Odonata
Odonata Richness
%EOT
EOT rich
Non-Chironomid Diptera Richness
% Chironomidae
% Orthocladiinae
% Chironominae/Chironomidae
% Orthocladiinae/Chironomidae
% Tanypodinae/Chironomidae
% Oligochaeta
Oligochaeta richness
% Oligochaeta, Annelida, Chironomidae, Planaria
% Amphipoda
Crustacea and Mollusca Richness
% Crustacea and Mollusca
% Crustacea
% Crustacea and Gastropoda
% Gastropoda
Gastropoda richness
% Physidae
% Sphaeridae
% Zooplankton
% Ostracods
% Cyclopoid
% Calanoid
% Cladoceran

Appendix 4.II. List of 116 taxa encountered in the survey with tolerance values (TV) and functional feeding group (FFG) designations. TV and FFG sources included Southwestern Association of Freshwater Invertebrate Taxonomists (Richards and Rogers 2006), Appendix B from Barbour et al. (1999), and Thorp and Covich (2001).

P = Predator (all types), MH = Macrophyte/Herbivore, CG = Collector/Gatherer, SH = Shredder, CF = Collector/Filterer, SC = Scraper

Phylum	Subhylum/Class	Order	Family	Taxa	TV	FFG
Arthropoda	Insecta	Coleoptera	Dytiscidae	*Agabus sp.*	8	P
Arthropoda	Insecta	Coleoptera	Dytiscidae	*Cybister sp.*	5	P
Arthropoda	Insecta	Coleoptera	Dytiscidae	*Dytiscus sp.*	5	P
Arthropoda	Insecta	Coleoptera	Dytiscidae	*Hygrotus sp.*	5	P
Arthropoda	Insecta	Coleoptera	Dytiscidae	*Laccophilus sp.*	5	P
Arthropoda	Insecta	Coleoptera	Dytiscidae	*Neoclypeodytes sp.*	5	P
Arthropoda	Insecta	Coleoptera	Dytiscidae	*Stictotarsus sp.*	5	P
Arthropoda	Insecta	Coleoptera	Haliplidae	*Apteraliplus sp.*	5	MH
Arthropoda	Insecta	Coleoptera	Haliplidae	*Peltodytes sp.*	5	MH
Arthropoda	Insecta	Coleoptera	Haliplidae		5	MH
Arthropoda	Insecta	Coleoptera	Hydrophilidae	*Berosus sp.*	5	P
Arthropoda	Insecta	Coleoptera	Hydrophilidae	*Enochrus sp.*	5	CG
Arthropoda	Insecta	Coleoptera	Hydrophilidae	*Tropisternus sp.*	5	P
Arthropoda	Insecta	Coleoptera	Hydrophilidae		5	P
Arthropoda	Insecta	Collembola	Entomobryidae		5	CG
Arthropoda	Insecta	Collembola	Isotomidae	Isotomidae	5	CG
Arthropoda	Insecta	Collembola	Onychiuridae		5	CG
Arthropoda	Insecta	Collembola	Sminthuridae		5	CG
Arthropoda	Insecta	Diptera	Ceratopogonidae	*Bezzia/Palpomyia sp.*	6	P
Arthropoda	Insecta	Diptera	Ceratopogonidae	*Dasyhelea sp.*	6	CG
Arthropoda	Insecta	Diptera	Ceratopogonidae		6	P
Arthropoda	Insecta	Diptera	Chaoboridae	*Chaoborus sp.*	7	P
Arthropoda	Insecta	Diptera	Chironomidae	Chironominae	6	CG
Arthropoda	Insecta	Diptera	Chironomidae	Orthocladiinae	5	CG
Arthropoda	Insecta	Diptera	Chironomidae	Tanypodinae	7	CG

Arthropoda	Insecta	Diptera	Culicidae	Culex sp.	8	CG
Arthropoda	Insecta	Diptera	Culicidae		8	CG
Arthropoda	Insecta	Diptera	Culicidae	Anopheles sp.	8	CG
Arthropoda	Insecta	Diptera	Dixidae	Dixella sp.	2	CG
Arthropoda	Insecta	Diptera	Ephydridae		6	CG
Arthropoda	Insecta	Diptera	Limoniidae	Limonia sp.	6	SH
Arthropoda	Insecta	Diptera	Psychodidae	Psychoda sp.	10	CG
Arthropoda	Insecta	Diptera	Stratiomyidae		8	CG
Arthropoda	Insecta	Ephemeroptera	Baetidae	Callibaetis sp.	9	CG
Arthropoda	Insecta	Hemiptera	Belostomatidae		8	P
Arthropoda	Insecta	Hemiptera	Corixidae	Cenocorixa sp.	8	P
Arthropoda	Insecta	Hemiptera	Corixidae	Corisella sp.	8	P
Arthropoda	Insecta	Hemiptera	Corixidae	Hesperocorixa sp.	8	P
Arthropoda	Insecta	Hemiptera	Corixidae	Sigara sp.	8	P
Arthropoda	Insecta	Hemiptera	Corixidae	Trichocorixa sp.	8	P
Arthropoda	Insecta	Hemiptera	Gerridae		10	P
Arthropoda	Insecta	Hemiptera	Notonectidae	Notonecta sp.	5	P
Arthropoda	Insecta	Odonata	Aeshnidae	Aeshna sp.	10	P
Arthropoda	Insecta	Odonata	Aeshnidae	Anax sp.	5	P
Arthropoda	Insecta	Odonata	Aeshnidae		8	P
Arthropoda	Insecta	Odonata	Libellulidae	Erythemis sp.	5	P
Arthropoda	Insecta	Odonata	Libellulidae	Sympetrum sp.	9	P
Arthropoda	Insecta	Odonata	Libellulidae/Cordulidae		9	P
Arthropoda	Insecta	Odonata	Coenagrionidae	Coenagrion/Enallagma sp.	9	P
Arthropoda	Insecta	Odonata	Coenagrionidae	Ischnura sp.	9	P
Arthropoda	Insecta	Odonata	Coenagrionidae		9	P
Arthropoda	Insecta	Odonata	Lestidae	Lestes sp.	9	P
Arthropoda	Insecta	Trichoptera	Hydroptilidae		4	MH
Arthropoda	Arachnida	Acari	Arrenuridae	Arrenurus sp.	5	P
Arthropoda	Arachnida	Acari	Hydrachnidae	Hydrachna sp.	5	P

Phylum	Class	Order	Family	Genus/species		
Arthropoda	Arachnida	Acari	Limnesiidae	*Limnesia sp.*	5	P
Arthropoda	Arachnida	Acari	Pionidae	*Piona sp.*	5	P
Arthropoda	Arachnida	Acari	Oribatei		5	P
Arthropoda	Branchiopoda	Anostraca	Chirocephalidae	*Linderiella occidentalis*		CF
Arthropoda	Branchiopoda	Spinicaudata	Cyzicidae	*Cyzicus sp.*	8	CF
Arthropoda	Branchiopoda	Laevicaudata	Lynceidae	*Lynceus brachyurus*	8	CF
Arthropoda	Branchiopoda	Cladocera	Bosminidae	*Bosmina sp.*	8	CF
Arthropoda	Branchiopoda	Cladocera	Chydoridae		8	CG
Arthropoda	Branchiopoda	Cladocera	Daphniidae	*Ceriodaphnia sp.*	8	CF
Arthropoda	Branchiopoda	Cladocera	Daphniidae	*Daphnia sp.*	8	CF
Arthropoda	Branchiopoda	Cladocera	Daphniidae	*Scapholeberis sp.*	8	CF
Arthropoda	Branchiopoda	Cladocera	Daphniidae	*Simocephalus sp.*	8	CF
Arthropoda	Branchiopoda	Cladocera	Macrothricidae		8	CG
Arthropoda	Branchiopoda	Cladocera	Sididae	*Sida crystallina*	8	CF
Arthropoda	Branchiopoda	Cladocera	Sididae	*Diaphanosoma sp.*	8	CF
Arthropoda	Copepoda	Cyclopoida	Cyclopidae	*Acanthocyclops sp.*	8	CG
Arthropoda	Copepoda	Cyclopoida	Cyclopidae	*Macrocyclops sp.*	8	CG
Arthropoda	Copepoda	Cyclopoida	Cyclopidae		8	CG
Arthropoda	Copepoda	Calanoida	Candoniidae		8	CF
Arthropoda	Copepoda	Calanoida	Diaptomidae		8	CF
Arthropoda	Copepoda	Calanoida	Diaptomidae	*Leptodiaptomus sp.*	8	CF
Arthropoda	Ostracoda	Podocopa	Cypridae		8	CG
Arthropoda	Ostracoda	Podocopida	Cytheridae		8	CG
Arthropoda	Malacostraca	Amphipoda	Crangonyctidae	*Crangonyx sp.*	4	CG
Arthropoda	Malacostraca	Amphipoda	Hyalellidae	*Hyalella sp.*	8	CG
Arthropoda	Malacostraca	Amphipoda	Anisogammaridae	*Eogammarus confervicolus*	6	CG
Arthropoda	Malacostraca	Amphipoda	Gammaridae	*Gammarus sp.*	6	CG
Arthropoda	Malacostraca	Decapoda	Palaemonidae	*Exopalaemon modestus*	8	SH
Arthropoda	Malacostraca	Decapoda	Cambaridae	*Procambarus clarkii*	8	SH
Arthropoda	Malacostraca	Mysida	Mysidae	*Neomysis mercedis*		CF
Mollusca	Bivalvia	Veneroida	Sphaeriidae	*Sphaerium sp.*	8	CF

Mollusca	Gastropoda	Basommatophora	Lymnaeidae	*Physa sp.*	6	SC
Mollusca	Gastropoda	Basommatophora	Physidae	*Ferrissia sp.*	8	SC
Mollusca	Gastropoda	Basommatophora	Planorbidae	*Gyraulus sp.*	6	SC
Mollusca	Gastropoda	Basommatophora	Planorbidae	*Menetus sp.*	8	SC
Mollusca	Gastropoda	Basommatophora	Planorbidae	*Planorbella sp.*	6	SC
Mollusca	Gastropoda	Basommatophora	Planorbidae	*Erpobdella sp.*	6	SC
Annelida	Hirudinea	Arhynchobdellida	Erpobdellidae		8	P
Annelida	Hirudinea	Rhynchobdellida	Glossiphoniidae		8	P
Annelida	Oligochaeta	Tubificina	Enchytraeidae		10	CG
Annelida	Oligochaeta	Lumbriculida	Lumbriculidae	*Lumbriculus sp.*	8	CG
Annelida	Oligochaeta	Tubificina	Naididae	*Dero sp.*	10	CG
Annelida	Oligochaeta	Tubificina	Naididae		10	CG
Annelida	Oligochaeta	Tubificina	Naididae	*Nais sp.*	10	CG
Annelida	Oligochaeta	Tubificina	Naididae	*Paranais sp.*	10	CG
Annelida	Oligochaeta	Tubificina	Naididae	*Pristina sp.*	10	CG
Annelida	Oligochaeta	Tubificina	Naididae	*Slavina sp.*	10	CG
Annelida	Oligochaeta	Tubificina	Naididae	*Stylaria sp.*	10	CG
Annelida	Oligochaeta	Tubificina	Tubificidae	*Aulodrilus sp.*	10	CG
Annelida	Oligochaeta	Tubificina	Tubificidae	*Chaetogaster sp.*	10	CG
Annelida	Oligochaeta	Tubificina	Tubificidae	*Limnodrilus sp.*	10	CG
Annelida	Oligochaeta	Tubificina	Tubificidae	*Spirosperma sp.*	8	CG
Annelida	Oligochaeta	Tubificina	Tubificidae	*Tubifex sp.*	10	CG
Annelida	Oligochaeta	Tubificina	Tubificidae		10	CG
Annelida	Oligochaeta	Tubificina	Tubificidae	*Varichaetadrilus sp.*	10	CG
Tubellaria	Tricladida	Planariidae	Planariidae		4	P
Tubellaria					4	P
Nematoda					5	P
Cnidaria	Hydrozoa	Hydroida	Hydridae	*Hydra sp.*	5	P

CHAPTER 5

IDENTIFYING REFERENCE SITES AND QUANTIFYING BIOLOGICAL VARIABILITY WITHIN THE BENTHIC MACROINVERTEBRATE COMMUNITY AT NORTHERN CALIFORNIA STREAMS

Identifying reference sites and quantifying biological variability within the benthic macroinvertebrate community at Northern California streams

Abstract

Identification of minimally disturbed reference sites is critical step in developing precise and accurate ecological indicators. I compared procedures to select reference sites, and quantified both site-level and temporal variability among reference conditions using a macroinvertebrate dataset collected from mediterranean-climate streams in the San Francisco Bay Area, California (USA). First, I determined that a landscape level GIS-based screen combined with a local stressor screen was necessary to identify high quality reference sites. The biological communities at (1) landscape-disturbed, (2) locally disturbed, and (3) least-disturbed reference sites were significantly different according to NMS multivariate ordination (A = 0.051, $p < 0.001$) and scores from two indices of biotic integrity (IBIs) developed for adjacent regions (ANOVA, $p < 0.05$). Second, within least-disturbed reference sites, inter-site variability was associated with flow status (i.e., perennial vs. non-perennial), supporting the need develop a unique IBI for non-perennial streams. Although the two IBIs, their component metrics, and four common metrics showed a wide range of natural variability at all reference sites (CV range: 17–150%), metrics were less variable among perennial than non-perennial streams. Third, among sites sampled more than once, the biological community showed moderate interannual variability, with IBI scores ranging from 12 to 15 points out of 100. Variance components analysis indicated that site-level variability was approximately six times greater than interannual variability. This study demonstrates the value of multi-year bioassessment data for determining the condition of a particular stream, such as classifying impairment according to Clean Water Act 303(d) standards.

Key words: biomonitoring, interannual variability, temporal variability, reference condition, IBI, mediterranean,

INTRODUCTION

Biomonitoring is used worldwide to assess the ecological condition of streams and rivers based on the presence or abundance of aquatic organisms. With this approach, government agencies, citizen groups, and research institutions can determine the cumulative effect of multiple stressors (e.g., urbanization, agriculture, logging, hydropower operations) on stream condition by developing responsive indicators based on in-stream biological communities (Karr, 1999; Resh, 2007; Resh and Rosenberg, 1989). Of the potential groups organisms used for assessments in aquatic habitats (e.g., diatoms, benthic macroinvertebrates, zooplankton, and fish (Hellawell, 1986)), benthic macroinvertebrates (e.g., insects, crustaceans and snails) are the most widely used to assess stream condition because they are ubiquitous, diverse, and species have unique responses to specific stressors (Resh, 2008).

Because the biological communities found at reference sites represent the target ecological condition and form the basis for the evaluating sites of unknown condition, proper identification of a high-quality reference sites is a critical step in developing an effective biomonitoring tool or indicator (Stoddard et al., 2006). The majority of biomonitoring indicators are developed using the reference condition approach, whereby reference sites are presumed to be in "good" ecological condition and provide a type of "control" to compare with sites of unknown ecological condition (Bailey et al., 2004; Barbour et al., 1999). These reference sites are assumed to represent the full range of natural variability in biological communities where anthropogenic disturbances are absent (Hughes, 1995; Reynoldson et al., 1997; Stoddard et al., 2006). Biomonitoring programs commonly ensure that three major requirements are met related to reference conditions: 1) reference sites that represent the biological community at sites with minimal anthropogenic stress can be identified in the region; 2) site-level variability in the biological community among reference sites is limited, or can be reduced by grouping sites with similar environmental variables (e.g., ecoregion); and 3) the interannual variability at reference sites is limited compared to the effect of anthropogenic disturbance. Precision and accuracy of a biological index are optimal when a suite of high-quality reference sites with low inter-site and low interannual variability can be identified, thereby improving the effectiveness of the monitoring program (Barbour et al., 1999; Southerland et al., 2007). If an indicator of ecological condition experiences substantial natural variability, detection of changes resulting from anthropogenic activities will be problematic (Osenberg et al., 1994).

Reference sites are often identified using explicit screening criteria based on available data. For example, criteria at the landscape level are based on land use land cover information in geographic information systems (GIS), whereas local criteria rely on hydrological, chemical, and habitat indicators at the reach scale. Additionally, poor quality sites can be differentiated from reference sites using best professional judgment (BPJ) of knowledgeable individuals who are aware of watershed or stream stressors such as small dams, water diversions, cattle grazing, and invasive species, all of which are stressors that may not be included in GIS databases or reach-level assessments. In practice, programs often use combinations of these three approaches (e.g., Barbour et al., 1999; Collier et al., 2007; Sanchez-Montoya et al., 2009; Stoddard et al., 2006; Yates and Bailey, 2010).

Although there are many approaches to selecting reference sites, few studies have compared how different approaches affect the quality of the reference sites identified by the selection process. Whittier et al. (2007) found that the use of BPJ alone could result in the misclassification of many poor quality sites as reference sites, reducing the mean condition of the reference pool. Similarly, Chavez et al. (2006) found that a reference site selection process using map-based criteria plus a field-oriented screening step were necessary to identify a suitable reference pool. Both of these examples indicate the importance of using criteria based on different geographic scales.

In addition to the choice of methods for selecting reference sites, accurate determination of reference conditions also requires an understanding of the natural variability of benthic macroinvertebrate communities in the region of interest. Because invertebrate communities are known to vary spatially and between stream types (Resh and Rosenberg, 1989), the process of developing a biomonitoring tool such as a multimetric index of biotic integrity (IBI) (Kerans and Karr, 1994) should consider natural factors that affect the macroinvertebrate community in the absence of anthropogenic stress (Barbour et al., 1999). Spatial variability in macroinvertebrate communities occurs at multiple geographic scales, such as the patch scale (e.g., generally $0.01 <$ $10m^2$), within a stream section (i.e., at the reach level), between streams and watersheds, and at the landscape scale (Frissell et al., 1986; Gebler, 2004; Johnson et al., 2007; Li et al., 2001; Vinson and Hawkins, 1998). Consequently, the site-level variability of invertebrate communities can result from differences in geology, climate, water chemistry, stream morphology, biotic interactions, allocthonous inputs, temperature, habitat quality, and stream hydrodynamics (e.g., Minshall et al., 1983; Townsend, 1989). For example, stream order, ecoregion, and flow status (e.g., perennial vs. non-perennial streams) have been repeatedly identified as important factors that influence benthic macroinvertebrate community structure (e.g., Bonada et al., 2006; Feminella, 1996; Lake et al., 1994; Li et al., 2001). In order to improve the precision of an IBI, researchers analyze the biological variability among reference sites to see if the data should be divided into groups of streams with similar physical conditions and similar biological communities into classes called "strata", such as stream order or ecoregion (Bailey et al., 2004; Barbour et al., 1999; Southerland et al., 2007).

In addition, temporal variability in the macroinvertebrate community, whether seasonal or interannual, can also reduce the precision of an IBI (Bailey et al., 2004). Interannual variability resulting from climactic cycles such as El Niño Southern Oscillation (ENSO), climate change, or variability in temperature and rainfall can have a significant effect on macroinvertebrate communities and thus biological index scores (Gilbert et al., 2008; Hughes, 1995). For example, Milner et al. (2006) observed significant changes in macroinvertebrate community structure as well as composition-based metrics (e.g., % Ephemeroptera, Plecoptera, and Trichoptera individuals) throughout a 9-year study of reference streams in Alaska, demonstrating that some common invertebrate metrics were not suitable for that region. Within a mediterranean climate, Mazor et al. (2009) identified high interannual variability of multimetric index scores that was correlated with changes in the El Niño Southern Oscillation (ENSO) index, indicating the influence of climate on bioassessment indicators. Biomonitoring programs, especially those designed to measure long-term trends such as climate change impacts, must account for interannual variability and long-term weather cycles (Bonada et al., 2007; Lawrence et al., 2010).

The purpose of this study was to examine how reference-selection methods and inter-site variability between reference sites and interannual variability could influence interpretations of stream macroinvertebrate biomonitoring data. The first objective was to determine what process and data were necessary to select high-quality reference sites in this region with widespread urban development. Second, I sought to quantify the extent of inter-site variability in the reference pool, and to determine whether this variability could be reduced by grouping sites into classes of similar stream types. Third, I wanted to determine if the interannual variability of macroinvertebrate communities could significantly affect IBI scores and, if so, to determine if the sources of interannual variability were associated with disturbance or common environmental gradients.

METHODS

Study Area

The study region is the San Francisco Bay Area, including all or portions of Marin, Sonoma, Napa, Solano, Contra Costa, Alameda, Santa Clara, and San Mateo Counties, which spans 22,000 km^2 (Fig. 5.1). The region experiences a mediterranean climate characterized by wet, cold winters followed by dry, warm summers, with high variability in annual precipitation (Gasith and Resh, 1999). Average annual rainfall also varies spatially within the region, ranging from 35 cm in the interior of the region to 135 cm in the mountainous regions (Gilliam, 2002). The area is mainly divided into two Level III Omernik ecoregions, (1) the Coast Range and (2) the Southern and Central California Chaparral and Oak Woodlands, with minor portions of a third ecoregion, the Central California Valley (U.S. Environmental Protection Agency, 1996). The region is well-developed with a total population of 7 million people (ABAG, 2011).

Bioassessment Data

Benthic macroinvertebrate data were compiled from 731 bioassessment samples collected between 2000 and 2007 at 429 sites by local and state agencies (Fig. 5.1). Macroinvertebrates were collected with a 500-μm d-frame dipnet within wadeable streams (e.g., generally 1st to 4th order) during an index period of April and May. Although all samples in the compiled dataset were collected using targeted-riffle field methods (Rehn et al., 2007), several slight changes to field and laboratory methods were made about halfway through the study reflecting changes in the State of California standard operating procedures. Specifically, between 2000 and 2003 benthic macroinvertebrates were collected from three 0.27 m^2 samples taken from adjacent riffles (0.81 m^2 total sample area); 300 organisms were subsampled from each of the 3 riffle samples, for a total of 900 individuals (Harrington, 1999). In samples collected from 2004 to 2007, eight 0.09 m^2 samples (0.72 m^2 sample area) were collected from random locations in riffle habitats; the 8 samples were combined into a single composite sample from which 500 individuals were subsampled (Rehn et al., 2007). To standardize the data between the two methods based on the number of organisms that were subsampled, I used a consistent multiplier (500/900) on all taxon abundance values from the 2000-2003 dataset.

To store the data and calculate metrics, raw invertebrate data were entered into CalEDAS, a bioassessment database developed for the State of California. Taxonomic identifications were standardized using Level 1 Standardized Taxonomic Effort of the Southwest Association of Freshwater Invertebrate Taxonomists' (Richards and Rogers, 2006), which involves identifications to genus for most taxa. The first dataset stored taxonomic results at the site level (n= 429 sites). In addition, to determine the biological community at sites where more than one sample was taken over the study period, I took an average of the relative abundance for each taxon for that site, rounding down to remove the influence of taxa observed in only one year. This dataset was used to identify reference sites and analyze inter-site variability. The second dataset used to determine interannual variability contained the raw taxonomic information for 468 sampling events at a total of 184 sites.

In order to assess the ecological condition for each sample, I applied two IBIs that were recently developed in adjacent regions of California but have not been validated for use in the San Francisco Bay region. The North Coast IBI (NC-IBI) was developed for the northern coastal area of California, most of which is north of the San Francisco Bay region (Rehn et al., 2005). The Southern and Central California IBI (SC-IBI) was developed for the southern and central coastal watersheds of California, south of the San Francisco Bay region (Ode et al., 2005).

Landscape Data

Landscape variables were assessed at two spatial scales: (1) the entire watershed draining to the sample site, and (2) a proximate scale that includes only the watershed within a 1-km radius of the site. These scales were chosen because biological metrics may respond to anthropogenic stressors at various spatial scales (Brazner et al., 2007), and because the same scale was used to screen reference sites for the development of the NC-IBI (Rehn et al., 2005). The proportion of urbanization within these zones was calculated from the National Land Cover Dataset (NLCD) 2001 dataset (Homer et al., 2004) using ArcGIS 9.1 (ESRI, 2005). The NLCD categories of low, medium, and high intensity developed were aggregated into a single urban category. The road layer was acquired from the Bureau of Transportation Survey and used to calculate road density (BTS 2002). I used the ArcHydro tool within ArcGIS along with a 10 m^2 pixel digital elevation model (U.S. Geological Survey, 1999) to build the stream and watershed network. A pixel was considered to be a stream if more than 50,000 pixels (5 km^2) flowed into it based on the flow accumulation model. GIS sites were snapped to the DEM-derived stream network, and watersheds were drawn for all land draining to that sample location using the flow accumulation model. Omernik level III ecoregion was used to classify sites according to biogeography (U.S. Environmental Protection Agency, 1996). Average annual rainfall data were acquired from PRISM (PRISM Climate Group, 2010)

Reference Site Selection and Validation

To determine which sampling sites might be of reference quality and conform to a "least-disturbed condition" (Stoddard et al., 2006, pp. 1267), I used a two-step screening process that required information at both the landscape and local scales (Fig. 5.2). The first screen (hereafter referred to as the landscape screen) was based on landscape-scale measures of human disturbance calculated with ArcGIS (e.g., percent urbanization and road density within the watershed). Stressors and thresholds were similar to the NC-IBI and SC-IBI (Table 5.1). A site was excluded from further reference consideration if any single metric was above a given threshold.

The second screen (hereafter referred to as the local screen) required information based on local conditions derived from personal observations during site visits and knowledge of the area. I contacted individuals or organizations responsible for the macroinvertebrate data collection to obtain their best professional judgment (BPJ) as to whether these could be considered as reference-quality sites. Stressors such as heavy grazing, mining, small dams, proximate stream channelization, or hydrological impacts eliminated sites from the reference pool. This second screen was only performed on the sites that passed the landscape screen because the original sampling agencies were unable to provide local information on all the sites.

This two-step screening process created three classes of sites with varying levels of disturbance: "landscape-disturbed", "locally disturbed", and "least-disturbed" reference sites (Fig. 5.2).

Because hydrology can greatly affect biological community structure (e.g., Bonada et al., 2006), information on the flow status of the stream reach at sample locations was also obtained. In addition, because the NHD+ designations of flow status have inaccuracies exceeding 40% in the western US (Olsen and Peck 2008) and similar inaccuracies in Southern California (R. Mazor, unpublished data), direct observations of flow were used to classify reference streams as perennial or non-perennial. Flow status was classified as perennial if the stream had surface flow during late summer (August-September), when mediterranean-climate streams typically have the lowest flow; any other conditions (e.g., no flow, disconnected surface pools, etc.) were classified as non-perennial. Flow status of non-reference sites was not determined because this data request could not be fulfilled by the original sampling programs.

To determine if the macroinvertebrate communities at landscape-disturbed, locally disturbed, and least-disturbed sites were significantly different from each other, I performed multivariate analyses on the raw taxonomic data followed by ANOVA tests on IBI scores. First, multivariate analyses of taxonomic data were conducted using non-metric multidimensional scaling (NMS) ordinations in PC-ORD (McCune and Mefford, 2006) with the following settings: ≤ 6 axes; 200 runs of real data; 20 iterations to evaluate stability; and 100 maximum iterations; Sorenson distance metric. Taxa present at 5 or more of the 429 sites (> 1.1%) were included in the analysis (n = 201 taxa included). Taxonomic counts were transformed using the natural log with a correction factor for zero count data (ln (1 + count)). I then compared overall taxonomic differences among the three groups identified in the reference selection process using multi-response permutation procedures (MRPP) (McCune and Grace, 2002). Second, I compared the NC-IBI and SC-IBI scores across the three disturbance classes (landscape-disturbed, locally disturbed, and least-disturbed) using ANOVA in JMP (v 8, SAS Inc, Corey NC) followed by Tukey's pairwise comparisons.

To evaluate the quality of the least-disturbed class as a potential reference site group, I examined the proportion of perennial stream reference sites that were below impairment thresholds according to both the SC-IBI and NC-IBI, which are 39 and 52 out of 100, respectively (Ode et al., 2005; Rehn et al., 2005). Because these impairment thresholds were originally set at 2 standard deviations below the reference group mean, I expect approximately 2.5% of normally distributed high-quality reference sites within to score below the impairment threshold (Ode et al., 2005; Rehn et al., 2005).

Inter-site Variability of the Macroinvertebrate Community

I analyzed the degree of variability in community structure among least-disturbed reference sites and determined if this variability was associated with environmental variables independent of anthropogenic activity. These analyses were performed on reference sites because these sites are less susceptible to confounding effects with anthropogenic stressors (Bailey et al., 2004). The influence of continuous explanatory variables (i.e., average annual rainfall, elevation, watershed size, and stream order) was evaluated using vector correlations with NMS ordination axes. NMS ordinations were run in PC-ORD using the same settings as listed above. Categorical explanatory variables (i.e., flow status, ecoregion) were compared using MRPP (McCune and Grace, 2002). No rare taxa were excluded from either the NMS or MRPP analyses (186 taxa included). To determine if differences in macroinvertebrate community structure resulting from natural variability could influence bioassessment indicators, I calculated the coefficient of variation (CV) for reference sites based on the NC-IBI, SC-IBI, each component metric, and other metrics commonly used within the United States (Resh and Carter, unpublished data). These CVs were compared to expected ranges of variation for those values similar to Resh (1994) and Sandin and Johnson (2000).

Interannual Variability of the Macroinvertebrate Community

To document interannual variability among the three disturbance groups (landscape-disturbed, local-disturbed, least-disturbed) and interpret how temporal variance affects precision, I quantified the standard deviation (SD), root mean square error (RMSE), and minimum detectible difference (MDD) in NC-IBI and SC-IBI scores among the 184 sites where more than one sample was taken during the study period. Although the MDD is often based on replicate samples taken on the same day (Rehn et al., 2005), I applied this estimate of precision to incorporate interannual variability because this dataset provided a unique opportunity to do so. To calculate the MDD, I followed methods described in Rehn and others (2005). I determined RMSE by regressing the IBI score against the sites within each disturbance class, and used the power analysis formula for a two sample t-test following Formula 8.23 in Zar (1999) to determine the MDD. A sample size of $n = 3$ for each sample, $df = 4$ (total $n - 2$), $\alpha = 0.1$, and $\beta = 0.1$ was used in the power analysis formula to be comparable to other California stream assessments (Mazor et al., 2009; Ode et al., 2005; Rehn et al., 2005).

In order to identify site-level characteristics that influence the degree of interannual variability, I compared the SD of IBI scores among sites in the reference pool to potential explanatory variables. For example, I tested for associations between SD and categorical variables (i.e., ecoregion, flow status) using t-tests, and continuous variables using ordinary least square (OLS) regressions (i.e., elevation, watershed size, precipitation, stream order, seasonal variation). Watershed size and elevation were natural-log transformed. Effects of seasonal variation were quantified by determining the Julian date for each sample collection and then calculating the maximum difference in the Julian dates at each site. Results were examined using a family wise Bonferroni-corrected alpha value of 0.01 for each IBI.

Comparison of Interannual and Environmental Variability

I performed a variance components analysis to determine if inter-site or interannual variability was a more significant source of the total variability in bioassessment data. This method was chosen in addition to a comparison of CVs because CV scores are affected by mean values, and because variance components are directly related to the sums of squares used in ANOVA tests (Larsen et al., 2001). Only sites with multiple sampling events could be included in this analysis. This analysis was performed individually for each of the three disturbance groups and with all sites treated as a single group. The amount of variability in both the NC-IBI and SC-IBI was attributed to *year*, *site*, and the interaction of site and year (*site*year*). In this model variability of *site* represents the variance resulting from natural environmental variables affecting inter-site variability. Because of the lack of replicates within single sampling events, residual error was indistinguishable from the interaction term. Restricted Maximum likelihood (REML) was used to calculate variance components because of the unbalanced design (e.g., sites were not sampled consistently across all years) and JMP software was used for all calculations (Larsen et al., 2001).

RESULTS

Reference Site Selection and Validation

I classified each of the 429 sites into landscape-disturbed, locally disturbed, and least-disturbed groups by applying two screens of anthropogenic stress (Fig. 5.2). The first screen identified sites that were subjected to landscape and watershed scale disturbances and identified 312 sites that were classified as landscape-disturbed based on *a priori* criteria also used for the SC-IBI and NC-IBI developed in adjacent regions (Table 5.1). The remaining 117 sites were subjected to a screen for local stressors, and those that failed and were classified as locally disturbed (n = 56). The sites that passed both screens (n=61), were considered least-disturbed and examined to see if they were reference quality.

There were significant differences in macroinvertebrate community structure between the three groups with varying degrees and types of anthropogenic stress (landscape, local, and least-disturbed). For example, according to results from non-metric multidimensional scaling (NMS) ordination each reference selection screen resulted in selecting sites with a biological community tending towards the right side of the two axis solution (Fig. 5.3). The ordination explained 80.8% of the variance in multidimensional space with a two axis solution (Sorensen distance method, stress = 18.34, instability = 0.0033). MRPP confirmed that the biological communities differed between the three disturbance classes (A statistic = 0.051, p <0.0001). In addition, both the IBI indices (NC-IBI and SC-IBI) showed significant and consistent increases in ecological condition with decreasing anthropogenic stress, and an overall good condition for sites in the least-disturbed group (Fig. 5.4). The initial landscape screen removed a majority (88% and 92%) of the sites in poor condition and subsequent application of the local screen successfully eliminated nearly all sites (97% and 99%) that were in poor condition. This result is evidence that the sites in the least-disturbed condition are reference quality.

Flow status was associated with significant differences in IBI scores. For example, average NC-IBI and SC-IBI scores were 17 and 15 points higher among perennial streams compared to non-perennial streams ($p < 0.01$; Fig. 5.5). The number of sites classified as poor condition according to the IBIs decreased when assessing only perennial streams, for which these two IBIs were initially developed: Only 3 (8%) and 2 (5%) of the 37 perennial reference streams scored below impairment thresholds based on the NC-IBI and SC-IBI, respectively. Of the 3 perennial sites classified as impaired according to the NC-IBI, 2 were also identified as impaired according to SC-IBI, meaning there was agreement between the two IBIs in identifying the low quality sites in the reference group.

Inter-site Variability of the Macroinvertebrate Community

Among reference sites with minimal anthropogenic disturbance, benthic macroinvertebrate community structure was correlated with particular environmental variables. For example, results from the NMS ordination (stress = 18.19, instability < 0.0001, total variance = 80.0%) indicated that non-perennial streams supported distinct macroinvertebrate communities compared to perennial streams (Fig. 5.6). MRPP tests confirmed that flow status had twice the explanatory power compared to ecoregion, the only other categorical environmental variable (Fig. 5.6). This same ordination showed that mean annual precipitation was the only continuous variable highly associated with differences in community structure, whereas elevation, watershed size, and stream order were not.

The variability in community structure observed in the ordination analysis affected biomonitoring indicators. For example, CVs for NC-IBI, SC-IBI, and their sub-metrics ranged from 22% for Ephemeroptera, Plecoptera, and Trichoptera (EPT) taxa to 158% for Percent Non-Gastropoda Scrapers (Table 5.2). Seven of the 15 unique sub-metrics were highly variable, defined as having CVs above 50%. Variability was lower for the IBIs compared to their sub-metrics and was lower among perennial streams for 13 of the 17 metrics (Table 5.2).

Variability of the Macroinvertebrate Community Among Years

The metrics and IBI scores describing the macroinvertebrate community exhibited moderate interannual variability. The average maximum difference in NC-IBI and SC-IBI scores at the 184 sites that were sampled more than once (two-five times) during the study period was 12 and 15 IBI points, respectively (Table 5.3). However, six sites had SC-IBI scores that ranged more than 50 points, which is half of the entire 100 point scale.

Anthropogenic stress was not correlated with the amount of interannual variability. For example, the difference in the standard deviation (SD) of IBI scores among the landscape-disturbed, locally disturbed, and reference groups showed no trend for either index ($p > 0.05$, Fig. 5.7). The SD of IBI scores, RMSE, and corresponding MDD values were similar for all three site classes with varying anthropogenic stress (Table 5.3). MDDs ranged from 30-40 IBI points, which roughly correspond to breaking the 100 point scale up into three distinct categories (Fore et al., 2001).

I found no relationships between interannual variability and natural environmental gradients or stream classes within the least-disturbed sites. For example, there was no significant association between SD scores of IBI scores and the two common ecoregions or between perennial and non-perennial streams (t-test, $p > 0.4$). Similarly, there was no association between SD of IBI scores and average annual precipitation, watershed size, elevation, or stream order (OLS regression, $p > 0.1$). In addition, within season variability, quantified as the maximum difference in Julian collection date, was not useful in explaining the source of interannual variability (OLS regression, $p > 0.6$).

Comparison of Interannual and Environmental Variability

Variance components analysis showed that the overwhelming majority of variability in the both NC-IBI and SC-IBI scores was associated with inter-site differences (*site*), and that the interannual component (*year*) was consistently less than 10% (Table 5.4). These patterns were consistent for all three disturbance groups and both the SC-IBI and NC-IBI. The interaction term of *site*year* explained 20 to 30% of the variability, depending on the IBI and disturbance group.

DISCUSSION

Because reference sites are the standard against which test sites are examined, selection of high quality reference sites with biological communities that are distinct from disturbed sites is a critical step for developing biological metrics and assessment tools. Variability in the biological community between reference sites and between years influences the precision and accuracy of a biological index, and requires critical analyses when developing a biological index (Barbour et al., 1999). Consequently, this study evaluated the process of selecting least-disturbed reference sites, and quantified the interannual and inter-site variability in the macroinvertebrate biological community. Identifying appropriate reference sites and stable biological indicators in this region is a challenge because of widespread anthropogenic activity and the strong interannual variability in weather patterns owing to its mediterranean climate.

The combination of landscape and local disturbance criteria worked well to identify a suitable pool of least-disturbed reference sites for streams in the San Francisco Bay Area. Moreover, information from the local screen based on observations of physical habitat and knowledge of local conditions, was essential in this process. For example, the use of only the landscape level criteria would have left too many poor condition sites within the reference pool (15-31% depending on the index). This proportion is far greater than the 2.5% of poor quality sites expected from a normal distribution of reference sites, and is also higher than the 9-14% of least-disturbed sites found within handpicked reference sites by Whittier et al. (2007). The presence of 15-30% of poor quality sites in the reference pool would substantially alter the IBI development process by reducing the discriminatory power when screening for potential metrics, when scoring raw metrics and when validating the IBI with independent data (e.g., Ode et al., 2005; Rehn et al., 2005). One limitation in this study was that only local data were available at sites that passed the landscape screen (n=117). With availability of local stressor information from all 429 sites, I would be able to compare performance of the two screens independently.

Variability inherent in the biological community can substantially alter the interpretation of results from biomonitoring programs (e.g., Bailey et al., 2004). In this study, the natural variability among reference sites was partially explained by flow status (Fig. 5.5). In general, perennial streams had lower CVs for common metrics (Table 5.2), and were less dispersed in ordination space (Fig. 5.6), implying that the biological communities were more similar. An IBI developed for these perennial streams, therefore, has the potential to be more precise than for non-perennial streams, a problem for mediterranean regions that often have a high proportion of non-perennial stream miles.

Variability was lower for both IBIs compared to their individual metrics, a pattern that has been observed elsewhere (e.g., Mazor et al., 2009). This pattern supports the concept that multimetric indices are more useful than individual metrics (Karr and Chu, 1999). In our study, the majority of metrics analyzed had levels of variability similar to those observed in other studies (e.g., 30-60) and was not much greater than CVs observed in studies within a single catchment or region (Collier et al., 2007; Gebler, 2004; Resh, 1979; Resh et al., 2000).

Differences in the interannual variability of IBI scores were not correlated with site level differences in anthropogenic stress or common environmental variables (Table 5.4). Although sites in the landscape-disturbed group had a larger range of variance in biological condition (Fig. 5.7), I believe this result stems from the large sample size of this group compared to the locally disturbed group. The lack of association with anthropogenic stress suggests that measurements of interannual variability can be assessed by long-term monitoring at disturbed or reference sites in this region. Similarly, (Scarsbrook, 2002) observed no significant difference in reference quality and disturbed streams over a 9 year study. However, Collier (2008) found that impacted and reference streams varied the most, while moderately stressed sites showed the least annual variability in community structure.

Inter-site variability within the reference sites was a much greater source of total variance compared to interannual variability. For example, approximately 60% of the total variability was attributable to the site-level differences, and 40% was attributable to either annual variation or the interaction of site and time (Table 5.4). IBI scores for individual sites did not respond uniformly between years, which is why the *year* term only explained at most 10% of the total variation. The *site*year* term, which was also the same as the model error, explains the variation whereby some sites increased IBI scores in a single year while others decreased. On average, the unexplained temporal variability in the model was three times greater than the average annual changes in IBI scores. Thus, the major cause of interannual variability was not a uniform annual change over a single year.

I were unable to identify variables in this dataset that explained why some sites exhibited higher interannual variability than others. For example, reference sites and disturbed sites all had similar levels of annual variability for IBI scores. This result agrees with the study of Collier et al. (2007) that found no significant differences in CVs of a local multimetric indicator with natural and anthropogenic factors. Similarly, in this study I saw no differences in annual variability based on flow status, a result that contrasts with a different study in Northern California which found higher temporal variability among intermittent streams (Béche et al., 2006). The observed differences in interannual variability may result from local, site-level factors (e.g., slope, substrate) that were not measured in this study. The full range of temporal variance was certainly underestimated at some of our sites with only 2 to 3 sample events (Zar, 1999), because I noticed a positive relationship between sites with more interannual sample events and standard deviations of IBI scores.

There are number of possible sources of interannual variability that are important to consider for biomonitoring programs. For example, variability may result from inter-operator error because repeat visits are often conducted by different field personnel, which can result in metric variability (Hannaford and Resh, 1995; Needham and Usinger, 1956). Some error may be attributable to patchy distributions of organisms within the same reach (Nichols et al., 2006; Resh, 1979), although the lack of replication within a sampling event prevented analysis of this variance component in this study. Lastly, it is unlikely that subsampling error and invertebrate identification error (Nichols et al., 2006) were significant contributing factors to overall variability in this study because these processes followed a stringent QA/QC process to limit identification error and identified 500 organisms per sample, which has been shown to reduce the effect of subsampling error (Doberstein et al., 2000; Lorenz et al., 2004).

Implications for Bay Area IBI Development

This study precedes an effort to develop an IBI for streams in the San Francisco Bay Area region. Our results provide evidence that both the NC-IBI and SC-IBI were useful in evaluating the biological condition of streams outside their development range. Therefore, these indicators may have some applicability to streams and creeks of the San Francisco Bay Area. Perennial reference-condition streams in this study had similar IBI scores to the NC-IBI reference sites. In contrast, when reference sties were scored by the SC-IBI, the mean of 85 was nearly 20 points higher than reference sites used to develop the SC-IBI (Ode et al., 2005), which indicates that the SC-IBI may over-score sites in this region. Although this study was not designed to formally validate either IBI for this region, I do feel both indices were useful indicators and, because of their reduced inter-site variability, are a better choice for evaluating ecological status than using a single metric (e.g., EPT richness). The potential application of a multimetric index outside of its development scope contrasts with another study in California, which found that sampling methods and resulting index scores developed for high gradient streams performed marginally in low gradient streams (Mazor et al., 2010).

Our results strongly indicate the need to develop a unique IBI for non-perennial streams in this mediterranean climate. Non-perennial reference streams scored 15 to 7 IBI points lower than perennial reference streams. This result is not completely unexpected because these indices were developed using biological data from perennial streams, and their applicability to non-perennial streams even within their development region was unknown. Multiple studies have identified taxa that are adapted to the seasonal drying regime by evolving desiccation resistant life stages, or dispersal and colonization mechanisms (reviewed in Wiggins et al., 1980; Williams, 2006). Non-perennial streams support unique biological communities in this region in particular, which is likely to be a factor for all mediterranean climate streams (Bonada et al., 2006; Gasith and Resh, 1999). Despite these reasons to develop separate IBIs based on flow, to our knowledge no other biomonitoring programs have done so.

Most of the metrics that are part of the NC-IBI and SC-IBI had reasonably low variability within the reference pool (e.g., < 40%) and thus could have good applicability in this region (Rosenberg and Resh, 1982). However, the most variable metrics such as Percent Non-Gastropoda Scrapers and Percent Tolerant Taxa could reduce the overall precision of an IBI in this area. Although the CVs of the two IBIs were similar, the SC-IBI was slightly lower, which might be a result of the higher mean for this group. It should be reiterated that no data from this study were used to develop either the SC-IBI or NC-IBI, although the geographic range sampled partially overlaps with the NC-IBI (i.e., Marin County).

Broader Implications for Bioassessment Tiered Aquatic Life Uses

Our analysis of interannual variability indicates that minimum detectable differences (MDDs) calculated from multiple years of data will generally be higher than when calculated with replicate samples taken on the same day. For example, the MDDs observed in the NC-IBI and SC-IBI development process, which involved 3 replicate samples taken on the same date from the same riffle were 19.7 and 13.1 (Ode et al., 2005; Rehn et al., 2005). These MDDs incorporate patch level spatial variability plus variability in subsampling and identification error. In contrast, because this study involved samples collected in different patches, across different years, on different Julian dates, the MDDs more than doubled to 35 according to the NC-IBI and 42 for the SC-IBI. This would mean that instead of having five tiered aquatic life uses (TALUs), which are distinct classes of ecological condition (Fore et al., 2001; Ode et al., 2005), these metrics may only support two to three classes, resulting a substantial difference in the precision of the indicator. Most data in this study are not from the regions covered by the SC-IBI or NC-IBI, and thus an analysis of sites with multiple years of data in each respective region would be necessary to truly determine their respective MDDs when considering interannual variability.

A fundamental question asked of bioassessment data in the United States is whether a particular stream segment should be placed on the 303(d) list as impaired according to Clean Water Act standards (Barbour et al., 1999). Similarly, evaluations based on bioassessment are being conducted as part of the European Water Framework Directive in the European Union in order to protect or enhance the ecological condition of freshwater and marine ecosystems (e.g., Borja et al., 2004; Moss et al., 2003). Results of this study indicate that IBI scores based on the macroinvertebrate community typically vary over time by 10 to 15 points (and sometimes up to 50 points out of a 100 point scale). Thus, it may be unwise to list a stream segment as impaired using only a single year of bioassessment data, a concern that has also been raised by others in the bioassessment community (Collier, 2008; Milner et al., 2006; Scarsbrook, 2002).

www.ingramcontent.com/pod-product-compliance
Lightning Source LLC
LaVergne TN
LVHW021047100526
838202LV00079B/4765